Kings of Texas

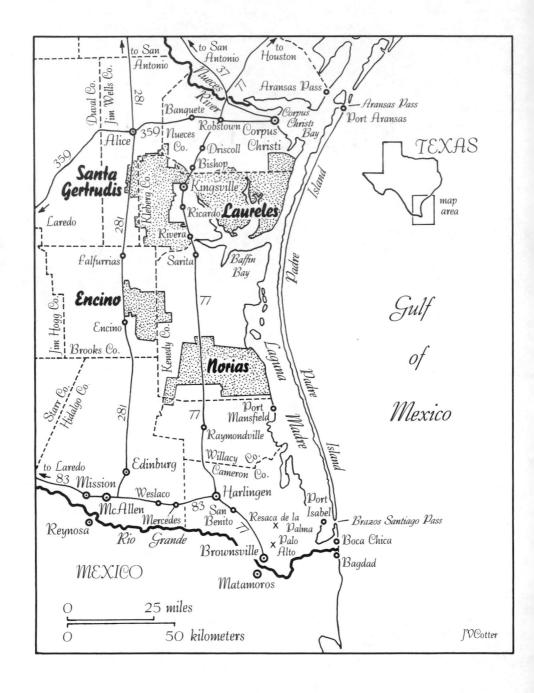

Kings of Texas

The 150-Year Saga
of an American
Ranching Empire

Don Graham

John Wiley & Sons, Inc.

Published by John Wiley & Sons, Inc., Hoboken, New Jersey
Published simultaneously in Canada

Design and production by Navta Associates, Inc.

Illustration credits: page ii courtesy of John V. Cotter, Ph.D.; pages 19, 207, and 210 courtesy of the Texas and Southwestern Cattle Raisers Foundation, Fort Worth, Texas; pages 23 and 24 Chapman [William WE.] Papers. CN Number 11163. The Center for American History, the University of Texas at Austin. Courtesy of Edward Coker; page 49 courtesy of the Photography Collection, Harry Ransom Humanities Research Center, the University of Texas at Austin; page 77 courtesy of Hildago County Historical Museum, Edinburg, Texas; page 135 courtesy of Western History Collections, University of Oklahoma Libraries, Norman, Oklahoma; page 203 courtesy of Texas State Library and Archives Commission, Austin, Texas; page 249 courtesy of Adair Margo.

For general information about our other products and services, please contact our Customer Care Department within the United States at (800) 762-2974, outside the United States at (317) 572-3993 or fax (317) 572-4002.

Wiley also publishes its books in a variety of electronic formats. Some content that appears in print may not be available in electronic books. For more information about Wiley products, visit our web site at www.wiley.com.

Library of Congress Cataloging-in-Publication Data:

Graham, Don, date
  Kings of Texas : the 150-year saga of an American ranching empire / Don Graham.
    p. cm.
  Includes bibliographical references and index.
    ISBN 0-471-39451-3 (acid-free paper)
    1. King Ranch (Tex.)—History. 2. King Ranch (Tex.)—Biography.
  3. Ranch life—Texas. I. Title.
  F392.K47 G73 2003
  976.4'47306—dc21   2002014036

Printed in the United States of America

10 9 8 7 6 5 4 3 2 1

Again, for my wife, BB

The crookedness of the Rio Grande cannot be exaggerated. It is extremely muddy, the banks low, and utterly without interest and passing up this stream the question arises: For what are we here? For such a country as this why expend such blood and treasure?

—HELEN CHAPMAN, LETTER, 1848

The cattle is a little thin and bitter water down in the rincon and no pens.

—RICHARD KING, LETTER, 1862

Contents

Acknowledgments

During the course of writing this book, I received a great deal of help from old friends and new ones made along the way. Herewith, my heartfelt thanks.

I am profoundly grateful first of all to Edward Coker of Charlotte, North Carolina, for his unstinting help. Ed was invaluable in helping me locate documents and better understand the complex background of his ancestors' relationships with Richard and Henrietta King. It was he who encouraged me to examine the records at the Edwards Legal Firm in Corpus Christi. In sum, Ed Coker's advice and aid made this project viable and exciting, and I am forever grateful.

At the beginning of my research, journalist Skip Hollandsworth turned over to me a large box containing all the background information and notes he had gathered for his excellent 1998 *Texas Monthly* article on King Ranch. Skip's generosity saved me a lot of time, and I am grateful.

In Corpus Christi at the Edwards Legal Firm, I was the beneficiary of many kindnesses from attorneys Michael G. Terry and William R. Edwards. I also wish to thank Janie Loa and Michelle Shircliffe of that firm for their help.

Thanks also to Al Lowman of San Marcos, who made available to me his collection of correspondence surrounding the publication of Tom Lea's *The King Ranch* and offered useful hints for research.

Tom Kreneck, associate director of Special Collections and Archives at Texas A&M University-Corpus Christi, was especially helpful in filling me in on the background of archival research in South Texas. I also wish to thank Bruce Cheeseman for agreeing to talk to me about his time as King Ranch archivist.

Others historians and writers who offered useful advice and counsel include Jerry Thompson, Andrés Tijerina, David Montejano, Rolando Hinojosa, David Gracy, John Leffler, Richard Holland, Bert Almon, and James Sanderson.

Thanks for various forms of help are extended to Cherrie Weatherford, Donald Avance, R. W. Hoover, Fred Berry, Yolanda Z. Gonzalez, Mimi Berry, Alan Alexander, and Freddee Berry.

Scholars and staff at the Texas State Historical Association at The University of Texas were very helpful, and I am grateful to George Ward, Ron Tyler, and Sandra Gilstrap for their aid.

Don Carleton, director of the Center for American History, offered crucial advice in the early stages of this project and supported my research. I am grateful to him and to the staff who handle the daily flow of information at the center's library: Ralph Elder, Evan Hocker, Paulette Delahoussaye, John Wheat, Alison Beck, Brenda Gunn, Stephanie Malmros, and David Dettmer.

I am also grateful to Tom Staley, director of the Harry Ransom Humanities Research Center, who has always been very supportive of my work.

Mark Busby brought to my attention a number of valuable articles and documents, for which I am grateful.

And a special thanks to cartographer John Cotter for his splendid map.

For the photographs, I wish to thank Dr. Cheri L. Wolfe of the Cattle Raisers Museum in Fort Worth; Steve Lomas of the Hidalgo County Historical Museum in Edinburg; John Anderson of the Texas State Library and Archives in Austin; Linda Peterson and Janis Olsen of the Center for American History, University of Texas at Austin; John Lovett of the University of Oklahoma; Linda Briscoe of the Harry Ransom Humanities Research Center at the University of Texas; Adair Margo of the Adair Margo Gallery in El Paso; and, again, Edward Coker.

For the cover photo, I wish to thank photographer David R. Stoecklein; Carrie R. James of his office; and Kathy Marcus of *Texas Monthly* for steering me in that direction.

I wish also to thank Evan Smith, editor of *Texas Monthly,* and Quita McMath and all the writers and staff at the magazine for their encouragement, goodwill, and support.

In the English Department at The University of Texas, chair James Garrison has been, as always, enthusiastically supportive, and I wish also to thank Ramona Van Loan, Geneva Walton, and Anda Wynn for their able handling of travel forms and other administrative matters. And special thanks to Mary Blockley for help with a Latin translation.

Richard Lariviere, dean of the College of Liberal Arts at The University of Texas, has been very supportive of my research initiatives, and I wish to thank both him and the university for granting me a Faculty Research Award to complete this project. I wish also to thank Dean Lariviere for a Research Award. I am very grateful to Joey S. Walker of the dean's office for her invaluable help as well.

I also wish to thank the Summerlee Foundation in Dallas, headed by John Crain, for a research grant. Their support is much appreciated. My thanks to The Writers' League of Texas for acting as my sponsor for the Summerlee Foundation Grant, and a special thanks to Sally Baker of The Writers' League for her help.

In New York, Emily Loose had some good ideas about the early stages of the project, but my biggest debt, far and away, is to Stephen S. Power, who helped bring the book into its present shape. As they used to say in Texas, he would do to ride the river with.

My agent, Jim Hornfischer, who is always on the lookout for a good story, brought the possibility of this project to my attention, and he deserves a huge measure of thanks as well.

I would also like to say a word or two more about my wife, Betsy Berry, to whom this book is dedicated. She is a superb editor and as always was helpful in that regard, but more than that, she provided me some indispensable time to write by teaching my classes when I was under the deadline gun. When I returned to those classes, the question would always be "When will Dr. Berry be back?" My thanks to BB for her love and support.

If there are errors or mistakes of any kind in this book, I cannot blame a research assistant, for I had none; I can only blame myself.

Introduction

Deep in the heart of the blackland, cotton-farming country northeast of Dallas where I grew up, we learned about storybook Texas. Eight grades gathered together in one room, a separate grade planted on each row. We memorized the lumbering state song, "Texas, Our Texas"; we thrilled to the tales told in *Texas History Movies,* a simplified, comic-strip version of the state's past; we belted out the rousing "Yellow Rose of Texas." Everything was supposed to make us proud to be Texans. "Other states were made or born,/ Texas grew from hide and horn" was a truth sold us in a poem by a lady named Berta Hart Nance.

The poem, however, said nothing about the Texas we lived in, on shirttail farms or in the little towns where there was work at the five-and-dime or at the funeral home, jobs that my father held, among others, upon leaving the land. Although we lived outside the myth, we accepted its tenets: Texas was home-on-the-range country. The movies said so, the press said so, and the music on the radio said so. Consequently, those places where Texas grew from hide and horn seemed blessed, while the farms and towns where the rest of us lived did not.

We knew which place was most blessed, most powerful, most protected from the winds of change, from the vicissitudes of the economic forces that buffeted the rest of us. That was King Ranch, the biggest ranch in the biggest state in the union.

Texas, all 246,866 square miles of it, occupies almost 10 percent of the land area of the United States. Eleven states combined could fit inside Texas with room left over, and we could name them: Maine, New Hampshire, Vermont, Massachusetts, Connecticut, Rhode Island,

1

New York, Pennsylvania, New Jersey, Ohio, and Indiana. Texas was so big it was a "world in itself," as pulp novelist Zane Grey had declared. *New Yorker* author John Bainbridge wrote a book about Texans that he called *The Super-Americans*. John Steinbeck visited the state and solemnly declared, "Texas is a state of mind. Texas is an obsession . . . a mystique closely approximating a religion." He also noted the lofty status of the ranching aristocracy: "The tradition of the frontier cattleman is as tenderly nurtured in Texas as is the hint of Norman blood in England." If these things were true, and we believed they were, then King Ranch was the most Texas place of all—a great, sprawling realm of land and cattle and the men and women who made their living from land and cattle, ranchers, Texans strong enough to stand against nature's forces with grit and tenacity and more than their share of luck. *Fortune* magazine perhaps said it best, back in 1933: "It is a pleasant fiction that the King Ranch is a part of the U.S."

In the time I am speaking of, the 1950s, King Ranch consisted of slightly over a million acres. It occupied parts of six counties and stretched over sixty miles. But that was just in the United States. There were foreign holdings as well, in South America and Australia, that sent the total amount into the stratosphere of eight million acres. Equally impressive was the fact that King Ranch had been held intact by one family and its heirs down through the generations, while in our part of Texas families had a hard time hanging on to their property. With the small family farm headed for the last roundup, by 1960 the Grahams were landless in a state where nothing was more important than owning land. The Grahams weren't alone. In 1940, 60 percent of Texans lived on farms and ranches; in 1960, 40 percent. Today the ratio is 18 percent rural, 82 percent urban. During this period of radical transformation in population and economy, when the whole state was changing, King Ranch remained King Ranch.

In that era King Ranch was very much a living part of Texas history—unlike the long-dead tales of Indian fighters and buffalo hunters out of the old books. Stories of King Ranch rode high, wide, and handsome across the newsprint of that time. The overlord of King Ranch, Bob Kleberg Jr., graced the cover of *Time* magazine in 1947. The year before, a King Ranch horse, Assault, won the Triple Crown. *Giant,* the novel in 1952 and the film in 1956, was thought to be based on King Ranch. Tom Lea's celebrated history, *The King Ranch*, in two volumes, was published to great fanfare in 1957. In 1961 King Ranch was declared a National Historic Landmark.

It stretched wide across the landscape of our imagination, a burning brand so fixed in our minds that it was impossible to live in the state and not dream of the great ranch. Because the interstate highways had not yet been built, distances seemed farther and places more remote—so far away that the thought of going to them was like traveling to a foreign country. With its aura and mystery, King Ranch was the most remote and inaccessible of them all.

The legend of the ranch was second only to that of the Alamo, except that it was still a going concern while the Alamo was a shrine, an old refurbished mission in the heart of San Antonio, encrusted with layers of mythology so thick that half the boys who visited there, it seems, became Texas historians. Everybody went to see the Alamo, but I didn't know anyone who had ever seen King Ranch. On a family vacation in the 1950s we traveled from Dallas to Beaumont—a long trip on those old two-lane highways—then to San Jacinto to see the monument there, and on to Corpus Christi. Somewhere southwest of Corpus we drove alongside a fence that ran forever, it seemed, and Dad said, "That's the King Ranch." We looked out the window at the brush and the miles of grass and thought, "Gee, that's the King Ranch," and didn't know any more about it than we had before. The mystery endured—and as I would later find, mystery is one of the ranch's most refined products.

King Ranch unscrolled alongside the road for so long that we forgot about it, but every time we looked out the window, there it was, endless. While I tried to be impressed by the brush and fence scrabble whizzing by, my brother, Bill, just a little kid, warbled a couple of lines from some ditty he had heard on the radio while we drove on through King Ranch country: "The sun's done riz and the sun's done set, an' I ain't offen the King Ranch yet."

Imaginatively, I never was "offen the King Ranch" just as, literally, I never was on it. But King Ranch never went away. Old rumors about King Ranch circulated among historians of my acquaintance. Tales of stolen land in South Texas surfaced now and then in the press and in new books about the region. Then, in 1998, a story in *Texas Monthly* by Skip Hollandsworth about the removal of Stephen "Tio"

Kleberg from his position as head of King Ranch's cattle operations spurred my interest even more.

And so I began the winding, rabbit-trail journey of reading, researching, and the fixing of one's concentration upon a subject that forever eludes it. As Texas continued to change and the population became transformed by newcomers to the state, the idea of what was lost and what was constant became for me a central theme. This involvement with the past was in no sense a matter of nostalgic chauvinism—I had always wanted to leave rural Texas, I had always preferred cities, preferably far away, in Europe or Australia, and, failing those, in Texas—but I was also interested in knowing the truth about the past, not the legendary past but the actual past, specifically the nineteenth century and, more specifically, King Ranch.

To start, I finally visited that place of myth and childhood wonderings—and there I took the seven-dollar tour.

Kingsville, founded in 1904, located about forty miles southwest of Corpus Christi, is a dusty little town possessed of a water tower with the words "A Living Legend" inscribed thereon, a small university (Texas A&M at Kingsville), a population of 25,575, and, nearby, the gigantic ranch that has been, since 1853, the locus of land, power, and desire in South Texas.

Once in Kingsville, signs everywhere indicate that you are in King Ranch country. Kingsville is the county seat of Kleberg County, its main street is named King, a parallel street is named Kenedy (after Richard King's longtime friend, patron, and partner, Mifflin Kenedy), and other streets of King Ranch–inspired names crisscross the town: Kleberg, Gertrudis, Henrietta, Caesar, Richard, Etta, Alice, Nettie. People bank at the Kleberg First National Bank, and when they die, they are buried in the cemetery named Chamberlain Memorial Park (after Henrietta King's father, Hiram Chamberlain). From cradle to grave, Kingsville is a company town.

The entrance to King Ranch is on Highway 141, just past the city limits of Kingsville and a couple of miles from downtown. Palm trees line the short entranceway that leads you to the King Ranch Visitors Center. The standard tour—Daily Historical Tour—takes about an hour and a half. The one I took was conducted by J. B., who had his guide patter down pretty good. There were about ten of us, and we watched out the windows of a small van as J. B. drove us around to different sites and told us what we were seeing. On the way to points of interest he covered the history of the ranch's development, drawing all of his stories and dialogue, it appeared to me, from Tom Lea's *The King Ranch*, the standard history that has the authority of the Old Testament with most King Ranch people and a majority of Texas historians.

King Ranch is so big that you're not always entirely clear where you are, but near one complex of outbuildings we were asked to observe a small field enclosed by a fence and covered in tall grass. This was an "old *Kineño* cemetery," we were told, where men, women, and children who had worked on King Ranch were buried. There were no markers or names. Nearby, however, was a plaque with an engraved picture of Peppy San Badger, one of King Ranch's famous quarter horses.

J. B. explained the dimensions of King Ranch as it exists today. The ranch is not one giant parcel of land but rather four large divisions. North to south, King Ranch stretches some sixty miles and comprises 825,000 acres, an area larger than Rhode Island (one of the mantras of KR publicity). The four divisions are Santa Gertrudis (203,468 acres), the original site from 1853; Laureles, the largest, at 225,026 acres, twenty-two miles south of Corpus Christi and fronting the gulf on two sides; Norias (237,348 acres), way to the south, reaching down some seventy miles north of Brownsville and site of a famous raid against King Ranch in the disturbances of 1915; and Encino, the fourth and smallest (a mere 131,017 acres), northwest of Norias. The four divisions encompass more than 1,300 square miles. The ranch, home to 60,000 head of Santa Gertrudis cattle and 1,000 registered quarter horses, is surrounded by 2,000 miles of net wire fences, enough to stretch end to end from Kingsville to Boston. King Ranch has 424 water wells, 300 windmills, 27 solar-powered mills, and 2,730 oil and gas wells. These numbers—or numbers like them—are trotted out in virtually every article and book ever written about King Ranch.

The tour van sent up spirals of dust as we drove past objects of interest: a gigantic root plow used to shear off the roots of mesquite trees, which periodically threaten to take over the land, and a huge funnel plow for pushing over brush. We see silos, an old chuck wagon, stables, barns, corrals, pastures, Santa Gertrudis Creek, Santa Gertrudis cattle in one field, non-KR cattle in another, brought in to "feed out" before being sold for slaughter. Of special interest are the "bump gates," developed by Exxon to permit entrance to a pasture by driving slowly through the gate, pushing it open with one's vehicle. Bob Kleberg did not like cattle guards, a more traditional method of separating pastures, involving a grid of round metal poles embedded in the ground that discourage livestock from crossing. Lying in the shade of the low-slung trees are "some more of them bulls" that J. B. has been promising us we would see. We drive past the building that houses the Santa Gertrudis Independent School District, built to educate the children of King Ranch. We pass a grassy sward where a small herd of longhorns, reminders of the old days, are supposed to be on view, but they are hidden this day and we do not see them.

We pass near a deserted grandstand, built in the long-ago days of the 1940s, and used in the manner of Bedouin chieftains, to view the thoroughbreds going through their paces on a fine racing course. It was here that Assault, the 1946 Triple Crown winner, trained as well as Middleground, who won two of the big three, and all the other King Ranch horses that ran for glory in those years when King Ranch challenged Kentucky as a site for training thoroughbred champions. Today the track is grown over with grass, the bandstands long emptied of owners and observers.

There was land, and land, always the land, and an air of faded glory that one could not ignore. We were witnessing a dusty, old-looking working ranch that was largely devoid of life. Not once did we espy a cowboy or vaquero—where were they, the cowboys, the vaqueros, our hearts' desire? The closest we came to glamour was a slow progress past the Main House, the famous ranch home built in 1915 to replace the one that burned in 1912. White stucco with redbrick trim, it rises above the trees, commanding the landscape of brush and pastures stretching away to the southwest. A line of ceiling fans runs the length of the long open gallery in front—a reminder of how hot it gets here in South Texas in the summer, which lasts only six to seven months. The Main House is plenty big, 33,000 square feet, with an open patio, seventeen bedrooms, and nineteen baths—the dimensions of a mansion, or a small hotel. The kitchen occupies a separate structure.

Although fully staffed, the Main House is no longer anyone's home. The extended family of KR descendants uses the Main House as a hotel during visits to the ranch, calling ahead to reserve rooms. The annual spring stockholders' meeting of KR, Inc., whose headquarters are two hundred miles away, in a Houston highrise, is held in the Main House.

Of the adjacent buildings, two afford some interest. One is the former commissary where Richard King had his office, a building that always impressed nineteenth-century visitors because of its great store of rifles and other hardware useful for staying alive in South Texas. Farther on is a sturdy stone stable built in 1909—Mrs. King's carriage house.

The emptiness of King Ranch is what struck me most. The whole scene, on a workaday Tuesday morning in November, had the appearance of a deserted movie studio lot, all the players, all the color and action and purpose strangely absent, leaving only structures and machinery, the dust and leached-out light of a fall day when the countryside is poised to decline into that weather-beaten harshness of South Texas in the winter season, the land at rest.

When we got out of the tour van, a woman asked J. B. if he knew why cows wouldn't eat the round bales of hay we had seen in the pastures. You could tell she had been saving it up. When J. B., as earnest as the day is long, allowed as how he didn't, she said, "Because they can't get a square meal." J. B. said he'd never thought about it like that.

Leaving Kingsville, I drove down Highway 77 toward Brownsville, the route laid out by Taylor's Army of Occupation in the spring of 1846. The road runs like a plumb line, mile upon mile, through tightly fenced properties, King Ranch on the right, King Ranch on the left. When this highway was first proposed, back in the 1930s, King Ranch fought hard to keep it from being built. Bob Kleberg and Johnny Kenedy (grandson of Mifflin Kenedy) didn't want the public driving through the middle of their property. Instead they urged the state to build its highway down the narrow hundred-mile strip of Padre Island, where King Ranch didn't own any land. Public criticism of the ranch mounted, and journalists seized on the image of the "Walled Kingdom" to characterize King Ranch's power and privacy. The name stuck, and the effort to stop the highway from being built was one fight that the Walled Kingdom lost. Hugh Best in *Debrett's Texas Peerage* put it this way: "Getting into the King Ranch is like getting into China before they lifted the curtain."

At Sarita, a tiny village (pop. 250) just off 77, is the office of the Kenedy Pasture Company. On down the road, past Armstrong (another ranch of note), announced by a small post office, the country feels empty except for the trucks and automobiles, and Kenedy County *is* empty (pop. 414 in 2002). On the gulf side of Kenedy County, where the shallow waters of the Laguna Madre provide shelter for a rich ecosystem of bird, plant, and animal life, the U.S. Navy, in 2001, seriously considered using the coastline for military exercises to replace the much-disputed Vieques site off Puerto Rico. Still farther south, the highway passes a small sign, Norias—the southernmost section of King Ranch land. I have been driving for sixty-odd miles and I am still in King Ranch country. On this road nothing seems to have changed since the 1950s. All around there is the inescapable impression of King Ranch, its immensity and impenetrable grandeur.

But eventually even that ends, and the ranching gives way to farming and the towns of the valley begin to appear: Raymondville; Harlingen, that most American of towns with its statue of the Marines at Iwo Jima and its airport and its Chamber of Commerce boosterism; and finally, Brownsville on the border, unofficial capital of the lower Rio Grande Valley, a true delta consisting of alluvial soils congenial to agriculture and composed of four counties—Cameron, Hidalgo, Starr, and Willacy—that make up a mass of about 43,000 square miles of the levelest land you ever saw. It is not really a valley, as even Gertrude Stein understood, who had never visited the region when she wrote about it her book *Everybody's America:* "The valley of the Rio Grande spoken of by all Texans as the valley is perfectly flat miles of flat land just of the same flatness on either side and yet just at one moment begins the valley, only a Texan has the feeling he knows when it is just ordinary flat land and when it is a valley." (Stein based her description on what Sherwood Anderson had told her.) A Texas writer, John Houghton Allen, who lived on a ranch in Hidalgo County, nineteen miles from the Mexican border, described the area in his book *Southwest* as "hard country, brush country, mean country, heartbreak country." The seasons, he wrote, were different only in degrees of appearance: "Ugly in summer, drought-stricken, dusty, glaring, but in winter it is hideous." A "cul de sac of a country," "the endless purgatory of the southwest," he called it.

On the tip of Texas, where the flatness of the "valley" ends at the sea, the United States seems to form a kind of natural funnel at the mouth of the Rio Grande, where the polluted, dirty, hydrilla-infested formerly Great River dies by inches into the Gulf of Mexico. It is the southernmost part of the center of the country, and across the river is that other country, Mexico, so that along the Rio Grande there is both a boundary and a constant crossing of boundaries, legal and illegal. The border is a down-and-out sort of place, a dingy, exhilarating, and depressing flux of poverty and cheap gaudiness, at once dangerous, mundane, exotic, and threadbare, backlit with a kind of shabby glory.

This has always been so. The border is one of the things that makes Texas different from many other states in the union—a foreign nation living on the south side of that river, a different country entirely, of a different race, religion, history, and culture. And that nation once owned all of the land on the Texas side of the river. It makes a difference, which is why the border region, much like Ireland, has experienced its own Troubles for more than a century and a half.

South Texas, an area larger than the state of Arkansas, is a province within a province, and largely foreign to the rest of Texas. Poorer, less healthy, and distant from the large cities (San Antonio, Houston), South Texas has striking demographics. The percentages in the last census, 2000, for Cameron County (Brownsville) are 14.73 Anglo, 0.30 black, and 84.34 Hispanic; Nueces County (Corpus Christi), 38.32 Anglo, 4.24 black, and 55.78 Hispanic; and Kleberg County (Kingsville), 29.03 Anglo, 3.69 black, and 65.4 Hispanic. Thus Spanish competes with English as the dominant language of South Texas, and literacy in English is a huge problem. So are basic amenities in the *colonias,* makeshift settlements without adequate (or sometimes any) paved streets, indoor plumbing, and the other hallmarks of a first world country. Because of pollution from chemical wastes and other sources, the cancer rates in some areas of the valley are off the charts. The figures are dramatic and depressing. Women die of cervical cancer at twice the national rate; the statistical average for death from diabetes is much higher in the Rio Grande Valley than in the rest of the state; diseases long considered confined to third world countries—dengue fever and cholera, for example—continue to surface; and alarming clusters of nightmare birth defects such as anencephaly (babies born without a brain) have appeared along the border, in 1990 and 1991 and again in 2000 and 2001.

The remoteness of South Texas from the rest of the state—and from America—has been reduced somewhat in recent years. Even so, going to South Texas can feel a bit like leaving the United States, and if you come back from there, as I did in the fall of 2001, sick as a dog from an intestinal parasite, you will find that the medical community is unsurprised. The doctor at the emergency room asked me if I had been traveling in a foreign country. When I replied, "South Texas," he did not blink.

Back in Kingsville, I visit the King Ranch Saddle Shop in the heart of the small commercial downtown, where the selling of brand has taken on its twenty-first-century cast. The wide array of KR items to purchase includes fine leather goods, sturdy shirts, hats, boots, blankets, home furnishings, travel accoutrements, what have you. A King Ranch rocking chair goes for $278, King Ranch twill shirts for $55, King Ranch cooler and ice chest, leather, for $245, Kleberg wallet for $140, El Vaquero briefcase for $195 in tan cordura or $225 in King Ranch leather, Running W wristwatch for $68, Cattle Baron's laptop briefcase for $548. Most items bear the famous Running W insignia, the King Ranch brand. Anybody with cash or credit card can feel a part of King Ranch, Inc.

One of the most popular items is the *King Ranch Cookbook* (1992), which gives you the flavor of KR chow on the range, with recipes for Pan de Campo de Santa Gertrudis (bread cooked over coals), Palomas à la Flaco (doves "fresh from the field, cooked over a mesquite campfire, seasoned with tall tales"), Nigali Stew (Asian antelope introduced on King Ranch in 1940), Barbacoa de Cabeza (cow's head wrapped in a potato sack and cooked in a hole in the ground all night), and Fried Deer Heart Slices (again, open fire recommended).

A novelty item, a postcard made of wood, contains a recipe for King Ranch Chicken Casserole.

At the turn of the twenty-first century, King Ranch, Inc. was busy selling the legend, branching out in the world of entrepreneurial possibilities, going where no ranch had gone before. There was talk of a new line of perfume called King Ranch Cologne. In 2001 King Ranch made a deal with Ford Motor Company to franchise the Running W brand on a line of Ford pickups.

Every fall King Ranch hosts an old-fashioned King Ranch Chuck-wagon Breakfast in downtown Kingsville. People in Kingsville remember the old days when the Klebergs lived in the Main House and there were public events held on the grounds, in the spreading shade of the live oaks that had been there forever, it seemed. In those days King Ranch was a vital part of the community. Now things are different. But the land remains, and King Ranch has always done well with the land. The vast interior lands of King Ranch have been managed in a way that is very protective of the flora and fauna of South Texas. This is part of the record, too, and must be understood.

The best time to see it is in the spring, when winter's bleakness gives way, by early March, to the subtle traceries of spring in South Texas as the country begins to come alive. Huisache trees, with their delicate yellow blossoms, create a kind of shower of color. Mesquites burst into flower. The strange anaqua, or so-called sandpaper trees, produce bark that feels like a cat's tongue. Yuccas, as large as small trees, shoot their white columns of bloom upward. Blankets of daisies, daffodils, pink primroses, Indian paintbrush, and bluebonnets cover the pastures.

King Ranch is a kind of paradise of birds. The birds seem ecstatic in spring. Green jays, with violet-blue crowns, flash like rubies among the huisache and mesquite trees. Lemony-yellow kiskadees (or Derby flycatchers), found only in South Texas, dart through the foliage. Yellow-rumped warblers (winter residents) linger among the burgeoning green. The vermilion flycatchers are simply astonishing. To attract females, the male, a showoff with a black mask and intense red crown and body, flies straight up, a hundred feet, and flutters there like a helicopter, drawing attention. There is also the dazzling pyrrhuloxia, a bird so named because of its bright red stripes that make it look like it's on fire when it takes off from a perch. There are mourning doves and meadowlarks and teals and ibises and ground doves and Eastern bluebirds and red-winged blackbirds and scissor-tailed flycatchers and on and on. There is a plenitude of hawks: Cooper's hawks, a major predator; red-tailed hawks; and Harris hawks, which hunt in packs, four of them, for example, surrounding a rabbit in hiding while another walks through the brush to flush out the prey. There is the sensational crested caracara, a "vulture in a tuxedo," so called because of the white markings on its tail and the ends of its wings. There are butcher birds (loggerhead shrikes), notorious for impaling their prey on cactus. There are roadrunners in abundance, called *paisanos* by the Mexicans, large birds that spend most of their life on the ground and are adept at killing rattlesnakes. There are the ferruginous pygmy owl, quite rare though plentiful on King Ranch lands, and the tropical parula. But perhaps the greatest bird of all in that country is the great horned owl. In the spring the great horned owl inhabits a nest constructed and abandoned by some previous large bird and there it sits, high atop the tallest, bushiest tree in the pasture, feeding its young by regurgitating some quarry eaten earlier, looking more like a bobcat than a bird. Over three hundred species of birds thrive on King Ranch lands.

There are animals aplenty as well. White-tailed deer bed down under huisache trees, whose uplifted branches leave inviting open spaces beneath. Javelina, strange, stumpy little creatures with long faces, travel in small packs called sounders. They look like animals you would expect to find in Australia. The Spaniards gave them their name because the tips of their teeth recalled a javelin's teeth. Although they are often considered wild pigs, they are actually collared peccaries. The young follow their mothers around like adorable little pets. They give off a musky smell, especially when afraid, and have poor eyesight. They are considered a great delicacy if dressed properly so as to avoid contamination from the musk gland.

Antisocial old badgers lurk in holes and seldom show themselves. Fierce little bobcats hunt by night and keep hidden by day. Larger cats, panthers, are said to be returning to the land. Red and gray foxes sometimes show themselves, then are gone. Coyotes, taller, stringier, more like fast dogs, but from another world, trot into the open, then vanish. They pose a danger to calves and have been known to attack and kill them as they are being born. Elusive and smart, the coyotes would be there for the long term. Deer in great number graze delicately at the edges of open fields. And there are the cattle, in the fenced pastures, cherry-red Santa Gertrudis with the embossed Running W brand. In its interior, King Ranch can still seem very enclosed, far away from the world of the cities and marketing and modern America.

◇ ◇ ◇

There is something about King Ranch that escapes the eye alone, that can't be sold or even branded. Apart from the pastoral, agrarian world arranged like a stage setting for tourists, all around, one feels the immensity. Nearly 150 years after its founding, King Ranch continues to exude a sense of mystery and power. The real King Ranch is hard to know. To understand it is to confront the history of ranching in the American West. Ranching is vastly important because it is the only new pastoral activity to be created in the New World. The production of beef cattle helped create modern America. The cattle industry helped bind the nation together following the close of the Civil War. It fed an entire nation of urban dwellers. It created an original body of American folklore, music, painting, and narrative. King Ranch was there at the beginning, and it is still there, whipping past the car window if you're in that country or, if not, purely in the eddies and swirls of one's imagination.

The story of King Ranch has much to tell us about Texas and America, reaching deep into the heart of intertwined desires of land, ownership, and destiny. Here is the pulse of the national epic of cattle and cowboys, ranchers and horses, a vast fortune created out of the oldest source of wealth there is, land and cattle. Here, too, is a sometimes unstable ecology of two distinct peoples, white and brown, living in unequal partnership on a plot of the contested earth where notions of ownership and inheritance are both distinct and intertwined. For to contemplate King Ranch is to do nothing less than ask ourselves, Who owns history, Texas, and memory? To understand King Ranch is to understand the very idea of human will exerted against the forces of nature, time, other claimants, and change. Above all, the story of King Ranch is the story of an American empire.

The Henrietta Memorial Center, on Lee Street, near downtown Kingsville, is my last stop. Originally an ice house, it was converted into a combination museum, banquet hall, and library archives. In the museum, the visitor can admire artifacts from the past—a wagon of the type that transported Richard King and his bride to their honeymoon bower on the wild prairie of the Santa Gertrudis rancho, in December 1854, or the magnificent customized Buick hunting car built for Bob Kleberg in the 1950s, or trophies and photographs of majestically antlered deer killed by men and women of the King and Kleberg families.

Two tall wooden doors mark the entrance to the archives, where the old records are stored, but no visitors are admitted inside. The archives are closed. In early 2000, I asked for permission to use the archives. Lisa Neely, the current archivist, enjoined me to write a formal letter stating my research aims, and after I did so, she wrote to inform me (June 9, 2000) of the decision of King Ranch, Inc.: "While we appreciate your scholarly interest in our history, we cannot grant your request for two reasons." The reasons were: (1) "The King Ranch family, at this time, is not prepared to participate in the creation of an additional narrative on the history of King Ranch" and (2) "The breadth of your work renders the project impractical at this time. We are simply not in a position to do justice to the important subject that you have taken on." The letter ended by asking me to keep them "apprised of [my] work as it progresses."

The closed archives seem but the latest avatar of the Walled Kingdom, and it is here that my narrative of King Ranch begins and ends. It entails the story of a lawsuit of historic proportions, filed in 1995, that led to the closing of the archives and that threatens the very sovereignty of the ranch's founding. History, it turns out, is only somewhat more stable than nitroglycerin. If jostled, it, too, has a tendency to blow up in our faces, shattering old received truths, exploding sagas of long-reverenced repute.

CHAPTER 1

Manifest Destiny's Children

The Rincón de Santa Gertrudis, an old Spanish land grant, lies at the heart of King Ranch, for it was here, on these untenanted lands, that Capt. Richard King, in 1853, first laid claim to a dream of ownership that would make his nascent rancho the envy of the world. The site on the Santa Gertrudis Creek, which ran prettily in seasons of rain and dried to caked mud in the frequent droughts of that land, was 125 miles north of Brownsville on the border and 45 miles southwest of the little gulf seaside town of Corpus Christi. What was true of an adjacent, larger tract (the Santa Gertrudis de la Garza land grant), which King would buy the next year, was true of all this land—in the grandiloquent language of Spanish deeds, it was "unappropriated, waste and unpopulated."

Originally the land had belonged to no one, lying on the floor of the Late Cretaceous seas a mere sixty-five million years ago; in the full-ness of time the waters receded, leaving behind deposits of oil and salt domes and subhumid plains of varying soils and grasses and plants, and an ecology that would support human beings. Small Indian groups, designated later by ethnologists as Coahuiltecans, hunted or gathered such food—various roots and tubers, deer, shellfish, pecans along the Nueces (Nut) River—as they could find in the sparse, unforgiving country that the Spanish, when they arrived in the sixteenth century, called *El Desierto de los Muertos,* the Desert of the Dead.

Cabeza de Vaca, the first European to spend any length of time in Texas, passed this way during his seven-year sojourn of surviving half-naked among the peoples there to greet him. De Vaca recognized an agrarian future awaiting this country: "All over the land," he

15

wrote, "are vast and handsome pastures, with good grass for cattle; and it strikes me the soil would be very fertile were the country inhabited and improved by reasonable people." Eventually Spain flung its northernmost settlements across the Rio Grande and Spanish land-grant holders reached as far inland as the Santa Gertrudis Creek, but Indians in the area resisted the Spanish as they later resisted Anglo incursions, and the Spanish abandoned these holdings and were content to stay along the border in the towns built in the eighteenth century.

When Anglos began to stream into Texas from the 1820s on, and after the Texas revolution in 1836, settlements remained east and south of the Nueces country. Stephen F. Austin, the father of Texas settlement, looked with disfavor upon the region because it did not fit the prototype for cotton plantations. After a trip to Matamoros in the 1820s, he wrote of the land that English speakers were now calling the Wild Horse Desert: "the poorest I ever saw in my life. It is generally nothing but sand, entirely void of lumber, covered with scrubby thorn bushes and prickly pear." As late as 1839, the following notation appeared on maps depicting South Texas: "Of this section of country little is known."

But it was here in this inhospitable wasteland of grass and sweltering heat that Richard King assembled his empire piece by piece. To do so he hired the best legal talent available. The successive transfer of ownership from Spanish to Mexican to Anglo meant a very tangled history of land titles and taxes paid and unpaid and dispossession and new ownership, a lengthy and knotty process with new laws cantilevered over older ones. One Spanish deed holder on the Rio Grande spoke to the problem of title: "I have traced the [land] title back to the King of Spain, who got it by right of discovery and conquest, and since he ruled by Divine Right, that takes it back to God Almighty himself, and that is as far as I can go."

King did not have to go that far and did not. In all, King made over sixty purchases of land in his lifetime, so that by the time of his death in 1885 he owned over a half-million acres and was the richest man in Texas, the archetypal cattle baron whose fame would increase with the passage of time. What in the beginning had seemed a fool's errand into a wilderness acquired instead the patina of myth, the aura of legend. "Buy land; and never sell" were words of wisdom uttered, the family maintained, by the sainted Robert E. Lee himself. They became King's motto and stood him well from first to last.

Fifty years ago I could have traveled, as the great chronicler of the King Ranch, Tom Lea, once did, upstream from the mouth of the Rio Grande all the way to Roma, 150 miles to the west, to get the feel of the Rio Grande and the region as it might have been experienced by Captain King. *No más.*

Today the closest I can get to the river's mouth is a few miles away, on the windblown beach at Boca Chica (Little Mouth). The road from Brownsville to Boca Chica, State Highway 4, gives a glimpse of just how desolate the country still is. Northeast of Brownsville there is almost no development at all, and four or five miles from the coast, there is nothing but salt flats to the east and flat, empty scrub country to the west. The last historical marker signifies the site where Camp Belknap once stood, about a mile west of S. H. 4, on a stretch of "high ground," a long narrow belt of land only slightly elevated above the low-lying plain. General Zachary Taylor established a camp at this spot to receive volunteers who in the summer of 1846 poured into Brazos Santiago a few miles away, on the coast. Many men never left Camp Belknap, dying instead in that pestilential, mosquito-plagued hellhole, the camp averaging two to three burials per day.

S. H. 4 ends a hundred yards from the water. To either side stretch dirty, taupe-colored beaches where the families of the poor gather beside their pickups and four-wheel-drive vehicles to grill chicken and steaks while the kids play in the sand and water, the radios and CD players pumping out the sounds of conjunto music. A few miles to the northeast rise the condos and hotels of South Padre Island, but along the Boca Chica beach there is nothing at all except dirty sand, dead seaweed, the strange purple and green cellophanelike remains of jellyfish, and the quiet slap of waves.

South of where I am standing, a few miles away, is the mouth of the river, only in 2002 there is no river. Where once the Rio Grande entered the Gulf of Mexico, today it does not. A newly created sandbar caused by wave action from the Atlantic Ocean plus the sluggish flow and pooling upstream marks the river's end. Although it is possible to walk across the mouth of the river, it is probably not such a good idea, for this is drug smuggler country and anybody poking around in this isolated place, a true borderland, vague and undefined, is asking for trouble. It is also no longer possible to take a boat from Boca Chica to Brownsville. Today the only boats on the river belong to the Border Patrol.

At the edge of the gulf at Boca Chica, waves lapping at one's feet, looking west away from the gulf, toward Brownsville, thirty miles distant by land, all one can see is the overarching blue sky, the shimmer cast by blazing sunlight, an irregular line of low sand hummocks tufted with sea-blown grass, and beyond, a blurry haze created by the sun's glare and mist from the gulf. From here, one sees Texas as it appeared to those who first came to these shores, from the Spaniard de la Pineda in 1519 to the youthful future founder of King Ranch three centuries later. From this perspective Texas is all possibility, formless and blank. Those with a taste for the picturesque, as many cultivated nineteenth-century newcomers were, would have had to travel far up that river to find anything that would appeal to their sensibilities. Extreme South Texas was extreme in its lack of picturesqueness. There was an end-of-the-world feeling here—there still is—as though America seems to drain away and something else begins. South Texas in the mid-nineteenth century was a place where, from the American point of view, there was nothing else to do except try to find a way to get rich.

In May 1847, when Richard King stepped ashore at Brazos Santiago, the place hummed with activity generated by commerce and its handmaiden, war. But apart from its vital economic function, nobody ever had anything good to say about Brazos Santiago. Major Luther Giddings, who hated the "suffocating atmosphere of that sandy waste at the Brazos," enumerated the panoply of pests like some Darwinian Dante: "snakes, tarantulas, ants, centipedes, lizards, horned toads, scorpions, fleas, spiders,—*et id genus omne*" [and it is all types]. Lieutenant William S. Henry told a tall tale to capture the deplorable conditions that he observed during the summer of 1846, telling about a man who swallowed a sandbar and saying to his doctor, "Well, then, I am a *gone sucker*. I've got a sand-bar in my innards, upon which every thing grounds, and I can't get any thing up nor down." A Pennsylvania volunteer named Jacob Oswandel described his impression from aboard ship on January 28, 1847, just four months before Richard King arrived in Texas: "A miserable looking place it is; two or three shanties and a few tents along the beach, and the harbor full of vessels of all descriptions anchored around the beach."

Whatever its shortcomings as a site of pleasurable human habitation, Brazos Santiago was a crucial port of entry where ships unloaded passengers and goods by means of lighters (smaller boats) that trundled cargo, human or otherwise, from ships anchored offshore to Brazos Santiago or Brazos Island. So important economically was Brazos Santiago—the only northern seaport for trade with Mexico—that controlling it was a vital factor in the war that brought men like Richard King to Texas in the first place.

Who *was* Richard King? He was a pure product of America, an orphaned youth without family, money, or pedigree, with only his wits and determination and pluck to carry him through the world. His childhood had been brief. He was born on July 10, 1824, in New York, of Irish parentage, which meant, unspoken, a great deal. It meant a history, back in Ireland, of hunger, need, oppression, and flight to America. The year he fetched up at the mouth of the river in

Richard King. The once beardless young steamboat captain as Victorian patriarch.

South Texas, Ireland was being emptied of its hungry, suffering masses. That historical process, the slow leaking of Ireland's people, was now a cascading, frantic, giant exodus forced by the failure of the potato crop—and a dozen other ills. It had been going on since the turn of the century. Nothing is known of Richard King's parents except that like other Irish immigrants, they must have come to New York for a fresh start. But there they perished instead, and their son Richard King, at age five, found himself placed in the care of an aunt and then, at age nine, apprenticed to a jeweler. The young King did not like being an apprentice, sweeping, running errands, taking orders, and in 1835, when he was eleven, like that archetypal American, Benjamin Franklin ("I dislik'd the Trade and had a strong Inclination for the Sea"), the boy bolted from his apprenticeship and took to sea, hiding away on the *Desdemona,* a ship bound for the Gulf Coast.

At some point in its passage south, down the Atlantic coast, around Florida, and into the tranquil waters of Mobile Bay, the boy was discovered and brought before the captain of the *Desdemona.* Something in King's look, some spirit, some keenness of intellect or physical promise, led the captain to take an interest in the boy's welfare. He became a "cabin's cub," and under the tutelage of Capt. Hugh Monroe he learned the ins and outs of riverboat navigation. In 1837, at age thirteen, he went to work on Capt. Joe Holland's boat, which operated on the Alabama River from Mobile to Montgomery. From Holland he learned still more, including an eight-month stint at a school in Connecticut—the only formal schooling he ever had—and afterward returned to work on the Alabama River. He became a pilot in 1840, when he was sixteen.

Rivers were crucial to America's future. Before railroads, they offered the key to commercial development. Rivers were the underlying reason for the Lewis and Clark expedition. Thomas Jefferson envisioned a river route from the Mississippi all the way to the West Coast; the Northwest Passage was thought to be a waterway. At about the time the Lewis and Clark expedition returned from the west, Robert Fulton was revolutionizing river transportation. The steamboat would be the first big breakthrough of the machine age in travel. So in learning the craft of riverboat piloting, Richard King was riding the wave of the present and the foreseeable future. The mighty Mississippi wasn't the only navigable river in the country.

Richard King added a new page to his growing frontier résumé when he went to Florida in 1841 and received a crash course in American imperialism. The Seminole War (1835–1842) was a bloody exercise in conquering and depopulating a people who had lived in that aboriginal land for centuries.

Not that there wasn't plenty of hatred to go around on both sides. Halleck Tustenuggee, one of the leading Seminole chieftains, hated whites so much that it was said he killed his own sister when she advocated compromising with the enemy. On the American side, the purpose was plain. Col. William J. Worth, who took command of the army in Florida in May 1841, issued orders to "find the enemy, capture, or exterminate." There was nothing new about this policy except its brutal succinctness.

The Americans resorted to savage tactics against the "savages." At one point the army purchased thirty-three Cuban bloodhounds to track down the elusive Seminoles and to wage war against what Governor Robert Reid called "beasts of prey." Reid, incidentally, was considered a gentleman, an intellectual, and a humanitarian. There were military-type battles, to be expected in war, but there were also instances of guerrilla-type tactics. Out of a desire to avenge an embarrassing surprise attack by a band of Seminoles, Lt. Col. William Harney later captured several Seminole men and ordered them hanged in front of their wives and children.

The methods that seemed to work the best were those of duplicity and betrayal. Army officers would invite groups of Seminoles to friendly powwows, then arrest them and ship them west. To many Seminoles, forced emigration was as bad as death. It was in such a manner that Colonel Worth deceived Halleck. Colonel Worth invited him and his warriors to a feast, then ordered them surrounded, bound in chains, and hauled away in wagons to the embarkation point at Tampa. Brokenhearted, Halleck said, "I have been hunted like a wolf, and now I am to be sent away like a dog."

Richard King saw some of these methods firsthand. In 1841 he served on the steamboat *Ocochobee* under the command of Capt. Henry Penny. Once again it was Colonel Worth who sprang the trap. He invited Chief Hospertarke, eighty-five years old, on board, along with eighteen warriors. He offered them whisky and supplies, but as soon as they were safely on the boat, they were arrested.

Many of the men who played a role in the Seminole War would later wind up in Texas: General Zachary Taylor, General Winfield Scott, Colonel Worth, many others. Lt. George Gordon Meade remarked in a letter to his wife that in Texas he was happy to meet "many of my old fellow-campaigners in Florida." Some of the most important men in King's future took part in the Seminole campaigns. One of them was Mifflin Kenedy. Another was William W. Chapman.

The friendship between King and Kenedy that began in Florida was one of those that shapes lives. Born to Quaker parents in Pennsylvania in 1818, Mifflin Kenedy taught school, sailed to India, and saw a bit of the world before settling on river navigation in 1836. For the next several years he worked on the *Champion* on the Apalachicola and Chattahoochee rivers in Alabama. Following their days in Florida, Kenedy and King pursued their riverboat careers in Alabama, and in 1846, during a visit to Pittsburgh, Kenedy met an army engineer who was rounding up boats to work on the Rio Grande. Kenedy saw an opportunity and invited the younger King to join him. For the rest of their lives Kenedy and King would be closely associated in many ventures, and both would rise to prominence in the frontier of South Texas.

The friendship of W. W. Chapman (1814–1859) and Richard King was another matter entirely. A graduate of West Point, Chapman also saw duty in Florida, in 1838, and later in Mexico was brevetted a major for gallantry displayed at the Battle of Buena Vista (1847). Afterward he served as army quartermaster in Matamoros and later Brownsville during the yeasty years of 1847 to 1852. He became friends with Richard King at some point, and he and his very interesting wife, Helen Blair Chapman (1817–1881), were deeply engaged in the life and times of that era. An inveterate writer of letters, Helen Chapman had a lively mind, a good education, and a novelist's capacity for characterization and evocative detail. Together and separately, their lives were intertwined with those of Richard King and his wife-to-be, Henrietta Morse Chamberlain. And they remain intertwined today, a century and a half later, in ways that the Kings certainly would not have wanted and that present-day heirs and assigns do not, either, as will be shown in these pages in the fullness of time.

The Mexican War, like the Seminole War, was a consequence of American expansionism. Its roots were more complex, however, as

William W. Chapman and son
Willie, ca. 1849.

Mexico, unlike the Seminoles in Florida, constituted a sovereign
nation. As did Texas itself, until January 1845, when the United
States annexed Texas as the twenty-eighth state. Now the interests of
the United States and those of Texas were officially one and the same.
President James K. Polk was committed to expanding the territory of
the continental United States, and he did so through artful diplomacy,
military plans, and a general overarching rationale with a compelling
name: Manifest Destiny.

In 1845 the phrase appeared for the first time in an article for the
Democratic Review. It caught on immediately. The writer, long
thought to be John L. O'Sullivan but recently identified as Jane
Cazneau (indefatigable journalist and author of *Eagle Pass; or Life on
the Border,* 1852), proclaimed that "the fulfillment of our Manifest
Destiny" is "to overspread the continent allotted by Providence for the
free developing of our yearly multiplying millions." Manifest Destiny
was but a name for long-standing policy, exemplified by Thomas Jefferson's authorization of the Lewis and Clark expedition at the beginning of the century, the goal of which was nothing less than to lay
claim to territories that would offer "room enough for all our descen-
dents to the thousandth and ten thousandth generation."

Helen Chapman and son Willie,
ca. 1846.

Not everybody went west, however. New England intellectuals like
Emerson and Thoreau attacked the war, Emerson writing in one
poem, "Behold the famous states/Harrying Mexico/With rifle and
with knife." Even among those who prosecuted the war, there were
some who felt the United States was completely in the wrong. A
young lieutenant in General Taylor's command, for example, wrote in
his memoirs that the Mexican War was "the most unjust war ever
waged by a stronger nation against a weaker nation . . . an instance of
a republic following the bad example of European monarchies." His
name was Ulysses S. Grant.

But as long as there was a continent to conquer, the idea of Manifest Destiny would prevail. Frederick Law Olmsted, a cultivated
northerner who hated slavery—and who would later design New
York's Central Park—traveled through Texas in 1854 and, in his
laconic manner, put the matter for land acquisition more succinctly
than anybody: "We saw the land lying idle; we took it. This to other
nations is all that we can say. Which one of them can cast the first
stone?" Although very critical of the kind of racism and ignorance he
observed in Texas, Olmsted was yet moved enough to prophesy:

"Texas has an Arcadian preeminence of position among our States, and an opulent future before her, that only wanton mismanagement can forfeit."

The main geographical, territorial point of dispute over which so much blood was spilled in the Mexican War was the establishment of a boundary between Texas and Mexico. Texas regarded the Rio Grande or Rio Bravo or Rio del Norte—it went by all three names— as the boundary. The river runs nearly two thousand miles, looping down out of New Mexico to traverse the desert north of El Paso, knifing through the Big Bend country into the flat desert scrubland before the terrain yields to subtropical farming land and then on down to the sea, petering out in a slow, imperceptible dispersal of its waters into the Gulf of Mexico. Before dams the river flowed desultorily or swiftly, deep or shallow, threading its way southward, randomly shifting its channel, leaving *resacas* (sunken beds or depressions) to mark its former course. For centuries the river performed its natural functions, providing water and shade from trees along its banks. Aboriginal men and women used the river in all the ways they knew, but things changed with the coming of Europeans.

Following the bloody events of 1836, when Texas defeated Mexico and became an independent republic, Texas claimed the Rio Grande as its southern border, but Mexico refused to recognize that claim. Instead Mexico insisted that the Nueces River, 130 miles farther north, should be the boundary. The dispute, of course, had to do with land. It is easy to understand Mexico's view. All of Texas had once belonged to Mexico, and the area along the Rio Grande, on both sides of the river, had been thoroughly settled for almost a century. In 1749 José de Escandón acquired permission from the king of Spain to grant leagues of land in that part of northern Mexico stretching from the modern Mexican states of Coahuila, Nuevo Leon, and Tamaulipas across the Rio Bravo into Texas all the way to the Nueces River. Under his guidance and stewardship, families moved onto the lands and built ranchos and towns. Missions were established to convert or pacify the Indians.

The grants varied in size from narrow *porciones* that fronted on the river to huge tracts encompassing thousands of leagues of land. Escandón also established five *villas* or towns along the river, *villas del norte* as they were called. Four of them—Guerrero, Mier, Carmargo, and Reynosa—were on the south bank of the river, northwest of where Matamoros and Brownsville would later be built. The fifth, Laredo, was on the north bank of the river. Many of the ranchlands owned by citizens of the four south-bank towns lay on the northern side of the river. The point is emphatically this: the river was a river, not a boundary. What was being created here in this arid region was a civilization Spanish and Mexican in its articulations and institutions, and the people felt themselves separate from both interior Mexico and the rest of what eventually became Coahuila y Texas. About twenty thousand people lived on about a thousand ranches. Escandón's *entrada* (entrance) had been highly successful. Those original settlements and ranches nourished Tejano culture for a century before the occupation by Americans changed nearly everything. The other salient fact often ignored by Anglo historians, romancers of the West, is that the Tejanos had stocked the range with longhorn cattle. Thus the famed Texas longhorns, so celebrated in song, legend, and history, were in fact Tejano longhorns. South Texas was not an empty place on the map; there were Tejanos and their livestock, cattle and immense amounts of sheep, on that land, as there had been groups of indigenous peoples there before them and, though reduced in numbers, still there when the "Texans" came.

Almost all of the new land that became Texas descended from earlier Spanish or Mexican holdings. Fort Texas (later Fort Brown) was situated on a rancho. Downtown Brownsville was part of a rancho; everything the Anglo-Americans built (and usually renamed) was originally Spanish land-grant holdings descending through the generations to become the property of Mexican citizens following Mexico's independence from Spain in 1821.

The Anglo-Americans overran and eventually supplanted a century-long continuity of settlement, ownership, and community. The Rio Bravo/Rio del Norte/Rio Grande thus became a political and divisive boundary separating families in Matamoros, for example, from their kin on the other side of the river: two riverbanks, two countries. Such division seemed unnatural and wholly against the grain of a century of relative stability based on the ancient patterns of stock raising and farming, trade and religion, and a common language. The boundary seemed completely arbitrary to one nation and completely justified to another. Now all that land, owned by Mexicans and Tejanos dating back to 1749, was subject to new claims by the light-skinned Americanos.

It was into this complex arena of new American energy that Richard King came in 1847. There was nothing holding him in Alabama, and the whole country had been talking about Texas and Mexico for over a year. Back in the winter of 1845, when President Polk had sent out a call for 50,000 volunteers to help the U.S. regulars fight Mexico, young men from all over the country had jumped at the chance for adventure and glory. When King arrived the war had blown past the border into the interior, but it was still uppermost in everybody's mind and the events of the previous year were still fresh. King would have met plenty of officers and soldiers who had been part of General Zachary Taylor's "Army of Occupation," as it was called.

In August 1845, two years before King came to Texas, General Taylor, Old Rough and Ready, a wily veteran, "a gallant, brave old man," one lieutenant called him, brought a command of over two thousand regulars to the primitive new trading post of Corpus Christi on the Gulf of Mexico, about 170 miles north of Matamoros. There was an improvisational, up-for-grabs feeling about the entire American venture into darkest Texas that moved one of Taylor's officers, Colonel Hitchcock, to remark: "As for Texas, her original limit was the Nueces and the hills ranging north from its sources, and she has never conquered, possessed, or exercised dominion west of the Nueces, except that a small smuggling company at this place, living here by Mexican sufferance, if not under Mexican protection, has chosen to call itself Texas, and some of the inhabitants have chosen to call themselves Texans."

On March 8, 1846, General Taylor and his Army of Occupation began the long march from Corpus Christi to the border, following the road of the Arroyo Colorado, an old trail used by traders and smugglers. Thereafter it would be called Taylor's Trail. Taylor marched first to Point Isabel, then to the Rio Grande opposite Matamoros, a stone's throw away on the other side of the river. A raising of the flag on the banks of the Rio Grande prompted Lieutenant Henry to note that it proclaimed "in a silent but impressive manner that the 'area of freedom' was again extended." At first Matamoros seemed to Lieutenant Henry "like a fairy vision before our enraptured eyes," but then he admitted maybe he was laying it on a little thick. The Mexican women, however, fulfilled every dream. "Nearly all the latter have well-developed, magnificent figures," Henry wrote; "they dress with as little clothing as can well be fancied." Later he returned to the same theme: "If you are a lover of nature—*unadorned*—you can gratify your taste by walking up to Fort Paredes any pleasant evening, and witness the fair ones bathing in the Rio Grande; no offense is taken by looking at them enjoying their aquatic amusements." Excited, some soldiers dived in, only to be turned back by Mexican guards. One day, fourteen soldiers deserted by swimming across the river. After two soldiers were shot dead in the water by U.S. troops acting on orders, officers such as Colonel Hitchcock regarded such actions as "an unpleasant state of things."

Taylor ordered that a fort be constructed across from Matamoros; he named it Fort Texas. On the Mexican side preparations for war were obvious. Artillery was moved into place, and priests blessed the artillery pieces one by one. The main battles would not take place at the nascent fort, but rather eleven miles away, north of Brownsville, at Palo Alto, a broad, flat plain. At first, Taylor's army thought they would be opposed by Mexican forces led by General Pedro Ampudia, a man whose reputation preceded him in lurid terms. Ampudia was notorious for having boiled in oil the head of one of his foes in Mexico. But instead it was not Ampudia but General Mariano Arista, a man the Americans held in much higher regard, who led the Mexican army at Palo Alto on May 8. The decisive factor was the American army's superb light artillery, whose tactics were developed by Major Samuel Ringgold, who died from wounds suffered that day.

The Battle of Palo Alto ended indecisively when the prairie grass caught on fire and great billowing clouds of smoke forced both armies to cease firing. The next day, at a nearby site, Resaca de la Palma, the Americans routed Arista's soldiers. Arista and his men held good defensive ground, in the empty lake bed carved by the Rio Grande in one of its former channels, but the Americans prevailed, and Arista's army fell apart. There were many dead and wounded, many deserters, and some three hundred who drowned trying to cross the Rio Grande. A Mexican ferryman later described what he saw in the aftermath of the defeat: "They came in flocks, running and crawling like *torgugas* [turtles], and they fell into the water flat on all fours like *tortugas* and never stopped till they were in the brush of the *Republica*

Mejicana. They had been at the fight of what we call Resaca de la Palma, and I was very glad that I had not been with them."

News of these victories spurred enthusiasm for the war throughout the nation, and the names of heroes were kept alive on the border. Richard King would have known those names. Ringgold Barracks at Laredo was named in honor of Major Ringgold; Fort Brown, originally Fort Texas, was renamed in honor of Maj. Jacob Brown, who, left in charge of the fort by General Taylor, was killed by Mexican cannon fire from across the river; and the first boat Richard King commanded on the Rio Grande, the *Colonel Cross,* was named for a popular officer, Truman Cross, "a high-minded, chivalric gentleman" killed in April by unknown assassins. Reminders of the battles were vivid in 1847 when King arrived, and for years to come. After the war, American army officers and their wives dined on an ornate silver service set abandoned by General Arista during the pell-mell flight from Resaca de la Palma.

Though the Mexican War is now largely forgotten by the rest of the country, the memory of it along the border and throughout South Texas remains strong in the minds of some who feel a measure of ambivalence about the political identities forged by blood and treaty. Such feelings come out in all sorts of ways, even today. Yolanda Gonzalez, a librarian at The University of Texas at Brownsville, located on the grounds of Fort Texas/Brown, told me of the fight that occurred back in the 1980s when a new library was to be named. When the Mexican-American and Mexican communities learned that the library was going to be named after Zachary Taylor, objections were raised and it was called instead the Arnuflo L. Oliveria Library, after a prominent educator in the valley. According to Mrs. Gonzalez, Zachary Taylor arranged to rent the land on which Fort Texas/Brown was built from an ancestor of hers who owned the land (it was a rancho then), but Taylor's government had never paid a dime for it. Each year Yolanda Gonzalez totes up what the U.S. government owes her family.

Similary, in Corpus Christi a recent effort to memorialize the encampment of Zachary Taylor's army there in 1845–46 has collapsed in the face of opposition. Proponents planned to construct Artesian Park in downtown Corpus Christi, with a hundred miniature pup tents to symbolize the American army and a hill to symbolize Aztec pyramids. Anthony Quiroz, an assistant professor of history at

Texas A&M-Corpus Christi, said of the controversy, "I knew it was going to ruffle some feathers. The truth is there are still scars. For Mexican-Americans, this war represents stealing their homeland."

So it was in the late nineteenth century, after the conquest, after the dust had presumably settled. Late in his life, in 1892, Mifflin Kenedy wrote: "For many years, Captain King and myself tried to Americanize that portion of the country [in Cameron County, on the Rio Grande], but we failed; it is very little more American in feeling today than it was in October 1848 when the Americans evacuated Matamoros and crossed over to this side."

The war in Texas spelled golden opportunities for steamboat pilots on the Rio Grande. The army required a lot of shipping of men and supplies from the gulf upstream to Fort Brown and Rio Grande City, Roma, and Camargo. In fact, the needs of the army created the economic opportunity that would propel Richard King and Mifflin Kenedy into achieving wealth in Brownsville, which wasn't even built yet when King arrived.

Acting upon Kenedy's invitation, King arrived just in time to provide the U.S. Army with reliable transportation of both goods and men. On June 13, 1847, King secured a position as one of three second pilots on the *Colonel Cross,* a side-wheeler of 160 tons, built in Shousetown, Pennsylvania, in 1846, owned by the United States Quartermaster Department (USQMD). After just seventeen days he was transferred to the *Corvette* (149 tons, Brownsville, Pennsylvania, USQMD) as first pilot. Sometime later, just before he turned twenty-four, he was made captain of the *Colonel Cross.*

The twisty, shallow, sandbar-treacherous Rio Grande would put King and Kenedy to the test. Most newcomers to the region remarked upon the disparity between the river's impressive name and its actuality. Abner Doubleday spoke of the army's disappointment upon first seeing the river: "Our people too labored under the delusion that the Rio Grande being a thousand miles long must form near its mouth a deep and wide line of defense and that it would be good policy to take possession of it as soon as possible. In reality it can be forded at a great many points during the dry season, and its convolutions are so remarkable that in a line of twenty-five miles from Brownsville to the mouth of the river the distance is more than a hundred miles by water."

Major Luther Giddings, an Ohio volunteer who went up the river by steamboat in the summer of 1846, called it "the most crooked stream on the continent," and he didn't think much of the *tierra caliente* through which it flowed either, saying if the river "were but straight, its homeliness would be complete."

Problems faced in negotiating the river were formidable. Steamboats had difficulty getting enough power to go upstream against a strong current. Boats that made six miles per hour on the Mississippi were hard-pressed to make two miles per hour on the Rio Grande. The only wood available for power was mesquite, which burned slowly and with little blaze. Sandbars and shallow spots in the river were a constant threat. Swarms of mosquitoes tormented crew and passengers alike. There was always the danger of a boiler exploding. Boats more or less crept up the river, taking an average of four to six days to reach Roma, the northernmost point of navigability. Mifflin Kenedy made one memorably fast trip from the mouth of the river to Camargo (south of Roma, on the Mexican side) in three days, in 1846.

Although King and Kenedy left no accounts of their experiences on the Rio Grande, there were other observers in those years who did. Major Giddings described an ascent he made on a "frail and filthy little steamboat" in August 1846. The boat carried four companies from his regiment; their destination was Camargo, where General Taylor would assemble his army for the eventual campaign at Buena Vista in the interior.

It took the boat Giddings was on over a week to reach Camargo, slowed down as it was by high water, the ignorance of pilots, and lack of wood for the boilers. Soldiers had to be dispatched to bring back wood from picket fences, and in some places the river's banks were out and the boat wandered around until it found the proper channel again. On both sides of the river dwellers at the *rancherias* gathered to watch the boat's struggles. Flocks of waterfowl fluttered away when the boat came near, and sometimes the bloated carcasses of dead animals floated past in the flood-raised river. The whole trip, Giddings pronounced, was "more tedious than hazardous." The incompetence of the pilots that Giddings spoke of was a commonplace of army observers in 1846–47. That is why the coming of Kenedy and King, both excellent and experienced pilots who would learn the shifting subtleties of the Rio Grande quickly, was a blessing to the army, which relied on the steamboats to move men to the staging area at Camargo.

Teresa Vielé, army wife and journalist, sailed with her husband on the *Corvette* in 1852, the same boat Richard King had piloted back in 1847 when he came to South Texas. The journey from Brownsville to Ringgold Barracks at Rio Grande City where Lieutenant Vielé was stationed moved at the usual slow pace. They were afloat four days on the "serpentine" river and were stuck several times on sandbars, for which they were in a way thankful, she said, as these incidents were novel and relieved the dominant feeling of tedium.

In November 1847 a very famous passenger steamed down the Rio Grande aboard the *Colonel Cross:* General Zachary Taylor. Perhaps King was at the helm. Fresh from victory at Buena Vista, Taylor was on a journey that would take him to the White House. Richard King was on a journey, too, that would carry him beyond the river into the grasslands of the interior. But he still had many trips to make up and down the Rio Grande.

CHAPTER 2

The Quartermaster's Depot

From his post in Matamoros, Quartermaster Major W. W. Chapman saw the American town being thrown up on the other side of the river. Indeed, he had a hand in its growth and development, and he may even have been the one who gave the town its name. The June 24–28, 1848, issue of the local paper, the *American Flag*, celebrated the town's emergence: "The Quartermaster's Department here is busily engaged in erecting buildings and temporary sheds on the opposite bank of the river, preparatory to the transfer of quarters from this city [Matamoros]."

The *Flag* announced that the "embryo city" would be named Athens and that it already possessed "thousands of magnificent houses" and "thousands upon thousands of industrious and enterprising citizens." In the very next issue of the *Flag*, however, there appeared a letter that proposed another, better name: Brownsville, "in memory of the gallant Major Brown." Athens, the writer pointed out, was "stale and worn out," a name so overused that "a letter to Athens, generally makes the circuit of the whole Union in search of its proper destination." The letter was signed "C," leading some historians to believe it was the quartermaster who had penned it.

In any event, the name Brownsville stuck, and by January 1849, the newest city upon a hill rose up on the north bank of the river, built at impressive speed. Helen Chapman, the quartermaster's wife, adopting the rhetoric of Manifest Destiny, caught the drama of the scramble to build Brownsville in a letter to her mother: "It was that of an *old race* passing away—a n*ew race* pressing on its departing footsteps—a new scene in the *history of the Country, a possession by conquest.*" A

33

local correspondent described a similar scene in early 1850: "Buildings are going up every day; goods arriving, steamboats loading and unloading, and every person seems engaged to some useful employment . . ." By contrast, Matamoros, its neighbor across the river, founded in 1823, was older and larger, with a population of over seven thousand.

The hot blast of history had made Brownsville viable, and after the war ended, there was something of a boom in the newborn city. There was trade with northern Mexico, and there were also the new gold fields in California. Argonauts taking the overland route to California found Brownsville a convenient place for provisioning before the long trek west. When John W. Audubon's party of California-bound gold seekers arrived in Brownsville in March 1849, he was struck by its typicality as a Southern village—the heat, the lethargy. At three o'clock in the afternoon "the rolling of bowling-alleys and the cannoning of billiard balls was all that seemed to enliven the village at that hour." The more Audubon saw of Brownsville, the more typical it seemed: "Like thousands of others in our Southern states; little work and large profits give an undue share of leisure without education or refinement, consequently drinking-houses and billiards with the etc. are abundant."

Teresa Vielé, arriving in 1851, called Brownsville a "curious, half-breed town." Like other travelers who recorded their impressions, she was struck by the apparent contrasts between the new American presence and the older Mexican element. The "rudely constructed huts" where "five generations" of a "vanishing people" (Mexicans) lived together were giving way to the "red brick stores, and white frame shops and buildings of every description," all of which, she said, "bore the marks of inevitable progress, or go-aheadativeness, otherwise called 'manifest destiny.'" Vielé's vernacular definition of Manifest Destiny as "go-aheadativeness" cannot be improved upon.

Boosterism aside, Brownsville had plenty of vice to go around. Abbé Domenech, who was "struck with the animation of Brownsville," recognized in the new town the same characteristics of all the towns scattered along the Texas border frontier: "The Americans of the Texian frontiers are, for the most part, the very scum of society—bankrupts, escaped criminals, old volunteers, who after the treaty of Guadalupe Hidalgo, came into a country protected by nothing that could be called a judicial authority, to seek adventure and illicit gains." Teresa Vielé held similarly dim views of the general state of things along the border: "There was never a country more unfitted by nature to be the home of civilized man, than this region of the lower Rio Grande in Texas. It seems to hate civilization." She went on, "It seems only to be intended as a home for desperate men, escaped refugees from the law; men who live in the saddle, and on the prairie seek their subsistence; such as give to Texas any bad reputation its population may have."

Law was erratic, and the Brownsville jail an easy one to escape from. Brownsville was a center for smugglers, and every sort of frontier hard case menaced its streets and the nearby countryside. In its gambling and drinking establishments men soaked themselves in alcohol, played billiards and cards, gambled, fought, and killed each other. The town was wild, bursting at the seams with men looking for a fast profit, legally or otherwise. Drunkards loitered everywhere, and some men died of drink. Abbé Domenech took note of public intoxication: "The greatest number of those I saw drunk were Mexicans who are not much accustomed to spirituous drinks, and Americans belonging to the temperance societies." According to the abbé, the Americans who pledged to stop drinking wine went right ahead with drinking spirits. In the grog shops, taverns, and barrooms drunken men fought duels over honor or over nothing. Instead of the law, men substituted the "Texas Code of Practice"—the sidearm—to settle disputes. Abbé Domenech related a story about an American merchant who killed an Irishman over some suspected slight. "At Brownsville, and along the entire Texian frontier, murder is very common," the abbé concluded.

Justice was sometimes brutal. There were floggings in the town square. To her horror, Helen Chapman happened upon one. Abbé Domenech spoke of Mexicans being flogged to the point of death when taken into custody for some real or imagined offense: "I saw at Brownsville Mexicans whom the sheriff was flogging to death with his ox-hide lash. They were bound, half-naked, their arms extended across the prison door, and then scourged on the sides and loins with the most brutal violence." Murderers were hanged if the case ever reached the courts, sometimes without benefit of a trial. Abbé Domenech described a lynching that he witnessed. A crowd in

Brownsville was asked to vote on whether to hang an American who had stabbed (fatally, it turned out) a Mexican at a fandango. The crowd voted enthusiastically in favor of the execution, and when the sheriff/hangman proved incompetent to tie the knot, the condemned man did so himself and made a short temperance speech blaming drink for his fate ("It is drunkenness that has put me into this cart").

Most men carried weapons in town, and certainly all did when traveling anywhere in the interior. The Avalos Banditti, a local gang, robbed with impunity. Indian raids all around Brownsville, north and south, kept citizens on edge. The Comanches made lightning assaults on Mexican villages, stealing and killing as they pleased, and on Americans when opportunity offered. In 1849, for example, Indians attacked the stage from Point (later, Port) Isabel, northeast of Brownsville, killing several people. An aged woman, pierced with lances and arrows, survived but, according to the local newspaper, was changed into a "maniac." The army was completely ineffectual in stopping the attacks, sending infantry on foot or in wagons, while the Comanches, on their fleet horses, rode like the best light cavalry in the world. Mexican authorities paid bounties for Indian scalps, and bloodthirsty scalp hunters like John Glanton and his outlaw gang took scalps indiscriminately, selling those of Indians and of Mexican peons—men, women, and children—for high prices to the government of Chihuahua in northern Mexico. The pay rate of $200 per scalp exceeded a soldier's wages for a year.

Bustling, violent, pestilential, corrupt, Brownsville displayed the tawdry edges of Manifest Destiny's westward sprawl. At night thousands of dogs barked in the streets, and mosquitoes tormented the sleepers. Teresa Vielé pronounced Brownsville the "birthplace of the flea" and said that "vermin are the scourge of this country." Cholera and yellow fever epidemics were still to be feared. In 1849 cholera ravaged the area. John W. Audubon lost ten men from his party to cholera in a camp opposite Rio Grande City, and Helen Chapman came down with the disease at Brazos Santiago but pulled through.

And this was where Richard King, like many another young man, cast his future. In the first six months of 1849, 475 Mexican passports were issued, three-fourths of them to single men with an average age of thirty. To such men, Richard King among them, Brownsville smelled of money, and a dozen years into its existence the town could boast of a surprising number of rich men, including two captains of steamboats, Richard King and Mifflin Kenedy.

For a time after the army departed, there was no work on the river because army supplies and troops provided the principal business, so King lived by other means. While waiting for the river traffic to revive, he operated a combination flophouse and grog shop at Brazos Santiago—doubtless one of these "common bars" mentioned by Helen Chapman. He was sole proprietor, bartender, bouncer, and bedmaker. The clientele was border riffraff, of which there was a seemingly endless supply. Smugglers operated openly on the other side of the river at the little village of Bagdad. King himself left no record of those days at Brazos Santiago. The port was still bleak and spartan, a way station for the flotsam and jetsam that always filter down to outlaw beaches and borders.

In the summer after the final acceptance of the Treaty of Guadalupe Hidalgo, in May 1848, the U.S. Quartermaster auctioned off the boats purchased by the army during the war. The prices were incredible, the best deal going. Richard King bought his old boat, the *Colonel Cross*, for $750, a fraction of the $14,000 the army had paid for it. The economy, stimulated by the war, did not fade entirely with the departure of the troops, and forts upriver still in operation required regular supplies. There was still a lot of money to be made on the river.

Together with Mifflin Kenedy, King freighted goods and passengers from Brazos Santiago to Matamoros, Rio Grande City, Roma, and other towns along the river. Kenedy engaged in other ventures, traveling inland into northern Mexico to trade goods for silver. In 1850 King joined with his close friend in a business venture that would prove highly lucrative in the years ahead. Along with some others, they formed a partnership named M. Kenedy and Co. Besides Kenedy and King, the other partners were Charles Stillman, who had believed in riverboat trade for years; Robert Penny; and James O'Donnell. They hoped to dominate steamboat trade on the river, but to do so, King felt, they needed new boats. To that end, he sketched a model of the kinds of boats that would be more efficient and easier to handle. Instead of using one style of boat for both the river and the gulf waters, two different types were needed. He envisioned a bigger, bulkier boat to perform the short hauling tasks from Brazos Santiago to the mouth of the river and Point Isabel, and a smaller, lighter, faster craft to negotiate the winding, deceptive river. Kenedy took the suggestions with him to Pittsburgh, and by 1852 the *Grampus* and the *Comanche* were performing the work assigned them just as King had imagined. The *Grampus,* at 221 tons, was used for the slower, heavier work at the coast, and the *Comanche,* at 164 tons, proved effective in plying the river upstream.

Even so, piloting the river was still a tough job. Abbé Domenech journeyed upriver sometime after 1850, aboard the *Comanche.* Although the boat was new, the conditions of travel on the river were still highly uncomfortable. The heat, he said, was "quite suffocating." In the daytime they were "smothered in an atmosphere of fire," and in the evenings they slept on deck to take such breezes as there might be. After three or four days on the water, the boat stuck so fast that the cargo had to be removed, and the travelers were forced to complete the rest of their journey by land.

But all difficulties aside, the steamboat business was profitable, and what really assured the success of M. Kenedy and Co. was the sweetheart deal they made with the government. Theoretically, capitalism thrives on competition, but what capitalists really like is a monopoly, and M. Kenedy and Co. had one. One of the chief agents of this monopolistic arrangement was Major Chapman. Through his help, M. Kenedy and Co. acquired a government contract to supply the forts along the river. What Chapman did was simple enough: He recommended to his superiors that the army award its contract with M. Kenedy and Co. without competitive bids. As a rationale for his recommendation, Chapman emphasized the desirability of using the new boats and praised their owners as being "responsible and reliable" men. At the end of one letter, he made the case for a complete monopoly on behalf of M. Kenedy and Co.: ". . . as they own the only good boats on the Rio Grande, *they are the only persons with whom it would be judicious to make a contract.*" It was not true that they owned the only good boats on the river, but they were his friends and they did have good boats.

Was there a quid pro quo? Did Chapman receive anything for his help? Although rumors persisted in Brownsville that he was also a partner in M. Kenedy and Co., this was never proven. Chapman seems to have benefited, however, from real estate ventures, and real estate was one of the specialties of M. Kenedy and Co. partner Charles Stillman. The city of Brownsville was Stillman's idea in the first place. When the Mexican War ended, Stillman looked around and saw the need for a commercial town to capitalize on the coming land boom. Fort Brown, situated upon a low bluff, was subject to flooding, but adjacent to it on the north side lay better ground, and it was here that Stillman commissioned a surveyor to measure out town lots. He established a store on Levee Street, close to the river. He named many of Brownsville's early streets, a succession of thoroughfares running north and south honoring presidents of the United States—Washington through Polk. For some other streets he drew upon personal history. Elizabeth Street, which would become the main street of Brownsville, he named after the woman he would marry, and St. Charles Street he named after himself. It was on Elizabeth Street that he built a brick house, the first in Brownsville. Here his wife joined him in 1849.

Chapman, a friend of Stillman's, was also involved in these years in real estate speculation in Brownsville. Helen Chapman was worried enough about it in April 1849 to caution her mother emphatically: "*Do not say to any one that William has been speculating.*" In 1850 Chapman plunged into more real estate investments under the helpful eye of Stillman, the craftiest entrepreneur in Brownsville. A warehouse that Chapman owned somehow became the official U.S. Customs House. In January 1851, Helen again spoke of her husband's penchant for speculation: "The Major is very sanguine that he will, before he dies, become a very rich man. I think the chances are about equal that he may become very rich or find himself all at once without a cent." William, on the other hand, adopted a rather jaunty manner regarding his speculation. In a letter to his mother-in-law on March 16, 1851, he mentioned the silver mine venture: "Now, Mother, please don't laugh about that *Silver mine*. For the end is not yet. I went into it with my eyes wide open, fully knowing it to be a perfect lottery, heads I win, tails I lose. It will be just $1,000 lost, or a 'Pile' made."

Locally, other businessmen complained about the handling of the contract with M. Kenedy and Co. One letter from a friend of Major Chapman's, written to President Fillmore, while trying to defend him, mentioned all of the suspicions about the major, especially the most harmful one, that he "owns part of these steamboats that has the contract to carry government freight now." At about the same time, a well-known Brownsville citizen and member of the Texas House of Representatives, Robert B. Kingsbury, laid out the case against M. Kenedy and Co. in a strongly worded letter sent to U. S. Congressman Volney Howard: "Great surprise and dissatisfaction here in consequence of the Quarter Master General having contracted at an enormous rate with a Steamboat Company for the transportation of Government Freights . . . The principal stock holders in this Company are Major Chapman and Charly Stillman although they do not appear as interested in the boats . . . Chapman so managed the deal that the government boats were not offered for sale until Captain Kenedy had gone to Washington and closed the deal with General Jesup. The company, it is understood, receive about double the rate that the contract would have been taken at provided there had been any competition. I think it is a damned corrupt and unhealthy state of affairs." Later, in a follow-up letter, Kingsbury hedged his bet and said he didn't want his name mentioned in any further connection with these events: "The masters of the Steamers are very clever men and friends of mine and perhaps would think very hard of me if they should know."

Chapman's role in the affairs of M. Kenedy and Co. continued, though from a distance, when he was assigned in 1852 to a new post at Corpus Christi.

When the steamboat contract expired in February 1854, a new one was not granted for several months, until July. The rates for shipping were cut, as the existing ones had been about double what they should have been, but there were still no competitive bids. However, the next year, Jefferson Davis, the new secretary of war, ordered in March that a new contract be negotiated—*with competitive bids.*

M. Kenedy and Co. entered a bid based on the same rates as their 1854 contract, but a new contender, Capt. James B. Armstrong, offered a bid that promised lower rates for every type of commodity. In June, J. P. Garesch, who had replaced Chapman in Brownsville, awarded the contract to the best bid—Armstrong's. There was already bad blood between Kenedy and Armstrong. With business booming on the river, Kenedy had hired Armstrong to pilot the *Comanche,* but they had quarreled and Armstrong had been demoted. Back in 1849 Armstrong and Chapman had a run-in; their mutual animosity was well known on the river. So against a background of personal dislike, intense behind-the-scene maneuvers on the part of M. Kenedy and Co. were launched to reverse the decision in their own favor instead of Armstrong's.

Kenedy mounted a campaign to undermine confidence in Armstrong. In a letter to Col. Charles Thomas, General Jesup's aide, Kennedy claimed that he, Stillman, and King were the only reliable bidders and that Armstrong lacked backing as well as sufficient boats. In fact, Armstrong's financial situation was strong and his boats in good condition. He also had the wherewithal to acquire more boats. But the biggest impediment was one insisted upon by Kenedy: Armstrong must be made to adhere to every point in the contract by the date set, August 1, a very short deadline. Such arguments won favor with M. Kenedy and Co.'s old friend in the army, General Jesup. Chapman, from Corpus Christi, was again deeply involved in the flurry of letters and lobbying, acting as an advocate, as usual, for M. Kenedy and Co. On July 15, Chapman informed Garesch that the agreement with Armstrong was suspended on the basis of doubts about his backing and ability to acquire suitable boats. Garesch stood firmly behind Armstrong. In a letter of July 24, Garesch made the point as emphatically as possible: "I am bound to say that . . . I think Mr. Armstrong quite as responsible, as reliable, and as capable of carrying out his contract as either Capt. Kenedy or Capt. King; and rather more so than one or two persons whose names I have heard mentioned as connected with the company." (O'Donnell, incidentally, thought so highly of Armstrong that he had at one time offered to sell him his share in M. Kenedy and Co. for $8,000, but Kenedy would not allow it because of the bad feeling between him and Armstrong.)

King himself made a trip to Corpus Christi to meet with Chapman in late July, and afterward Kenedy wrote another letter urging Jesup to ignore all of Armstrong's compliances in favor of his and his partners' track record. The war of words heated up when Brownsville citizens sent General Jesup a letter itemizing their complaints about Chapman's behavior, specifically that "it is believed that Chapman has used the patronage & influence of his office to the prejudice of private citizens, and has manifested undue partiality with honest competition for Govt. Service." The authors of the letter included documents related to Chapman's real estate dealings between 1850 and 1852.

More letters and more lobbying ensued. Chapman continued to push M. Kenedy and Co.'s cause at every opportunity, and Garesch became so disgusted that he resigned his post in Brownsville and was reassigned, with promotion, to Washington. As the months rolled by, the matter remained unsettled; in the meantime, the boats of M. Kenedy and Co. continued to handle all government shipping on the river. Finally in March of the next year, 1856, a board was appointed to inspect Armstrong's boats. The inspection was sloppy and unprofessional, but it rendered the judgment that Chapman and M. Kenedy and Co. wanted: The board said Armstrong was unsuited for the contract.

Always friendly to M. Kenedy and Co.'s interests before, now General Jesup instructed the new assistant quartermaster in Brownsville to ship government supplies on whichever boat was available at time of need, Armstrong's or M. Kenedy and Co.'s—a decision that virtually admitted that Armstrong should have been awarded the contract. But it still favored M. Kenedy and Co. because they owned two more boats than Armstrong and would therefore be in a better position to have a boat available when needed.

The army wasn't off the hook, though. Financial backers of Armstrong were angry about the suspension and the entire handling of the matter, and they wanted the suspension lifted. The lawyer they hired, the best in the valley, was Stephen Powers, who argued in a letter, "Certain it is that very extraordinary measures were taken to keep [the contract] out of Armstrong's hands." As remedy, Powers recommended damages for "past [breaches] of the contract." The result was an immediate appeal to the Court of Claims. When the decision came down, over a year later, in 1858, the court found that Armstrong had been wrongfully deprived of his contract. Damages were set at $17,000, the amount that was reckoned lost during the period of the suspension. But Armstrong wasn't around to enjoy the victory, having died the preceding year.

The advantages of doing business with the army become evident by looking at a typical army contract. In a contract dated November 14, 1856, Richard King and an officer of the 1st Artillery, U.S. Army, agreed that King would "transport on a good Steam Boat, or Boats, from Brazos Santiago, Texas, to Fort Brown, Texas, the companies of L and N first Artillery U.S. Army and twelve men, Band of 2nd

Cavalry with all their baggage, stores, and all other property of and belonging to Said Companies." For this service, King would be paid $960 upon completion. M. Kenedy and Co. made hundreds and hundreds of such contracts during the years they controlled the river. And the monopoly continued to draw fire from the press. A Brownsville correspondent for the *Nueces Valley* observed in March 1858: "The present monoply line are getting rich too fast, and too much at the expense of the people. They are clever men, but that does not justify them in making every body else hewers of wood and drawers of water for them."

The gold flowed on.

Ripples from the great steamboat monopoly case continued to be felt. Sometime in late 1856 or early 1857 General Jesup, Chapman's longtime champion, ordered Chapman to report to the Department of the Pacific immediately. But Chapman managed to forestall that exile and wound up at a series of postings on the East Coast. He testified in the Court of Claims in 1858, and in the fall of 1859, he died by his own hand. According to an officer who knew him, Chapman was "subject to fits of depression."

The years 1850 to 1854 were decisive ones for Richard King. By the end of this period he had made important strides in three areas: steamboating, ranching, and romance. These three strands of activity sometimes paralleled one another and sometimes intersected in very complex ways. On the Rio Grande the steamboat trade waxed and waned with the shifting currents of water flow and economic fortune, and beyond, in the Wild Horse Desert where the land lay waiting, he launched into the venture of a lifetime that would define his contribution to the history of Texas and the West. He also courted and won the preacher's daughter. In those years he moved steadily toward his own personal destiny, which often tallied nicely with the aims of Manifest Destiny.

CHAPTER 3

The Preacher and the Preacher's Daughter

In January 1850 Major W. W. Chapman wrote his mother-in-law a letter from the primitive port at Brazos Santiago, where he and his wife lived from time to time as he carried out his duties as quartermaster. Wanting to provide "a little idea of Texas life," he told her of having recently dealt with two men. One was a murderer, the other a preacher. "After I had secured and double ironed the prisoner," he wrote, "I sent the parson, his wife, three children with one at the breast in my carriage to Brownsville. I sent the prisoner to Brownsville yesterday after the parson to equalize the morals of the place." The parson was Hiram Chamberlain, the future father-in-law of Richard King.

The Chapmans—or Helen, at any rate—did not like Reverend Chamberlain's wife, who, when the Chamberlains arrived that day at Brazos Santiago, complained about the boat, the passage, and the bedraggled appearance of herself and her family caused by the difficult journey. Helen thought that she complained too much, that she didn't act the way a minister's wife should. In Helen's view, Mrs. Chamberlain spoke with "the languid drawling sort of tone of a spoiled woman of ease and fashion." She also left the task of tending the baby to her husband, so that Helen wrote bitingly that "it was easy to see that instead of poring over theology in his study, he held the Office of Baby's Arms." Of his children, Helen Chapman had this to say: "The eldest daughter was a bright, intelligent, pretty girl, and the other three were large healthy children, but undisciplined." The eldest daughter was Henrietta Morse Chamberlain, who would eventually marry Richard King.

Curiously, King family legend subscribes to an entirely different story of the arrival of the Chamberlains in Texas. According to Tom Lea and many other accounts, the Chamberlains came to Texas overland, wife and children in a coach, and the reverend riding alongside them on a mule. Helen Chapman's firsthand contemporaneous account obviously scotches the mule version. But why did it exist in the first place? Was this a conscious—or unconscious—effort to obscure the Chamberlains' early contacts with the Chapmans? Once recognized, the irony of Helen Chapman's role in bringing together the two people who would create King Ranch might be something one would not want to dwell upon, considering all that happened.

It had been in part Helen Chapman's avid desire to improve the morals and religious conditions of the new town of Brownsville that brought the Chamberlains to Texas in the first place. She had written letters back east asking for someone to come and preach to the flock in this faraway outpost. She was not alone. In a little book written by missionary Melinda Rankin published in 1850 and titled *Texas in 1850*, Miss Rankin asked, "Who among the highly favored of New England's products will come and cultivate the rich soil of Texas mind?" Near the end of her book she mentions the arrival of a possible answer, a Presbyterian clergyman "who promises great usefulness in this important field of labor." That clergyman was Hiram Chamberlain.

On paper, Reverend Chamberlain seemed to be exactly what the Protestants in Brownsville required. He had been a doughty missionary all his adult life. Born in Vermont in 1797, he had a solid education and a fervent commitment to spreading the gospel in benighted regions. His first wife, Maria Morse, Henrietta's mother, must have had doubts about the difficulties of being a missionary's wife, considering the letter he wrote her just prior to their marriage. In that letter he wondered "that there was self-denial enough in any female's heart to lead her to become the companion of a stranger in a strange land." Yet that is precisely what he required of her, and he spelled out the virtues she would need: "piety, self-denial, and a strength of affection." He pledged on his part to maintain her "comfort and her happiness with feelings of untenable tenderness." Together they would enter into "pagan lands" and perform "great work in the West." The West was first St. Louis and, following that, a series of pastoral duties in various towns in Missouri. In 1832, Maria gave birth to Henrietta and just three years later perished in childbirth, along with the baby. Hiram married twice more and had eight more children, but his first wife and the daughter she gave him remained strong in his affections.

As for the young Henrietta, she had to endure the nomadic upheavals of a missionary's daughter, along with the early deaths of her mother and first stepmother and several siblings. Life was a stern affair, a perfect exemplar of her father's rock-hard Presbyterianism. But the father and his family were prospering materially by the 1840s, enough so that the fourteen-year-old Henrietta was sent, in 1846, to a fine finishing school, Holly Springs Female Institute in Mississippi, where planters' daughters received instruction in grammar, algebra, moral philosophy, and French, and for more domestic uses, ornamental needlework in floss, chenille, worsted, beads, and gold and silver embroidery. While at school, she received letters from her father offering practical advice such as to sit up straight in order to achieve a "round chest" and thereby avoid the "horrors of diphtheria and consumption" and to learn to "spell all your words exactly right." In one letter he gave her a serious lecture about Life. The young girl had written home expressing her feelings of missing the "affectionate presence" of her three-year-old half-brother. Hiram Chamberlain went straight to the point: "You say you dream about him. This gives me some uneasiness. I fear you are getting nervous and unhappy in being away from home. This will never do." He told her to buck up and overcome such depressing thoughts. "It is your religious duty," he told her. "We were not made to be *perfectly* happy here." He went on to offer examples of the necessity of being away from home. He reminded her of her grandfather who had fought in the Revolutionary War, enduring frozen ground and bullets, and challenged her, "Can't you be a soldier for a few months?" Finally, he urged her to "put on a noble resolution." He signed it "your affectionate Father." Henrietta soldiered on, completed finishing school in 1848, and in less than two years found herself with her father and the rest of the family in a new pagan land, with much work to do. Texas was swarming with sin, and there were Catholics everywhere.

Helen Chapman attended the first sermon offered by Hiram Chamberlain, along with eighteen other souls, on February 23, 1850. The service was held onboard the *Whiteville,* an old, out-of-service boat that had been converted into a rental property because of housing shortages in Brownsville, which two years before had carried the Chapmans upriver on their maiden voyage to Matamoros.

Helen Chapman attended many of Reverend Chamberlain's services, but as a preacher he was a disappointment to her and to others. Just about everybody who ever heard Reverend Chamberlain preach thought he was dull. Helen Chapman compared him unfavorably to another minister, Neamiah A. Cravens, a Methodist, who built a small church and started preaching in May 1850. She said of Chamberlain, "His manner is not popular. He is prosy and monotonous in the pulpit and does not [talk] with the men like Mr. Cravens [does]." That was in August 1850.

Cravens went out among the people and worked hard to help down-and-out men stop drinking. Apparently there was a great deal of drunkenness to contend with. Helen Chapman reported many times on the evils of widespread drinking, saying at one point that "the young men of Brownsville are drinking themselves almost to death." In October 1850, Helen returned to the theme: "Mr. Cravens, the Methodist Minister, is really doing some good. Mr. Chamberlain with his slow and old fashioned jog trot preaching is not even looked at." Chamberlain, however, drew some favorable comment from the local newspaper when he attended the execution of a man convicted of murder and "made an impressive prayer in behalf of the prisoner." The last words of the murderer, Howard Slaughter, were in the spirit of the times: "Beware of Liquor, for it has brought me to this."

Others noted that Reverend Chamberlain preached mostly about the evils of Catholicism. Melinda Rankin wrote that Reverend Chamberlain's favorite sermons had to do with the "moral elevation of degraded Mexico and the dispersal of the darkened shadows of Romanism like dew before the morning sun." What drew the most unfavorable comment, however, was the fact that Chamberlain managed to get a large frame parsonage built in a hurry, his first year in Brownsville, at 9th and Elizabeth Streets. The new parsonage irked more than one observer.

Abbé Domenech, who considered Methodist and Presbyterian ministers the "most ignorant and the most intolerant" of the Protestant clergy he saw on the frontier, had a very low opinion of Reverend Chamberlain. In his book *Missionary Adventures in Texas and Mexico: A Personal Narrative of Six Years' Sojourn in Those Regions*,

Domenech sketches Chamberlain's actions and their consequences: "The Presbyterian . . . alienated the minds of his co-religionists by equivocal conduct in a rather serious case." The Presbyterian, Domenech continued, had raised money to build a church but had instead built his family a fine house. "Henceforth," Domenech wrote, "he was completely abandoned—his family and a few friends now constituting his entire auditory. His discourses were for the most part diatribes against the Pope and Papacy, subjects highly relished by the Presbyterians . . ." But the abbé did find one good thing to say about Reverend Chamberlain: "Notwithstanding his hatred of Catholic priests, he never was hostile to me personally; whenever I met him in the street, I saluted him, and he politely returned my greeting." Teresa Vielé also included a highly negative picture of Reverend Chamberlain in her memoir of the border. She spoke of a "wandering Presbyterian" who after collecting "an ample subscription from the people, for the purpose of building a church, invested it in a parsonage, built on a lot of his own ground!"

Not surprisingly, Helen Chapman also strongly disapproved of Reverend Chamberlain's demand for $1,200 per annum in addition to his house. Helen felt that Chamberlain's wife, with her "fine lady air," was much to blame. Helen was especially put out at Mrs. Chamberlain's complaint about the small rooms where she and her family were living and her desire to have a parlor as grand as Mrs. Chapman's. According to Helen, such complaints did not make the preacher's wife popular in Brownsville. Helen felt sorry for Reverend Chamberlain, though. "He looks feeble and dyspeptic, is undoubtedly worried and annoyed at home and altogether is much to be pitied."

Even so, Reverend Chamberlain forged ahead in his efforts to carry out the tasks of a man of the Lord come to a barbarous kind. He conducted church and Sunday school services, performed marriages, and prayed for the souls of those who were about to be hanged.

Sometime in February 1850, the same month the reverend preached his first sermon in Brownsville, Richard King, pilot of the *Colonel Cross,* had an encounter with the preacher's daughter. King meant to anchor his boat where he always did, but the way was blocked by the *Whiteville.* The story as it comes down to us, enshrined in Tom Lea's book and barnacled over with too much repetition (it's a staple of King Ranch tours), sounds like a scene from a Tracy–Hepburn

Henrietta King, the widow
of the famous Captain
Richard King, in May 1914
at age 81.

movie (or better yet, something out of *The African Queen* with Bogart
and, again, Hepburn). A gruff he-man type, a riverboat captain,
exhausted from battling the currents of the Rio Grande, comes puffing
into the purlieus of Brownsville, ready to dock at his accustomed place
when lo and behold, he runs smack into a vision of gentility, Victorian
propriety, and high-spiritedness that would make the toughest old salt
quail before her righteous indignation. He hurls imprecations at the
boat that's blocking his way, and she, all flounces and lace, appears on
deck and dresses him down, firmly, in correct English, and with that
spark of fire that sets a man's soul aflame. This is where she lives with
her family, she says indignantly, and she has never seen so rude a man
as the unkempt captain, et cetera. And so, although the roughneck
captain has to find another place to dock his boat, he cannot put the
image of the young woman out of his mind.

Smitten, the story goes, he set out to meet her and most probably
did so by attending Reverend Chamberlain's services. Family legend
tells a story of Mifflin Kenedy's bemusement at his younger friend's
sudden interest in religion.

Before Richard King's suit could proceed full steam ahead, however, there was another matter to be taken care of. At some point

either right before or after she met Richard King, Henrietta Chamberlain became engaged to another young man in Brownsville, W. N. Stansbury.

Who was Stansbury? Nobody seems to have recorded anything about him (he certainly does not appear in Tom Lea's book) except Helen Chapman. Helen knew him; she knew everybody (except, apparently, Richard King). On the basis of their first meeting, Helen considered Stansbury a "very excellent and well educated young man." A Methodist, he was superintendent of the Sunday school in Brownsville in 1850.

Later, when Helen Chapman became better acquainted with Stansbury, he confided in her, and she provided a short sketch of his character in another of those long letters she wrote to her mother. The portrait is fascinating in light of Stansbury's rival-to-be. Stansbury told her "all his stuggles and trials, hopes and fears." A member of the Methodist church, he had been raised with "severe notions of Christian decorum." Yet because his temperament was "lively and social," he constantly ran into conflicts between desire and Christian precepts. "He is constantly asked to take a drink, to go to fandangos and other places which his principles compel him to refuse." Brownsville was a tough town in which to be a teetotaler.

In a western, Stansbury would be the Casper Milquetoast type, a nice young man thrown over for a more worldly figure, a diamond in the rough like Richard King—which is exactly what happened. On the surface, Stansbury might seem the ideal match for a young woman of Henrietta Chamberlain's background. But he was familiar, tame, a known quantity. Henrietta had been around such young men all her life. Richard King was something new—rough and vital, like the land the two of them would eventually possess.

In a year's time, by May 1851, Stansbury's relationship with Henrietta Chamberlain had altered dramatically. So wrote Major Chapman to his wife, who was traveling in Mexico at the time: "There is no news in Brownsville, except that Miss Chamberlain has kicked Stansbury and the younger Miss Chamberlain danced like sixty at Mrs Fry's a few evenings since. The old woman made a great fuss and frightened all who came near her. The old man was absent at Galveston." (Anna Griswold Chamberlain, the "old woman," was then thirty-five. Her husband, Hiram, was fifty-three.) Obviously the Chapmans relished discussing the preacher's family and its foibles. Just as obviously, while dancing might be a cardinal sin in the eyes of the father, at least one of the Chamberlain daughters felt differently.

A few months later, in July, Major Chapman relayed final news of the Stansbury–Henrietta Chamberlain relationship: "The engagement between Stansbury and Miss Chamberlain is broken off *forever.*" Curiously, there is never any mention of Richard King in the letters of Helen or Major Chapman. This seems surprising in light of the Chapmans' close attention to the doings of the Chamberlain family. That Chapman and King were friends is certain. That Henrietta knew both of the Chapmans is certain. The odd thing is that Helen Chapman seems not to have known King. It is conceivable that they were both in attendance at the same time at one of Reverend Chamberlain's services. We can picture them there: Helen, irritated at the reverend's lackluster performance (his jog-trot rhythm), and Richard King, all eyes on the pious daughter of the pious preacher. But apparently they did not meet. Perhaps Richard King was simply too déclassé for Helen to want to meet him. It is one of the many lacunae in the private histories of those people. Helen Chapman left Brownsville in October 1852 to join her husband at his new post in Corpus Christi. Richard King was still a few years away from becoming a man you would have to notice.

In the meantime, Henrietta Chamberlain started teaching at a school for girls founded by the missionary Melinda Rankin. Henrietta taught an English course for Spanish-speaking children, and though Helen Chapman noted that in the first year Miss Chamberlain had only two or three students, by 1852 the enrollment had grown to forty. From Miss Rankin, Henrietta got a taste of Mexico, that colorful, Catholic-inflected, exotic contrast with familiar American Brownsville. There, in the company of Miss Rankin, Miss Chamberlain distributed Bibles and religious tracts to Mexican citizens hungry, they hoped, for the word of God, Protestant-style. She also began to learn Spanish, which would come in handy in the future. In 1854 Miss Rankin's school, with Reverend Chamberlain's help, became established as the Rio Grande Female Institute. But by then Henrietta Chamberlain had other plans for her future than continuing to be a schoolmarm.

What the Stansbury-Chamberlain breakup meant to Richard King is clear. With Stansbury out of the picture, the way was now open for him. Sometime before or after 1851, Richard King became a serious suitor. In rejecting Stansbury for King, Henrietta obviously chose a man from a world entirely different from her own. She selected the kind of man whom Helen Chapman found embodied in Harry Love, "our dashing and favorite express rider." Harry Love, veteran of the Mexican War, ranger, Indian fighter, scout, and explorer, struck genteel Helen Chapman as the very type of the western man. She admired Harry Love for reasons similar, one imagines, to those that drew Henrietta to the captain: "In describing the outward appearance of this daring, almost reckless, man, I can give you not the faintest conception of himself. I know nothing of his early history, but I presume he was not born a gentleman. There is, however, a kind of native nobility about him. His perceptions are quick and keen and his impulses are generous." She might just as well have been talking about Richard King.

Given King's roughhouse upbringing, it is perhaps surprising to find a man of his circumstances presuming an interest in a minister's daughter. But then, one should never, in that time and place, discount the power of Christian virtue embodied in a graceful young woman. Nice women upheld standards of rectitude and bore children. Helen Chapman felt sorry for men "who are not restrained by the finer moral sense of women." Such women lent grace to homes and helped civilize men, a formidable task. Women brought light and civilization to a sinful man's world. In the chaotic arena of frontier Brownsville, there really were only two kinds of women, and until now, King would have had more acquaintance with one kind than the other. To a woman like Henrietta Chamberlain, bright, educated, and morally serious, Richard King must have seemed like a project fit for a good woman: there was material to mold into a sound husband.

At first Hiram Chamberlain was not in favor of King's interest in his beloved daughter. It is easy to see why. King had no résumé to recommend him to a minister. When the two young people met in 1850, Richard King appeared to be like many of the young men who made of Brownsville a frontier hellhole. He had almost no formal education, he came from no known family, he was not a churchgoer, he had once owned and operated a place that sold spirits, he made his living piloting riverboats, he liked to drink and fight, and he had neither money nor prospects. The world King lived in could hardly have been more different from Hiram's religion-bound domestic circle.

Richard King was precisely the sort of churchless young man that

Hiram Chamberlain had come to Texas to save from drink, violence, and irreligion. Had he not had a nubile daughter, however, it is highly unlikely that he would have had any success at all with Richard King.

We know the kind of dress that Henrietta King wore on her wedding day because many years later she described it in intricate detail to her grandchildren. But we do not know what exchanges passed between the young lady and Richard King in their three years of courtship. Besides church services, where they were together, there would have been other occasions to commingle: perhaps balls held in Matamoros, which were common in those days; or public celebrations of national holidays such as Washington's Birthday; or visits in private homes like that of Charles and Elizabeth Stillman, a leading couple in Brownsville; or, a bit later, that of Mifflin Kenedy and his Mexican-born wife, Petra Vela de Vidal. Tours of the first battlefields of the Mexican War, at Palo Alto and Resaca de la Palma, were very popular with the citizens of Brownsville. Helen Chapman described just such an outing that took place in 1850: "On the 8th [of May] a large party rode down to *Palo Alto,* a distance of twelve miles, and returned to *Resaca de la Palma* in the afternoon where we dined. . . . On the 9th we went to *Resaca de la Palma* with the Light Artillery Company where a salute was fired at twelve a.m. We had dinner on the grounds and returned somewhat fatigued but very well pleased." The "consecrated and still ensanguined fields," as Major Giddings called them back in the summer of 1846, still held thrilling reminders of martial glory: broken muskets, rusting buttons from a tunic, the whitened bones of horses and men, uncovered by wind and weather.

There, on just such an outing or some other, Richard King might have told his dreams to the woman he wanted to marry, as she might have told him hers. They would have had plenty of time, traveling by carriage or on horseback, and during a long, languorous day under the brilliant sky, they could have spent hours talking, sharing their pasts. Richard King's history would not have taken long to relate, not the early part of his life, anyway.

For both of them, the future was what mattered.

CHAPTER 4

Sea of Grass

During the years of his courtship of Henrietta Chamberlain, Richard King's attention turned to the interior, to the sea of grass that stretched largely empty and untenanted under the sun for 160 miles, from north of the Rio Grande to the Nueces, the very land that the Mexican War had decided belonged forever to Texas.

He made his first trip inland in 1852, to attend the Lone Star Fair held at Corpus Christi. King's companion was James Durst, a friend from Brownsville. They rode near the old battlefield of Palo Alto north of Brownsville onto the coastal plain of the Wild Horse Desert, a land of waving grass, stunted, thorny undergrowth, and mottes of trees scattered in random fashion as far as the eye could see, and in that level country the eye could see far, the land stretching to the horizon under a blue, indifferent sky. Lt. George Gordon Meade described the grassy terrain after a short trip into the interior from General Taylor's army encampment at Corpus Christi: "Indeed, you would be surprised to learn that the country is very difficult to travel through. It is nearly all prairie, but having a most luxurious growth of long grass, as high as a man almost, which breaks you down in marching through it, so that starting a deer or other animal it is impossible to overtake him unless you are mounted on a horse."

The route King traveled was called General Taylor's Road or the old Taylor Trail because it was along this way that the general's army regulars had tramped in March 1846, on their way from Corpus Christ to Point Isabel. Ulysses S. Grant described the terrain in his memoirs: "The country was rolling prairie and from the highest ground, the vision was obstructed only by the earth's curvature. As far as the eye could reach . . . the herd extended." The herd was wild mustangs, so many, Grant reckoned, that together they amounted to a mass the size of the state of Delaware.

Two years after King rode along the Taylor Trail, Frederick Law Olmsted described the land as he observed it in 1854: "Along the coast lies a sandy tract, with salt lagoons and small, brackish streams. This is the desert country . . . It merges into the level coast prairies which, forty to sixty miles inland, become undulating and covered with a growth of prickly shrubs, upon a dry, barren, gravelly soil." Like Cabeza de Vaca of centuries before and Richard King of the present, Olmsted observed also that "the coast prairies have large districts of fertile soil, and, if supplied with water, might be available as pastures for rough cattle and sheep." These "pastures," he felt, "are a still greater source of future wealth, the production of beef and wool, if stimulated by the means of communication with a steady market, being almost incalculable." There, in a nutshell, was the future of the Wild Horse Desert—and of South Texas.

In 1852, King would also have seen evidence of pastoral failures, of abandoned ranchos along the way, crumbling reminders of the difficulties of establishing a home in that wilderness. Rancho Los Indios he would have passed, north of Palo Alto, and, farther on, El Sauz, which he would someday own, and Rancho La Parra, a little past midway in the journey, which his friend Mifflin Kenedy would eventually own. Together King and Kenedy would come to own much of the land that would make up three or four modern counties, one of them named, in fact, Kenedy, and another one named Kleberg after Richard King's son-in-law. North of Rancho La Parra the Taylor Trail skirted around Baffin Bay, which reached inland to within twenty miles of modern-day Kingsville.

Water was a decisive factor. General Taylor's troops had been parched for water, had gone thirty-six hours without any on their trek to the border. Lieutenant Meade remembered that bleak route in a letter to his wife: "The one hundred and seventy miles between Corpus Christi and this point [a camp opposite Matamoros] was the most miserable desert, without wood or water, that I ever saw described, and perfectly unfit for the habitation of man, except on the banks of a few little streams we crossed." So were King and his party in need of water these years later. They found it at Santa Gertrudis Creek, about forty-five miles southwest of their destination. They slept beside the creek and the next day rode on to the former smugglers' den and former army camp of Corpus Christi, where the fair was being held.

The fair was the brainchild of Col. Henry Lawrence Kinney, another of those sky's-the-limit promoters who flocked to the wide-open West, a man who looked into the future and saw the elongated shape of himself, rich as Midas. Kinney had a history of busted dreams. He had come to Texas in the first place because he had to flee Illinois when his land schemes collapsed in the financial panic of 1837–38. Texas looked like fertile ground, and he fetched up on the border, calling himself "Colonel" and claiming he had fought in the Seminole Wars, both excellent credentials but untrue. Still, he had a way about him. He helped found Corpus Christi, on land that was formerly part of an immense grant once owned by Enrique Villareal of the old Escandón settlement of Nuevo Santander. The little town became a hotbed of smuggling activities, and Kinney made himself well known to General Taylor and his command. Col. Ethan Allen Hitchcock caught Kinney's character in a thumbnail sketch: "Kinney seems to have a government of his own here, and to be alternately the friend and foe of Mexicans, Texans, Americans, and Indians, some-times defying them and meeting them with force and sometimes brib-ing and wheedling them. He lives by smuggling goods across the line." Kinney himself best explained his brand of diplomacy: "When Mr. Mexican came, I treated him with a good deal of politeness, par-ticularly if he had me in power; when Mr. American came, I did the same with him; and when Mr. Indian came, I also frequently disposed to make a compromise with him." During the Mexican War Kinney acquired a staff position with a U.S. Army command. He also ventured into politics, being elected for several terms to the Texas state senate.

The fair was his latest gambit, a scheme to sell town lots and make a killing. Like most of Kinney's dreams, the fair came a cropper, draw-ing only a thousand people, few of whom bought land from him. After that disappointment, Kinney went on to new doomed ventures. One was a plan to use camels to transport freight from Corpus Christi to San Francisco; another was a foolhardy attempt to establish a colony along Nicaragua's Mosquito Coast. All his grandiose dreams ended when he was shot to death on the streets of Matamoros in 1862, the fatal out-come of keeping a woman other than his wife in the Mexican city.

At the fair, King ran into his friend G. K. Lewis, who was King's age and well known in Brownsville for his many accomplishments. Lewis was already famous for having survived the Mier Expedition, back in 1842, an ill-planned and ill-executed paramilitary foray into northern Mexico by Texans that led to their capture and the infamous Black Bean Episode in which captives were forced to draw beans to determine who would live or die. The seventeen who drew black beans were shot by a firing squad. Needless to say, this event contributed strongly to the animosities still smoldering from the fires of the Texas Revolution of six years earlier. In the Mexican War Lewis fought with the Texas Mounted Rangers, adding further distinction to his name. Lewis met King at some point in Brownsville, and they hit it off. In 1852 Lewis started a newspaper in Corpus Christi, the *Nueces Valley*. Nicknamed "Legs," Lewis was a man's man, confident in the venues of love.

The young men probably enjoyed the fair. The ladies of Corpus Christi had baked cakes for sale, and there were lectures on philosophy and literature, and fireworks and cockfights and bullfights and windy speeches, and an assorted mix of hustlers like Kinney and at least one general from Mexico and friendly Comanche and Lipan Indians and blacks all stirred to a heady froth of conviviality in this place that Kinney billed as "Little Naples," the "Italy of America."

The fair had been designed to promote land sale and speculation and it did so, but not in the way Kinney had hoped. Eventually Richard King would own property in Corpus Christi, commercial and residential, and interests in several businesses, but that was a long way in the future, long after Kinney and his dreams were dead.

Upon returning to Brownsville, James Durst acted quickly to seize upon the new opportunities. On December 28, 1852, he purchased 92,996.4 acres of the La Barreta grant from the Ballí family for a price of 1,600 pesos. Part of that ranch survives today as the Armstrong Ranch in Kenedy County, south of King Ranch.

The next year, 1853, his friend Richard King set about buying a significant parcel of land on the most favorable spot he had seen, along the Santa Gertrudis Creek. Water from a seep spring fed the creek, and there was enough elevation on a rise of ground to suggest a perfect location for surveillance of the surrounding countryside. It was here that the main house of King's rancho would eventually sit. In the meantime, King knew that any attempt to build anything would require armed protection, and he made a deal with Legs Lewis to provide such aid. Legs got himself appointed captain of the Texas Mounted Volunteers and began patrolling the lonely, empty country southwest of Corpus Christi. At the same time, King set out to secure his holdings, which would not prove to be easy.

King's decision to buy the land marked a sharp break with his past. Up to now he had been a ship's pilot, a partner in a riverboat company, and a small-time investor in local real estate in Brownsville. He had no experience at all in ranching or in raising cattle or in anything related to ranching. But living in Brownsville and meeting all the men one met, on both sides of the river and in the towns scattered along the riverbank all the way to Camargo, 150 miles west, he would have observed much about ranching, for the whole border consisted of ranchos running along both sides of the river. At the end of the previous century, for example, there were 437 ranches and 17 haciendas in that region. The ranchos were a hundred years old, dating back to the original Spanish settlement of 1749, to the time of the *entrada* conceived of and carried out by José de Escandón. Escandón named the region Nuevo Santander after his native province Santander in Spain, and all the prominent Tejano families dotting the border sprang from those original families and grants of land from the king of Spain, his own lordly self. Some of the ranchos were immense, and the future king must have heard about them. At one time José de la Garza owned over 263,000 acres along the Rio Grande, and José Narisco Cabazos a whopping 600,000 acres in present-day Cameron, Willacy, and Kenedy counties. Given such magnitude, such extensive holdings, King's aspirations appear to be rooted in border precedent as well as in the southern plantation ideal. George Washington, Thomas Jefferson, Meriwether Lewis, Robert E. Lee (soon to become a friend of King's) all desired to own as much land as they could. Land was wealth; it lasted when other forms of wealth did not.

Moreover, King's friends were all going into ranching about the same time; the early to mid-1850s saw a rapid increase in land purchases in the remote interior. The interior made sense for a lot of reasons. Most of the land near the river was already owned and operated by Mexican rancheros, and the land, when available for sale, was much more expensive there than in the interior. Achieving clear title was also expensive and complicated, though as events would prove, the process was sometimes no less complicated in the interior. Land available for purchase along the river also tended to be in much smaller parcels than it was a hundred or so miles distant. About the only way to acquire a lot of land along the river was to marry a Mexican, which some Anglos did, most notably Mifflin Kenedy and Henry Clay Davis, founder of Rio Grande City, who married a woman with extensive landholdings.

Kenedy also invested in land for ranching operations. In 1852 he bought a tract of land at Valerio on the Nueces River, and two years later he bought the San Salvador del Tule grant closer to Brownsville, sixtysomething miles from the river. Charles Stillman, who usually led the way in all things related to moneymaking, had acquired the Laureles grant, south of Corpus Christi, back in 1844 and was now, in the early 1850s, to place stock on it. He also bought a tract north of Brownsville for the same purpose. Two lawyers, F. J. Parker and W. G. Hale, bought the Santa Rosa grant, only twenty miles south of the Santa Gertrudis area. All of these new rancho owners were absentee landlords. Such was the usual pattern of the day.

And such had been the pattern among some of the Mexican grantees as well. The Desert of the Dead was a lonely place, far removed from the comforts of the older settlements along the river. Capt. Enrique Villareal, who owned the Rincón del Oso grant on Corpus Christi bay, was typical. He was an absentee *patrón* whose operation was described in the following manner: "Enrique Villareal occupied the lands with *ganado mayor de vaca* (many cattle). . . . On the Oso Creek he had two pens, one large one and one small; he had servants, two vaqueros, and a *jacal,* a primitive Mexican-style house with walls made of sticks stuck together with mud and a thatched roof, in with the vaqueros lived on the land." But Villareal lived elsewhere and "came there usually at branding time and would leave again after branding; the two vaqueros lived there alone a very long time."

Richard King would change all that. He would live, with his retainers and family to come, on the land in the Wild Horse Desert.

King had a keen interest in increasing his personal well-being and preparing to support a wife and family if Henrietta Chamberlain would have him. He could see that the riverboat business might not continue to flourish as once it had. Drought years limited the flow and left boats dry-docked and producing no revenue. Farming practices upstream reduced the flow, as well, with water being diverted into Mexico. This became a recurring issue on the river, one that additional treaties have failed to resolve. As recently as the summer of 2002, Texas farmers in the Rio Grande Valley were complaining bitterly about Mexico's questionable appropriation of water from the Rio Grande.

The sea of grass looked more promising than the river of commerce.

The land King meant to purchase was part of the Rincón de Santa Gertrudis grant. Originally surveyed in 1832, it was granted to a Mexican citizen from Camargo, Juan Mendiola, in 1834. He died without improving the land, and his family never occupied it or improved it because the Texas Revolution of 1835–36 intervened, and south of the Rio Grande was a much safer place to be than in the middle of foraging troops, whether Mexican or Texan made little difference, and all the chaos of war. King traveled to Camargo, one of the old towns founded during the days of Escandón, to seek out Mendiola's widow and three sons. He wanted to buy the land, and they were eager to sell. On July 25, 1853, he agreed to pay $300 for three and a half leagues, 15,500 acres—less than two cents an acre. Two years before, W. W. Chapman had written to his wife that land was selling in the Corpus Christi area for $1 an acre, considered an excellent price. King had struck an extraordinary bargain.

Exhilarated by his purchase, King himself assisted the surveyor from Corpus Christi who in November marked off the official boundary lines of the 15,550-acre tract.

Next, King sold a half-interest in the property to his friend Legs Lewis for $2,000, in consideration for Legs having organized that Ranger Company to patrol the region. Lewis himself bought several leagues of land and then sold a half-interest to King for $1,000. Lewis had already purchased several lots in Corpus Christi. With so much land to be had so cheaply, it was like a game, like playing Monopoly before Monopoly was invented. But there were problems that no game contained: the problems of sure title and of developing the land into a working, profitable ranch. There were problems enough to occupy a lifetime.

The Wild Horse Desert had always offered more promise than fulfillment to those Euro-Americans who sought to convert its wilderness to a pastoral economy. Comanches, Lipan Apaches, and other tribes empowered by the advent of horses—like cattle, another Spanish contribution to New World culture—were a strong deterrent. They extended their raiding territory all the way to the coastal plains, and by the time Mexican settlers under Spanish rule tried to settle these lands, horse Indians were a dangerous problem. Juan Mendiola never occupied the San Rincón grant for just such reason. Everybody knew this was so. The abstract of the title purchased by Richard King spoke of the "disturbances of the time." Such disturbances had indeed proved calamitous on another highly desirable parcel of land, the de la Garza Santa Gertrudis grant, twelve square leagues, or 53,000 acres, adjacent to the Rincón de Santa Gertrudis. The de la Garza family of Camargo, in Tamaulipas, had secured the grant in 1808. At that time Spanish soldiers offered protection to such far-flung outposts of settlement, and the de la Garzas, father and two sons, set out to build a rancho. Buildings and corrals were erected, cattle were brought to the pastures, and a working hacienda was created. Soon trouble befell the distant rancho in the wilderness. Mexico revolted against Spain in 1810, and the Spanish troops withdrew, leaving the way open for new incursions from warring tribes bent on driving out the Europeans. In 1814 the *hacendado,* Don José de la Garza, was slain "whilst shaking hands with barbarous Indians."

The de la Garza sons wanted nothing more to do with their father's grant and used its title to settle a debt owed to Don José Perez Rey, who owned the Laureles grant on the shore of Laguna Madre, on the landward side of Padre Island, which stretched south of Corpus Christi a hundred miles to just above Brazos de Santiago at the tip of the state. Ultimately King Ranch would own both the de la Garza grant and part of the old Laureles grant. Like the de la Garzas, the Reys were harassed by Indian raids and eventually retreated from their isolated rancho to the safety of the border. The buildings fell into ruin, the corrals collapsed, and the cattle reverted to the wild.

Not long after Richard King was established on the Santa Gertrudis, he saw the value of adding the de la Garza holdings. The only heir of the Reyses, it turned out, lived in Matamoros. His name was Praxides Uribe and he had no intention of ever doing anything with the land, but he also did not possess the correct documents to prove clear title. King and Legs Lewis entered into negotiation with a man appointed by Uribe to handle the details and get clear title. The long and the short of it is that King and Lewis agreed to pay $1,800 for 53,000 acres of some of the best grass in South Texas. The deed was recorded in Corpus Christi on May 20, 1854.

The original cow camp of Richard King and Legs Lewis, set up in 1852 even before title had been secured, was the beginning. King brought to the Santa Gertrudis men he trusted from his riverboat years, men like Vicenti Patino and the amazing Faustino Villa, a giant of a man who was fiercely loyal to King and would live to a vast old age and, at one hundred, would swim the swollen Santa Gertrudis to deliver the mail. King also sought the help of his nearest neighbor, Francisco Alvarado, who operated the Bodedo Ranch, twelve miles south. Alvarado and his men, along with help from King's, built *jacales* and, for the livestock, rough corrals of mesquite, from the gnarly, twisted, stunted trees that grew in that country. To stock the rancho, King bought cows and a cinnamon-colored bull from two brothers who lived in Guerrero in Tamaulipas, and he bought from other men a mare and a stallion.

King took measures to defend his holdings. When Legs Lewis's company of Rangers disbanded in 1853, King and Lewis hired Capt. James Richardson, late of the Mexican War, a gunman noted for his bravery and skill in fighting Indians. Richardson in turn sometimes added the services of another captain from that war, William Gregory. (There were as many captains in the Texas of that day as there were colonels in the old South. So said Oscar Wilde upon visiting Galveston in 1882, and Wilde was right.) King ordered the building of a crude stockade and blockhouse, to be constructed on the highest spot near the Santa Gertrudis Creek, and he had cannons taken from M. Kenedy and Co. steamboats carted to the rancho and mounted on the ramparts. The cow camp was becoming a small fort. Rip Ford, Texas Ranger and longtime friend of Richard King, visited the camp early on and noted a special quality already in evidence: "This cattle-camp became a stopping-place of wayfarers, a sort of city of refuge for all classes, the timorous and the hungry. The men who held it were of no ordinary mould. They had gone to stay. It was no easy matter to scare them."

King had to spend a lot of money to get the rancho going those first few years. He could buy cattle pretty cheaply, thanks to the drought, and he could buy mustangs for $6 a mare, very cheap, but stallions, good stallions, cost a great deal more. He bought American stallions at prices ranging from $200 up to, in November 1854, a sorrel stud that cost $600, twice what he paid for the original Rincón de Santa Gertrudis grant. The sum of all this buying of cattle and horses and other operating expenses for the year 1854 toted up to a substantial outlay: $12,275.79.

In just two years King had accomplished a great deal. He had bought his original piece of land, then had more than quadrupled those holdings. He had made the raw prairie into a place where one could live. He had stocked his pastures with cattle and horses and sheep and goats. In 1854 he would do two more things that together would lay the foundation of an empire to come. The first was his decision to create a Mexican-style hacienda in South Texas. Only a handful of other such attempts were made elsewhere in the West, and King's was by far the most successful and long-lasting.

As someone who had not grown up in Texas, King did not share the often inbred hatred that many Texans of that time felt for Mexicans. Newcomers to South Texas in those days were struck by the intensity of Texan prejudice toward their near but distant neighbors. The always acute Helen Chapman spoke of the problem in a letter of 1852: "The old and deadly feud between Mexicans and Texans will exist so long as the imperfect civilization continues or so long as they can remain in the position of oppressor and oppressed. You can scarcely make an old Texan regard a Mexican as anything but a wild beast." Frederick Law Olmsted encountered the same attitudes during his travels in Texas. "Mexicans were regarded in a somewhat unchristian tone, not as heretics or heathen to be converted with flannel and tracts, but rather as vermin, to be exterminated." At a sugar plantation near Victoria, he met a woman who "was particularly strong in her prejudices. White folks and Mexicans were never made to live together, anyhow, and the Mexicans had no business here. They were getting so impertinent, and were so well protected by the laws, that the Americans would just have to get together and drive them all out of the country."

Racism in the modern sense was doubtless part of the equation, but the specific events of the spring of 1836 certainly played a large role in the creation of and fostering of deep divides between Mexico and

Texas. Two places became the flashpoints of hatred: the Alamo and Goliad. Approximately 200 men died at the Alamo, and approximately 400 were massacred at Goliad. A rough total, then, of 600 in a population that has been estimated at 30,000 works out to a ratio of 50 to 1 in terms of impact. Consider this against the approximate numbers killed in the September 11, 2001, attacks on the World Trade Center and the Pentagon: 3,000 dead out of a population, in 2000, of 281.4 million: a ratio of 1 to 94,000. Then consider the impact of the September 11 attack on the consciousness of the nation, and weigh that against the events of 1836. It is no wonder that a long legacy of dislike and mistrust came out of the Texas Revolution. Also, in any calculus of hatred, one must not overlook the payback slaughter of Mexican troops by Sam Houston's army at the Battle of San Jacinto, where, after the eighteen-minute battle was over decisively in Texas's favor, the killing of 600 or more Mexican troops went on into the afternoon.

Like Helen Chapman, Richard King came to Texas free of such prejudices, and he seems never to have taken up the prevailing views of the Mexican-hating Texans. In his heart of hearts, like most nineteenth-century imperialists, he might have felt himself, his race, superior to that of Mexicans, but early on, he acted more as a *patrón,* a familiar model of authority in Mexican ranching culture, than simply a rancher who hired Mexican labor.

In the years to come there would be numerous threats to the safety of King and his family stemming from Mexico, but King did not magnify the actions of a few Mexicans into an indictment of a people. Business trumped race in King's view and in the view of most of the successful businessmen along the border, men like King's friends and partners Charles Stillman, Mifflin Kenedy, and W. W. Chapman. Class was important, too. Mifflin Kenedy married, in 1852, a Mexican woman of degree, Petra Vela de Vidal, a widow from a distinguished family in Tamaulipas. They lived in a fine house on Elizabeth Street, and in time King and his wife would eventually live in a cottage of their own next door to the Kenedys.

Had King shared the prejudices of old-time Texans, he would likely never have had the imagination to create the world he did create, beginning with the *entrada* of 1854. Although King understood transportation and markets—the business of carrying freight on the river—he knew very little at all about ranching, managing livestock, breeding, all the science and lore of animal husbandry. He could learn, but he needed somebody to teach him. It so happened that a culture with a hundred years of experience in ranching in the semidesert lands of northern Mexico and southern Texas lay at hand.

There was a density, a thickness of cattle culture in South Texas that many historians, from Walter P. Webb on, have consistently overlooked or erased in their dramas of the rise of the cattle kingdom. The way Webb tells it, at the close of the Civil War, millions of cattle in South Texas stood around waiting for Anglo ranchers and cowboys to rope 'em and brand 'em and send them north to railheads in Missouri and Kansas. It is all rather like a John Wayne movie, like *Red River,* for example. But the map of Texas before the Anglos came was not a tabula rasa waiting to be written on with a branding iron. In 1821, three years before Richard King was born, fifteen years before San Jacinto, Nuevo Santander had a population of 67,434 persons living on ranchos and in the six towns strung along the Rio Bravo, five of them on the south side and only Laredo on the north side of the river. Livestock, cattle, horses, sheep, and goats numbered in the thousands. There was a country there, a culture.

Richard King was living in history and not in a history book or film, and so it was that in early 1854 he rode into northern Mexico to buy cattle for what he was already calling King's Rancho. He came to Cruillas, a small village in Tamaulipas, located at the foot of the Sierra Madres, southeast of Monterrey. It was an obscure, lost little village that had good cattle but no prospects otherwise. King bought the cattle and looked around, saw the village in all its bleak, nondescript meagerness, saw the villagers, good people though poor, and he had an idea. He offered to move the entire village, one hundred people in all, from the desert of Tamaulipas to another desert where there was water, at the rancho that he was building at Santa Gertrudis. The elders held a council and decided to take their possessions, such as they could carry; packed their belongings on two-wheeled carts and donkeys and such horses as they had; and marched like a small army the several hundred miles north to the new land. It was like an old Spanish *entrada,* an entrance. The Spanish and later the Mexicans had been making *entradas* from the days of Cortez, whose first hacienda, the whole Valle de Oaxaca, was a gift from the king of Spain for conquering the Aztecs.

Thus King set about to create an American version of a Mexican hacienda. A hacienda is a feudal system of pastoral economy based upon the raising of cattle, an animal so valued that its root meaning goes back to chattel and, distantly, to capitalism itself. A hacienda is a world complete unto itself. The head of a hacienda is called the *hacendado,* and King was the hacendado, though the men on King's Rancho did not call him that, but El Capitan or *el patrón,* or, later, El Cojo, because of a limp that he developed, from causes unknown whether on the river or on the ranch.

King's decision was a major innovation in its departure from the usual Anglo pattern. Anglo ranchers typically kept a small number of foremen on salary and hired cowboys on a seasonal basis. King adopted the Mexican model, which meant year-round, lifetime support for one's vaqueros and families. What King offered the former dwellers of Cruillas was houses, food, regular wages, and security. What they offered in return was knowledge and skill in the handling of livestock and horses, a capacity for work, and loyalty. This last was very important. The system bred mutual respect and loyalty. Together the Anglo hacendado and the Mexican vaqueros and their families would create a world of their own. The people of Cruillas soon became known as *Kineños,* King's people.

In creating his own world, feudal in organization, King in some fundamental way was fulfilling the destiny of his patronym. There are other ranches in South Texas, such as the O'Connor Ranches near Victoria, where Mexican-American families have lived for successive generations, providing a continuity based upon work and year-round support. But the Kineños, because of their association with King Ranch, acquired a kind of luster of their own. Always in the stories and books about King Ranch they are celebrated for their skills as vaqueros (those centaurs that Tom Lea writes of), their steadfastness down through the generations, their loyalty. But in modern South Texas such figures are not always called Kineños. Often, by other Mexicans and Mexican-Americans, they are called "Ranch Mexicans"—a term of disapprobation applied to those who have let themselves be held back by Anglo patriarchy. Certainly the Kineños held only the lowest positions in the ranch hierarchy. It was not until 1926 that a Kineño was made a foreman, when Lauro Cavazos, from a very old family that had owned a large Spanish land grant from the eighteenth century, was promoted to that position.

The second important event of 1854 was Richard King's marriage, after four years of courtship, to Henrietta Chamberlain.

On November 2 of that year, Hiram Chamberlain wrote his daughter one of those fatherly Presbyterian letters that make the nineteenth century seem so remote from the present. Issued like a papal bull from the parsonage at Brownsville, the letter set forth a few of the reverend's thoughts on the occasion of the "deeply interesting event"—the impending marriage of his daughter. First of all, he wrote, it would be necessary for Henrietta to "divest [her] mind of all romantic and foolish notions in regard to the married life, and view it as it really is, as a serious and solemn relation." Next he urged her, as a Christian, to seek "sufficient grace" to carry out her "whole duty to God and man." If the marriage turned out to be a happy one, all the better. If not, then her faith would have to sustain her. Even better, if it were a happy union, there was one more possible blessing: if "your way be prosperous, it will cause you to sing with joy and gladness."

They were married on Sunday, December 10, in Brownsville, at the First Presbyterian Church, Rev. Hiram Chamberlain presiding. In the past four years the reverend had changed his views of the upstart, unpolished riverboat man. He had come to appreciate "this young captain's sterling upright qualities," his beloved daughter later recalled.

There is a fading photograph from that time, circa 1854, made in a studio in Brownsville, of two men staring solemnly into the camera, in the accustomed protocols of that age. One is Mifflin Kenedy, standing, a man as plain in feature as Abraham Lincoln, with about the same amount of scraggly facial hair. His right hand is placed on the shoulder of a clean-shaven Richard King, thirty years old, dark hair combed tightly back, dark eyes staring intensely. Though sitting, King looks solid and compact. Above all, he looks serious.

This was the man Henrietta Chamberlain had chosen over the more conventional W. N. Stansbury.

Henrietta Chamberlain King remembered, as brides do, every detail of the gown she wore. In the years to come, she enjoyed telling her children and grandchildren about it. It was made of ruffled silk, peach-colored, set off by a white silk mull "shirred and trimmed with beading, and white baby ribbons under sleeves of white lace."

The most surprising thing about their wedding was where they honeymooned. They did not go to New Orleans, which would have been the most logical choice, an old, impressive city with fine hotels where the newlyweds might have been expected to celebrate their nuptials. They went instead to the nascent rancho at Santa Gertrudis. They traveled in an expensive carriage that King had bought in Corpus Christi; it cost more than a good stallion. They set out upon the broad prairie with four outriders as protection. All men carried firearms in those days of frontier South Texas. Back in 1849—and things were no different now—Helen Chapman had described a trip from Fort Brown to the coast: "The roadways are infested with robbers and all men go heavily armed. Whenever we approach on these roads our fellow men, the invariable habit is to elevate the guns into a conspicuous position. See that the pistols can at any instant be slipped from the holsters and draw up; the sword and sword case into full view." Mifflin Kenedy's wife, Petra Vela, traveled between Corpus Christi and Brownsville in a coach guarded by armed vaqueros. The Nueces Strip, as it came to be called by the Texas Rangers, was one of the most dangerous areas in the state.

Bride and groom camped at night, and a camp cook prepared meals in a skillet over a blazing fire. It took them four days to reach the rancho in the wilderness. In mid-December the land was turning toward winter, the days still mild, though the nights were growing chilly and cold in the predawn hours before light broke. The trees were largely barren of leaves except for evergreen shrubs. The sunlight shone thinly upon the land, the almost palpable thickness of summer leached out now, the grass browning and sparse. The young bride gazed upon the low jacales and the crude storehouse and the little fortress with its cannons pointing south; took in the rough corrals and the horses and cattle there enclosed; and observed the land, largely open except for trees lining the Santa Gertrudis Creek, the acres spreading as far as the eye could see, all of it owned by her husband and now mutually by her. She liked what she saw.

Did she will herself to like the land as it appeared in winter? Or see it through the colored lens of romance and marriage? For to other observers South Texas in winter is anything but romantic.

Not every woman would have responded to the landscape the way Henrietta King did. A young army wife named Lydia Spencer Lane, whose husband was a lieutenant of mounted rifles, journeyed through that region in the same year, two months before Henrietta. Lane wrote, "We travelled from Corpus Christi to the western frontier through a dreary, desolate country, where nothing lived but Indians, snakes, and other venomous reptiles, and I expected to see some dreadful thing whichever way I turned." Though she saw no snakes, her pet Saint Bernard, a puppy, fell from the wagon and was crushed to death by a wheel. She cried all day for that puppy.

Lane and her company ate mostly pan-made biscuits and molasses, and when they finally reached their destination, Fort McIntosh, north of Laredo, she summed up the experience: "No one travelled in that direction for amusement in those days. Nothing but stern necessity and duty took people to such a desolate place."

Yet this was the land to which Richard King had brought his bride. When she was in her seventies, Henrietta King, who was twenty-two that first year of marriage, still rhapsodized about her honeymoon. Tom Lea quotes from her own words, his source, he says, "Notes in Mrs. Henrietta M. King's writing, trembled with age—King Ranch vault." She and her husband, she wrote, "on horseback roamed the broad prairies," and when she grew tired he "would spread a Mexican blanket for me and then I would take my siesta under the shade of the mesquite tree." They dined on venison roasts and lived in a "mere jacal" for several months before returning to civilization. A mere jacale, remember, is a primitive dwelling made of mud, sticks, and straw. Lydia Lane lived in one and hated it.

Looking back many years afterward, Henrietta King doubted that "it falls to the lot of any bride to have had so happy a honeymoon." She must have conveyed a similar sense of joy in a letter to her grandfather back in Vermont, for in his letter to her, in November of the next year, he replied: "You speak of your conjugal union as very blissful." Like his son, he held a flinty view of man and woman's prospects: "In this dark world, full of evils consequent upon the introduction of sin, life is often embittered by 'unequal yoking,' and if you have found a mate of congenial tastes and sympathies with your own, you have abundant reason for gratitude to Him." The years ahead, as in any marriage, would test the character of husband and wife, but from the beginning the Kings possessed one of those unions that would prove durable, one in which a melding of different talents and tastes is achieved and great things result.

While Richard King was enjoying the early and multiple satisfactions of a good marriage, his friend and partner Legs Lewis was pursuing a different line of conjugal adventure. He was having an affair with a married lady, Mrs. J. T. Yarrington of Corpus Christi. Legs had his hands in business affairs, too, taking an active interest in the operation of King's Santa Gertrudis, and in early 1855 sought to purchase land on Padre Island from Guadalupe Ballí, a niece of Padre Nicolas Ballí, who held title to all of Padre Island. (King himself later bought 12,000 acres on Padre Island, though that parcel of land was never developed as part of King Ranch.)

The newspapers reported the incident in considerable detail. When Dr. Yarrington intercepted damning letters, he "put his wife away from him." Legs wanted the letters back. They could prove very embarrassing to his latest venture, announced earlier that year— Legs was running for a seat in the state legislature. He went to the doctor's office and demanded the return of the letters. Yarrington refused and hot words were exchanged. Legs came back two more times, demanding the letters, but each time the doctor refused, and the last time he issued a warning for Legs to keep away. Undeterred, Legs did return, and the doctor, armed with a shotgun, killed him. This was on April 14, 1855. Three days later the doctor, under custody, wrote a letter to the Gonzales *Inquirer* explaining why he had had the misfortune to kill Capt. G. K. Lewis: "The reason was, he seduced Mrs. Yarrington from me and my children, then added insult to injury by continually coming to my house, and also trying to steal my children from me, and for trying to force from my possession certain letters, which I intercepted, addressed to my wife." Legs Lewis was so well known and so well liked that a eulogy for him in a San Antonio newspaper reviewed his accomplishments and all but overlooked his shortcomings: "While the mantle of charity is thrown over his errors, let us drop a tear to memory of the boy-prisoner of Mier."

Lewis's death was no doubt a severe personal loss to King. After all, they had been friends for several years, and in the early days of the Santa Gertrudis, 1852 to 1854, they shared many common bonds connected with buying the land and starting up operation of the rancho. But Lewis's death posed a real dilemma. Because he died without a will and without heirs, the half-interest he had shared with King was at risk. Strangers could snap up the properties at auction, and King had to do something to prevent that. Also, King had a predilection for partnerships, ever since his days on the river and through his first decade and a half on the rancho.

Needing some financial aid, King turned to his old friend from Brownsville, W. W. Chapman, stationed in nearby Corpus Christi. His partnership with Chapman in 1856 set off the complicated sequence of events that today awaits final judgment by the courts.

Major Chapman, who was as interested in acquiring land as all his friends from the Brownsville days were, found the Santa Gertrudis area quite promising. In fact, Chapman had already acquired a tract of land and placed upon it both livestock and a manager, James Bryden, a Scot. The site was called the Chapman Ranch or the New Santa Gertrudis. Chapman furnished the land and improvements and an inventory of livestock that, in 1856, tallied 229 head of cattle, 1,109 sheep, 30 goats, and 25 horses, mules, oxen, and so on. His arrangement with Bryden was as follows: Bryden received one-half of the money from the sale of steers and bulls; one-third from the sale of mules, jacks, and horses; one-fourth from the sale of wethers; and one fourth of the net proceeds from the sale of each lot of wool. Bryden himself was not allowed to place his own animals on the ranch, except poultry and five hogs with pigs.

Partnering with Richard King would have been a natural way to increase Chapman's holdings on the promising Santa Gertrudis range. But something calamitous happened—or did not, depending on which account one believes. According to the official King version, as told in *The King Ranch,* Chapman, at King's behest, purchased the one-half Lewis interest at an auction held that summer. Not long afterward, Chapman rode from Corpus Christi to the Santa Gertrudis site and, finding Richard King absent, told James Bryden that "I have not the means to justify me in retaining a half interest and request the captain to release me from my obligation therein. Say also that I will write him shortly on this subject." Years later, James Bryden would testify that the major's widow, Helen Chapman, told him that she had found a memorandum to this effect among her husband's records. If so, that memorandum did not survive. Nor did the letter that Chapman was said to have written to King. Like nearly everything else about the Chapman-King partnership, all of this would be open to question in court, not once but twice. King must have thought that Chapman's sudden death in 1859 made the issue of ownership of Rincón de Santa Gertrudis a moot question—that is, until Helen Chapman resurfaced in the lives of the Kings two decades later.

After the arrangement with W. W. Chapman ended—or not—in whatever complex, ambiguous, and disputed circumstances there were, King was in the same bind he had been in before his partnerships with Legs Lewis and W. W. Chapman. He needed a partner. Partnership was part of King's MO. The new partner he selected was another M. Kenedy and Co. associate, Capt. James Walworth, who piloted a Kenedy-King steamboat on the Rio Grande. Walworth had also been involved in a commercial trading venture with Mifflin Kenedy back in 1849, in northern Mexico. That solved, King's other problem had to do with ownership of the large Rincón de la Garza Santa Gertrudis tract. No money had changed hands for it and would not until documents of clear title were received. So far that hadn't happened.

Walworth, acting on behalf of King, got in touch with Praxides Uribe, who had hired a new agent to handle the de la Garza Santa Gertrudis grant. By now, December 1856, the price had gone up to $5,000, and in early 1857 the new deal was accomplished. The old contract of King and Lewis was ended, and King, with Walworth's aid, had title to the large tract that was crucial if the rancho was going to succeed.

Between 1856 and the end of the decade, King was extremely busy, spending chunks of time at the rancho and the rest in Brownsville attending to business and family, which was made more sizable by the addition of two daughters and a son. Henrietta Marie (Nettie) King was born on April 17, 1856; Ella Morse King on April 13, 1858; and Richard King II on December 15, 1860. The local press clearly considered King still a resident of Brownsville, as so indicated in a comment in the *Nueces Valley* in December 1857 that "Capt. King of Brownsville" had recently visited Corpus Christi. On the border he continued to make friends who counted. In 1856 on a trip upriver on the *Ranchero*, a new M. Kenedy and Co. boat, King met Lt. Robert E. Lee, who came on board the *Ranchero* for the trip down to Brownsville. Lee, who had been sent to the border to preside over an army court-martial, had been in Texas before, during the Mexican War, and he would be back in Texas in 1859–60.

During his stay at Fort Brown, Lee and some junior officers called at the home of Captain King. Although the captain was absent, his wife, Henrietta, received them. Lee described the King dwelling in a letter to his wife: "The King cottage was removed from the street by well kept trees and shrubbery in the yard, among which were several orange trees filled with ripening fruit. Mrs. King's table was loaded with sweet oranges and many other things tempting to the eye."

There were other visits by Lee to the Kings', and visits to the Presby terian church where Hiram Chamberlain preached. There were also trips to the site of the Santa Gertrudis rancho. These were important to the Kings, and Henrietta King always cherished the memories of Lee's visits. "I am sure if General Lee were here to recall those days, he would say that a dinner served off our tin plates on this old ranch was more appetizing than many a banquet accorded him in later years," she wrote.

It was Lee whose advice, according to family legend, became virtually the motto of Captain King: "Buy land; and never sell." In the years ahead, King bought a lot of land—some sixty-odd purchases in all—and he almost never sold.

CHAPTER 5

Grandma's Cattle

On July 13, 1859, Juan Cortina was hanging out at one of his usual haunts, a small bar and coffeehouse owned by Gabriel Catsel, on Market Plaza in downtown Brownsville. He often came to visit with friends and find out the news. Five-six, red-haired, with green eyes, he was thirty-five years old, the son of the aristocratic Maria Estéfana Goseascochea Cavazis de Cortina. (Texas Ranger Rip Ford said her name was "nearly sufficient to break an ordinary sheriff's jaw to call.") Cortina was under indictment at the time for stealing cattle and transporting them to Mexico.

Despite any legal problems he might have, Cortina went where he pleased, heavily armed. He had friends in Matamoros, where he visited them at a billiards parlor, and in Brownsville. Indeed, he was already a very familiar figure on the border. Jeremiah Galvan, a businessman in Brownsville, said of Cortina that he "has always been considered a bold and daring fellow passing most of his time on horseback, trading in stock, driving stock for pay—acting as guide to travelers—and an influential man among his class of rancheros on account of his recklessness."

That humid day in July, sitting in the little bar, Cortina saw something through the window that made his blood boil. The newly appointed Brownsville city marshal, Robert Shears, approached a vaquero, who some said was drunk, and tried to arrest him. Cortina knew the vaquero well; the man had formerly worked for him and his mother. When the man resisted, the marshal pulled out his pistol and began pistol-whipping him. Outraged, Cortina rushed out of the bar and said to Shears, "Why do you ill-treat this man?" The marshal gave an insolent reply, and Cortina fired two shots at him, the second striking him in the left shoulder. Cortina later said of his action, "I punished his insolence and avenged my countrymen by shooting him with a pistol and stretching him at my feet." With the marshal lying bleeding in the dusty street, Cortina threw the vaquero onto the back of his mount, and together the two of them galloped out of town.

The sheriff, James G. Browne, arrived and raised a posse to go after Cortina, but most of the men grew faint of heart at the prospect, and nothing came of it. In days to follow, Cortina was observed frequently in Matamoros, but he did not return to Texas. Not yet, anyway.

Cortina's daring and the dash on horseback to safety were the stuff of local legend. Men with guitars composed *corridos,* border ballads, about Cortina's rescue of the Mexican vaquero.

This was the same Juan Cortina who, along with Richard King and others, had signed a separatist petition almost a decade earlier. In February 1850, the same month that King met Henrietta Chamberlain, he attended a political meeting held at the school of W. N. Stansbury (his rival for Henrietta's hand). It was a small world, Brownsville in 1850, and it was complicated and all mixed up, with two races intermingling in complex ways. The occasion was one of those outbursts of civil uprisings that characterized the volatile border, and interestingly, it had to do with the air of confusion and uncertainty that hung over the issue of land claims along the river. Old Spanish land grants conflicted with recent claims of American citizens. It was hard to obtain clear title, and certain citizens of Brownsville, among them Richard King, felt that the state of Texas was doing a poor job in the matter of land disputes. Mexicans felt the same way. Rafael Garcia Cavazos, for example, owned a huge tract of land in Cameron County that was threatened by the occupation of squatters and, more ominously, by the machinations of sharp lawyers. Eventually Cavazos was done out of his land for $33,000, which was never paid. The Brownsville Separatist Movement, as it was called, wanted essentially two things: for the United States to preempt Texas in the resolution of land claims and, seemingly a contradiction to that aim, to form a new political entity, the Republic of the Rio Grande. Such a republic would consist of land on both sides of the river and all of the state of Tamaulipas.

The idea of a republic had been around for a while, going back to the beginning of the previous decade, and it dovetailed nicely with the goals of José M. J. Carbajal, a Mexican revolutionary who enjoyed considerable popularity in Matamoros and among some elements in

Brownsville, including Richard King and the other partners of M. Kenedy and Co. King and his friends gave Carbajal supplies in return for which they expected, it appears, trade with Carbajal and his supporters. The Brownsville Separatist Movement sent two petitions to the U.S. Congress in February 1850. The first was signed by 106 persons, all but three of whom were Mexicans. One of the Mexican signatures belonged to J. Neppomuzeno Cortinas (a common variant spelling), who in a few years would become one of the most feared figures on the border and a personal adversary of King Ranch. But in 1850 Cortina and King were on the same side.

A second petition to Congress, dated March 11, 1850, bore the names of James O'Donnell, partner in M. Kenedy and Co., and Stephen Powers, the rising preeminent lawyer in the Valley, an expert in title claims and a future attorney of Captain King's. It also bore the name "R. King." King and his friends were among the most ardent-hearted young men in the valley. King's participation in this brief affair suggests the degree to which he was immersed in local politics. The activities of King and his fellow separatists were not popular with more conservative, loyal Texans. The separatist movement suggests how far King was willing to go in looking after the business interests of himself and his friends in the fluid, free-for-all atmosphere of Brownsville and South Texas in the run-up to the Civil War.

The Brownsville Separatist Movement dissolved in thin air when, that same February, the Texas legislature created a land commission that would make fair and equitable rulings regarding legal titles to land in the valley. The commission quieted things down and did its work successfully. By early 1852 landowners felt secure in turning to Texas for just titles—Anglo landowners, that is. The Tejanos thought their land was slipping away, thanks to shrewd lawyers and land-hungry Anglo-Texans with friends in Austin.

In 1859, though, Cortina and King were on different sides. Strangely, their lives bore some parallels. They were born in the same year, and they both were strong players in the post-Mexican War world of grab-and-brand that was South Texas in the years from 1849 to the 1870s. Both men lived through dangerous times; both were crafty survivors.

Born in Camarillo, on the south side of the river, on May 16, 1824, Juan Nepomuceno Cortina belonged to Tejano aristocracy, part

Formal portrait of Juan Cortina, whose actions made him a hero in Mexico and the scourge of cattle raisers in the Nueces Strip.

of the rich tapestry of landholdings and privilege that made up the culture of the century-old settlement along both sides of the river. His great-grandfather had been one of the earliest colonists in the area, a member of Escandón's settlement. Before the Americans came, Cortina enjoyed the status and privilege deriving from his family's vast landholdings. As a youngster, Cortina lived on the northern (later Texan) side of the Rio Grande, on the Rancho del Carmen, nine miles upriver from where Brownsville would be built. He felt a sense of entitlement, stemming from his family's wealth, and hence, under the new American order, a sense of injustice as well.

Cheno, as his family and friends called him, had little education, but he understood how to handle men. He could not read or write and did not learn to sign his name until many years later, when he was governor of Tamaulipas. But he was plenty smart. He became a popular leader along the border, especially among the poor, who regarded him as their champion. A local Anglo named Nesmith saw Cortina's natural savvy at work when one of Cheno's men came up to Cortina and asked for money to buy a suit of clothes. Cortina gave him twenty-five cents and said,

"Here, my man, take this money and go buy a suit of clothes."

"General, why do you fool with that poor fellow?" Nesmith remarked. "You know two bits will not purchase a suit of clothes."

"Yes, sir, I do, and so does he. I knew he only wanted money to get drunk on, and now he has it."

Rip Ford, who chased Cortina up and down the border for over two decades and never caught him, called him the black sheep of his family but still found things about him to admire: "He was rather fairer than most men of his nationality. He was fearless, self-possessed, and cunning. In some cases he has acted towards personal and political enemies with a clemency worthy of imitation."

Cortina's early experience with American power occurred in the opening days of the Mexican War, when he fought on the losing side at both Palo Alto and Resaca de la Palma (May 8 and 9, 1846) as a corporal in the Defensores de la Patria, a company from Tamaulipas.

Yet in the first few years after the war, Cortina seemed to accept American victory. In July 1848, he worked for a period as a kind of foreman of a mule team that carried goods into East Texas. His paymaster was none other than Major Chapman.

Cortina also took part in local politics, which became corrupt almost instantaneously, with politicians and businessmen seeking to influence, control, and own the Mexican vote. On election day in Brownsville, according to that tireless observer Abbé Domenech, democracy smelled like cheap liquor: "Tables are placed in the streets, garnished with bottles, full of whiskey, which is liberally distributed to such as take a ticket bearing the name of a certain candidate." Cortina hired out to the Anglos to bring Tejano peons to the polls to vote. He was always good for forty to fifty votes. The Mexicans voted by the "cross-mark" method—x's standing in for the names of those who could not write English. Cross-mark voting became a staple of political control in south Texas. In one instance mentioned in a local newspaper in the 1850s, ninety votes were cast by eight voters. It was fine for Tejanos to vote, but not to serve in office. Though they constituted a huge majority in Cameron County (Brownsville), local government was completely in the hands of a small ruling elite. This situation remained in effect well into the next century. In 1948 Lyndon Johnson bought his way into the U.S. Senate by hiring political bosses in South Texas to manufacture votes, causing him to win by a

razor-thin margin of eighty-seven votes and earn the nickname of
"Landslide Lyndon."

In the decade following the close of the Mexican War, Cortina saw
that much of the land owned by the Tejanos was falling into the hands
of the upstart newcomers. Everything, he felt, was rigged against the
Tejanos, those who had lived there for a century and whose ranchos provided the solid base of a stable, previously secure way of living. The
whole history of the border since the signing of the Treaty of Guadalupe
Hidalgo at the end of the Mexican War pointed to such a conclusion.

The odd pairing of Cortina and King on the same side, in the
Brownsville Separatist Movement of 1850, had to do with vexing
questions about land and titles to land. The outcome of that period of
unrest was the Bourland-Miller Commission, a panel sent to the border by the Texas state legislature in early 1850. William H. Bourland
and James B. Miller had the job of sorting out confusing and conflicting claims regarding Tejano land titles. Neither of them spoke Spanish,
a fact that understandably made Tejanos doubtful. The commissioners
themselves were well aware of Tejano suspicions, Miller writing the
governor that Tejanos felt that "the board was devised to destroy,
rather than to protect their rights." Later, Miller wrote Governor P. H.
Bell that "some action should be had immediately as the Mexicans are
anxious to sell a portion of their land and the Americans equally anxious to purchase." The governor agreed, assuring Miller that speed in
such matters would be certain.

Starting at Laredo, the commissioners worked their way south
down the river, stopping at Rio Grande City, then on to Brownsville,
putting the Tejano titles into a trunk for the trip to Austin. Their work
completed, they embarked on a government side-wheeler, the *Anson,*
but in November 1850 the ship went down in the gulf, opposite
Matagorda. The commissioners survived, but the trunk of titles did
not. Miller wrote to Governor Bell that he had "lost my trunk containing all of the original titles presented at Brownsville." The titles, a
hundred years old, were at the bottom of the Gulf of Mexico.

Miller and Bourland had to try to obtain duplicates, although in
many cases there were none. In lieu of those they took affidavits and
scoured old maps to try to reconstruct the titles of ownership. The
sinking of the government ship confirmed what the Tejanos had
feared all along—that the Anglos were conspiring to steal their lands.

Sharp lawyers set about transferring land titles into Anglo hands. The leading legal expert on land titles in Brownsville was Stephen Powers, a crack attorney with excellent connections. Born in Maine, Powers moved in international circles before coming to Texas. In 1839 he served as U.S. consul to Basel, Switzerland. He came to Brownsville in April 1847 (a month before Richard King) as a first lieutenant attached to General Taylor. Once in Brownsville, Powers became Mr. Everything. He specialized in interpreting Tejano land claims in favor of Anglo clients. He became a legal advisor to M. Kenedy and Co. In time he became one of Richard King's lawyers. He was also county judge and mayor of Brownsville in 1859 when Cortina shot the marshal, who was a Powers appointee. Powers and Cortina were also friends, a fact that further suggests the complexity of border society.

The land issue had a strongly personal side, too. Cortina had seen his mother lose thousands of acres of the Espiritu Santo Grant to Anglo lawyers, and he had watched with mounting fury as local bigwig Adolphus Glaevecke and a Cameron County judge deliberately undermined the estate of one of his aunts. His relationship with Glaevecke was especially complicated and personal. Glaevecke had come to Matamoros back in 1836 and married Concepión Ramirez, Cortina's first cousin. They had six children, and Glaevecke bought a ranch a few miles up the river on the American side. During the Mexican War Glaevecke acted as a courier for General Taylor. After the war he got involved in local politics, becoming a county commissioner and a city councilman. In the late 1850s he and Cortina rustled cattle together, but grew apart as Cortina became upset at Glaevecke's influence over Cortina's mother and his perceived mishandling of the property of one of Cortina's aunts. Things grew worse when Glaevecke had Cortina indicated for cattle theft, and Cortina swore to kill him. Glaevecke was also indicted at the same time for the same thing.

Despite Cortina's friendship with some Anglos and his employment by Anglos earlier in the decade, by 1859 the lines had hardened, and everywhere Cortina looked, he saw Tejano dispossession and Anglo domination. Texan racism and arrogance made him furious.

The racism extended beyond the border. A distinguished older Tejano named Lazaro Garza tried to take his case in person to the Texas legislature. In 1857 Garza traveled to Austin to assert his rights. But once there, he ran up against a committee rule that stated that Tejanos could not testify as U.S. citizens unless "their character for truth and veracity [was] established by the testimony of two white men." Lazaro Garza told the committee that "before he would submit to the indignity . . . he would willingly lose every cent of money and every inch of land to which he might justly be entitled."

Such was the climate and background of Cortina's actions. The loss of lands occasioned by the Mexican War and its long aftermath would no longer be accepted meekly, passively. At the end of the 1850s, Cortina had had enough.

It was also an advantageous time for action because in 1859 General David E. Twiggs, commander of the 8th Military Department, ordered the removal of U.S. troops from Fort Brown, Ringgold Barracks at Rio Grande City, and Fort McIntosh at Laredo. Against the protests of many of Brownsville's leading citizens, the border was suddenly left defenseless.

Following the daring rescue of his compadre in July, Cortina began rounding up a small guerrilla army. His actions had hit a nerve; it wasn't hard to find men to ride with him. Two months later, on Wednesday, September 28, 1859, Cortina launched the action that would reverberate for many years along the border of South Texas. Cortina and a band of seventy-five to a hundred men shattered the predawn quietness of a sleeping Brownsville and did the unthinkable: They seized control of the town. Americans returning from a late-night party in Matamoros saw clusters of armed horsemen riding through the streets shooting and crying "*Viva Cheno Cortina*" and "*Mueran los gringos*" and "*Viva la Republica Mexicana.*" It was all very exciting and very scary.

Cortina and his men rode down Elizabeth Street past the fine homes of the new ruling class, past those of Mifflin Kenedy and Richard King. He appointed sentinels with orders to shoot those who resisted, and he placed Tomás Cabrera, an older man and one of his principal lieutenants, in charge of the men along Elizabeth Street. Cortina went on to Fort Brown, where he intended to fly the Mexican flag but failed to because he couldn't find a rope.

He had mixed success with another purpose of his raid. He had made a list of Anglos to be killed. These included a blacksmith named George Morris who, according to Cortina, had committed numerous murders of Mexicans. Cortina's men killed Morris, and they killed

William Peter Neale, known for having killed two Mexicans recently. They killed the town jailer, Robert J. Johnston, when they broke into the jail and freed the Mexican prisoners being held there, and they killed Viviano Garcia, who tried to help Johnston. They killed a fifth man apparently by accident, an innocent Mexican cart driver.

But they failed to kill Cortina's two most hated names on the death list. Marshal Shears, who had survived the shooting in July, escaped death by hiding in an oven, and Adolphus Glaevecke, whom some of Cortina's men spotted, got away by fleeing down Elizabeth Street until he found his way to a store on Levee Street, where he remained hidden until the raid was over. Many years later, Glaevecke recalled how, from a vantage point in the store where he was hiding, he almost killed Cortina that day: "I brought the gun down to a rest, took good aim at the breast of Cortina, and in one second more he would have gone where he would never have troubled this border any more, if somebody had not thrown up the muzzle of the weapon and signed me not to shoot. Cortina got down from the window without realizing how near to death he had been."

By around seven o'clock that morning, important leaders in Matamoros, roused by the firing in the neighboring American city, had crossed the river to confer with Cortina. General Carbajal, who had played an instrumental role in border politics since the early 1840s, brought with him several other prominent men, including Cortina's cousin, Col. Miguel Tijerina. They succeeded in convincing Cortina to depart from Brownsville, and about seven-thirty he did so, riding slowly like some provincial Caesar from a conquered town, the poor of Brownsville following behind him as he and his men made their way to his family's Rancho del Carmen. In one stroke Cortina had brought a town of 2,500 to its knees. When the U.S. Army officer Major Samuel P. Heintzelman arrived a few months later, he marveled, "This is quite a good sized town & how they could fear the outlaws is more than I can see." One who did not fear him at first was Melinda Rankin, the missionary and teacher. In her book *Twenty Years Among the Mexicans* (1875), she stated that she continued holding classes in her school for the first two weeks after the assault because she knew his "murderous designs" were directed only at his enemies, but then as his ranks began to swell with "desperadoes from all parts," she felt a greater sense of danger.

Two days after the raid on Brownsville, at Rancho del Carmen, Cortina issued a proclamation printed in two languages and handed out on both sides of the river. The English translation is thick going. Addressed to the "inhabitants of the State of Texas, and especially of those of the city of Brownsville," he stated his intention: "To defend ourselves, and making use of the sacred right of self-preservation, we have assembled in a popular meeting." The cause was one of justice that was being denied by "a multitude of lawyers, a secret conclave, with all its ramifications, for the sole purpose of despoiling the Mexicans of their lands and usurp them afterwards." He underscored the nature of Tejano grievances by citing the conduct of his archenemy, Adolph Glaevecke, who, "invested with the character of deputy sheriff, and in collusion with the said lawyers, has spread terror among the unwary, making them believe that he will hang the Mexicans and burn their ranches, etc., that by this means he might compel them to abandon the country, and thus accomplish their object." Cortina's most memorable utterance was italized for emphasis: "*Our personal enemies shall not possess our lands until they have fattened it with their own gore.*" Although branded an illiterate bandit by Anglos, Cortina projected himself as a revolutionary. So it has always been in occupied territories. The terrorist of one generation becomes the statesman of the next.

The Cortina War had begun in earnest.

Cortina's case, historically, was quite strong, and in their heart of hearts the Anglos knew it. Why else their sense of wholesale panic, their continuously exaggerated claims of Cortina's strength, their fear of a massive Mexican retaliation all along the border? A letter appearing in the New Orleans *Daily Picayune* appealed for the return of federal troops to prevent the worst outcome imaginable. That was, quite simply, the changing of the boundary line. "Let the great guns again watch over our dear sister Matamoros, and the soldiers of Uncle Samuel keep marauders here in check, or practically the boundary . . . must be moved back to the Nueces." Another man, E. Basse, wrote to lawyer-rancher W. G. Hale in October 1859, telling him how ominous things were: "It is a much more serious affair than persons abroad think. Cortinas can head the whole Mexican population against us— it is the old feeling that existed before the war."

Anglos in Brownsville rallied to ward off the insurrection. A Committee of Safety was formed, and among its leading organizers were Mayor Powers and Mifflin Kenedy. The city prepared for a second attack, blocking off streets, building barricades of bricks. The committee members asked for help from their old friend in Matamoros, General Carbajal, and he sent some Mexican militia. The complexity of allegiances on the border can hardly be better exemplified than by these actions: a band of Mexicans from Matamoros sent to aid Anglos under attack by a man who had once been a member of the Matamoros militia himself and who also had considered himself a U.S. citizen.

In the meantime Cortina, with about 250 men, crossed into Mexico, taking with him as much Anglo livestock as he could find. People spotted him in Matamoros from time to time, where he was fêted as a hero. But Brownsville appeared safe enough so that the Mexican militia could be sent back home to Matamoros. The Cortina War might have dissolved into inconsequence if not for Anglo retaliation. On October 12, Sheriff Browne and a posse rode north toward Rancho del Carmen, and at nearby San José they arrested Tomás Cabrera, the sixty-five-year-old lieutenant of Cortina's who had played a role in the Brownsville raid back in September. They threw Cabrera in the Cameron County jail, and Cortina, in Matamoros, announced that if Cabrera were not freed, Brownsville would be put to the torch.

When the Anglos refused to release Cabrera, Cortina and about forty men rode back into Texas and set up camp at Rancho del Carmen. Every night, *Cortinistas* fired shots into Brownsville, and Cortina promised to leave the country if Cabrera were released.

The Anglo position hardened. Cortina, they felt, had to be defeated. They thought they could do it out of local enthusiasm. They formed a voluntary militia company of about twenty men and called themselves the Brownsville Tigers. Mayor Stephen Powers got his friend Mifflin Kenedy to donate a four-pound cannon from an M. Kenedy and Co. steamboat, the *Ranchero*. They got the Matamoros militia to rejoin them. The militia had a larger cannon that they brought with them, and together with some Tejano rancheros who sided with the Anglos, the Brownsville forces put together what looked like a small army.

But the Brownsville Tigers and assorted warriors proved no match at all for Cortina. On October 24, 1859, they moved upriver to apprehend Cortina and his men, but nothing worked out as they had hoped. Their muskets didn't fire because of a light mist and some wrong-sized cartridges that were too big for the muskets. The little cannon wouldn't fire, either, and the big cannon got stuck in the mud and had to be abandoned. Then, as William Thompson, leader of the Brownsville Tigers, put it, "Our retreat was in the utmost confusion." The men came straggling back to Brownsville on foot or riding double on horses, mules, and donkeys, their weapons left behind.

Hearing of such success, more Mexicans rushed to join Cortina's "army." His force grew to some four hundred strong.

On October 26 Cortina wrote a letter to Estevan (Stephen) Powers, telling him, as he had said repeatedly, that his target was not the whole of the Brownsville population, many of whom were "faultless," but certain bad men whom he named. Cortina wanted Glaevecke and Marshal Shears—the "squinting sheriff," Cortina called him—and some others turned over to him. Every day, people in Brownsville could see Cortina's men in the distance, and early every morning they could hear the boom of the captured cannons, which Cortina's men had recovered and made work. Brownsville had the nervousness of a town under siege.

King and his family's whereabouts from September 1859 to May 1860—the duration of the Cortina War and a few months afterward—have always been a matter of conjecture. Apparently they were not in Brownsville. Henrietta and the children were no doubt at the rancho, and there may have been a family trip to Kentucky. Richard King certainly stood to lose a great deal if the Cortina War went badly. He owned a house in Brownsville and obviously would not have wanted it put to the torch; he was a partner in a lucrative business whose operations were severely curtailed by the chaos and uproar of the times; he owned an interest in boats, which could be and were construed as military targets; he had many, many friends in business and in the Rangers and the army who were put at peril by Cortina's actions; and he had the entire future of his Santa Gertrudis rancho to think about. If Cortina succeeded in taking South Texas back for Mexico, King's rancho would be a prime piece of real estate to confiscate in the name of something. But undoubtedly the biggest threat had to do with his commercial holdings related to the riverboat trade. His friend Rip Ford estimated that $10 million worth of ordnance, residences, and businesses, including King & Kenedy's fleet of steamboats, were at risk if Cortina struck successfully at Brazos Santiago: "He would certainly have burned everything he could not have taken with him." King's financial well-being was most vulnerable, then, at the mouth of the river, and it was the collective aim of the military command to protect those combined private and government interests. All in all, King played a decidedly minor, background role in the Cortina War, mainly through exercising his generous hospitality at Santa Gertrudis and supplying, in one instance at least, good horses to a contingent of Rangers whose mounts were worn out.

Local methods having failed, Brownsville turned to the state government in Austin for help, and a company of Texas Rangers, led by William C. Tobin, was dispatched to South Texas. The Texas Rangers of this era were a mixed lot. Some were bold and brave, like Col. John "Rip" Ford, Jack Hays, and a dozen other legendary figures. But some were also corrupt and murderous, some were just plain incompetent, and not a few of them were racist to a degree that even by local nineteenth-century standards was hard to stomach. Their behavior in the Mexican War had earned the censure of most U.S. Army officers, and their behavior in the years following the war, in South Texas especially, all the way up to the 1960s, was the cause of much hatred, fear, and distrust by Tejanos and Mexicans alike.

Tobin's Rangers left San Antonio on October 25 and rode south. The road from San Antonio went to Corpus Christi; from there, the overland route to Brownsville was the old Taylor Trail from Mexican War days. Most Ranger units, passing near King's rancho, stopped at the captain's house, where they could always count on a hospitable reception. As Dock Burris, one of Tobin's young firebrands, told it, "We recruits overtook him [Tobin] at Banquette. Thence we started on a forced march to Brownsville, but some of our horses gave out and we had to stop at King's ranch to exchange them for fresh animals."

Freshly mounted, Tobin's band of a hundred unruly Rangers hurried to Brownsville, and no sooner had they arrived than new lawlessness broke out. They were barely in Brownsville for twenty-four hours before a bloodthirsty mob, under the cover of night, broke into the Cameron County jail, dragged Tomás Cabrera to Market Square, and hanged him. Some of Tobin's Rangers were almost certainly responsible for this crime.

Ad hoc Ranger groups continued to arrive. The sheriff of Karnes County, southeast of San Antonio, brought a command of thirty down to Brownsville, and another band from Live Oak County, southwest of San Antonio, came to lend their support. Clearly the Cortina threat was seen to extend to everywhere in South Texas, everywhere that Anglo cattlemen owned land or meant to own land. The Live Oak Rangers chased some Cortinistas into the brush near the old Palo Alto battlefield north of Brownsville, only to be badly shot up. A handful died, and the next day Captain Tobin and the sheriff of Nueces County (Corpus Christi) discovered the dead Rangers, stripped and mutilated.

The war was on in full. Tobin together with new Ranger companies from several south Texas counties moved upriver to find Cortina. At Santa Rita, a small village a couple of miles from Cortina's camp, Tobin's men burned the jacales of the villagers. Once Tobin saw Cortina's camp, though, estimated the size of his army, and observed the cover afforded by dense chaparral, he called off the attack and returned to Brownsville, after which about a hundred Rangers pulled up stakes and returned home without having ever fired a shot. So far Cortina was running rings around the Texans. On November 23, Cortina issued his second *pronunciamiento*. This time he made his case more political than personal. Addressing himself to "Mexicans," he stressed loss of lands and wholesale injustice: "Many of you have been robbed of your property, incarcerated, chased, murdered, and hunted like wild beasts, because your labor was fruitful, and because your industry excited the vile avarice which led them . . ." He ended by pledging to "offer myself as a sacrifice for your happiness." Such fiery words stirred more recruits to come forth. Sixty convicts in a prison at Victoria, Tamaulipas, broke out of jail and came north to join Cortina's army.

The seriousness of the threat posed by Cortina led to the decision, in November, to commit U.S. troops to South Texas, and on November 17 Major Samuel P. Heintzelman rode out of San Antonio in command of elements of the 1st Infantry, bound for Brownsville. Heintzelman, an observant and interesting man, knew or came to know most of the major players in the Brownsville drama. He knew, for example, Major Chapman. In 1857, in Washington, Heintzelman had met with the major and discussed the possibility of Heintzelman investing in a lead and silver mine operation at Vallecillo in Nuevo

Leon, Mexico, where Chapman already held stock in the venture. (Not surprisingly, Charles Stillman, Chapman's old kingpin friend in Brownsville, also owned some of that mining stock.) Chapman arranged a meeting with his friend Samuel Colt, inventor of the famous pistol that helped tame the frontier. Colt, too, was interested in those mines. A year later, on October 18, 1859, at Camp Verde, Texas, Heintzelman wrote in his diary: "Major Chapman committed suicide at Old Point [Virginia]. Nothing known as to the cause. He was subject to fits of depression. It is cool & uncomfortable today."

Details of Chapman's death, on September 28, 1859, were spelled out in a letter written by Major E. S. Sibley four days later to Chapman's older brother, Thomas F. Chapman: ". . . he was found by a couple of his brother officers dead in his bedroom, lying across the bed, evidently having committed suicide by cutting his throat, his hand still grasped the razor which rested in his wound. His death was no doubt instantaneous as the left carotid artery had been severed completely."

On the way south to Brownsville, Heintzelman made an important new acquaintance, Capt. Richard King. He and his infantry stopped at Fort Merrill on the Nueces River on November 22, as noted in his diary: "We recognized Cap. King who is encamped about half a mile below on the Ft. Merrill side. The Banks are bad & the water up to the buggy bottom. Our wagons did not get in till near 2 P.M. We are encamped close by King. He received us very hospitably." But King had no more news than they.

A week later, Heintzelman made camp "near Capt. King's Ranche." King stopped by for a visit, in the company of Capt. James Richardson and the "notorious Captain Henry." Richardson was a former Ranger and veteran of the Mexican War who seemed to Heintzelman like an "overseer or superintendent" of the captain's. He was basically a hired gun. Henry was a piece of work. He had been in the Seminole War, the Mexican War, and had been a filibusterer in Nicaragua and a city marshal and sheriff in Bexar County (San Antonio). Heintzelman considered him "notorious" because of his well-known criticism of the U.S. Army. Henry favored the "dirty shirt Texas Rangers" over the "tidy uniforms" of the regulars.

Heintzelman's next camp, that evening, was "3 miles beyond Captain King's ranche." In his diary he sketched what he knew of the captain: "He owns 15 leagues of land & foaled last year 1000 colts. He has just sent us two sheep. He runs boats on the Rio Grande."

More help came from Austin, only this time it was real help, unlike Tobin's crew. It came in the form of Rip Ford, a Texas-style renaissance man—doctor, lawyer, journalist, Indian fighter, veteran of the Mexican War, and as colorful a figure as ever lived in Texas. John Salmon Ford earned his nickname "Rip" from his habit, in the Mexico City campaign, of writing "R.I.P." after the names of fatalities. In Austin that fall of 1859, as Cortina's men tore up the Rio Grande region, rumors flew in the capital city. Corpus Christi, it was reported, had been sacked and burned. The governor grew very excited and told Ford, "Ford, you must go; you must start tonight and move swiftly." This was in November. By December Ford had a force of fifty-three men under his command. On the way to Brownsville, he swung by King's rancho: "About the first of December, 1859, camp was broken, and we made the ranch of Capt. Richard King, the baron of modern times."

Heintzelman in the meantime had pushed on to Fort Brown, arriving on December 6, 1859. He visited the local sites, such as they were, and in Matamoros admired "the pretty little square ornamented by Major Chapman, when the town was in our possession." His assessment of the general situation along the border underscored Cortina's successes so far: "The county from Brownsville to Rio Grande City, 120 miles, and back to the Arroyo Colorado has been laid waste, the citizens driven out, their horses and cattle driven across the Rio Grande into Mexico." Business all along the border had been disrupted for five months. Of Cortina, Heintzelman wrote to Col. Robert E. Lee, "Cortina was now a great man, he had defeated the Gringos and his position was impregnable; he had the Mexican flag flying in his camp and numbers were flocking to his standard. When he visited Matamoros he was received as the champion of his race— as the man who would right the wrongs the Mexicans had received; some thought he would drive back the hated Americans to the Nueces and some even spoke of the Sabine as the future boundary." Such was the threat posed by Cortina.

Rip Ford's assessment of Cortina's standing tallied pretty closely with the major's. Once Ford arrived in the Valley, he saw what Cortina had done. "Houses had been robbed and fired, fences burned, property destroyed or carried into Mexico. Settlements were broken up for the time being; the inhabitants had fled for their lives. Cortina had committed these outrages upon citizens of the United States regardless of race and upon Mexicans suspected of being friendly to Americans."

Heintzelman wasted little time in going after Cortina. On December 6 he attacked Cortina's camp at the Ebonal ranch north of Brownsville, but Cortina was not present. In less than two weeks Heintzelman was on the march again, headed upriver to engage Cortina. Although he had issued orders for Tobin and Ford to follow, there were problems with Tobin's Rangers. Heintzelman, an efficient, skillful officer, was appalled by the undisciplined behavior of the Rangers under Tobin. He regarded Rip Ford as much superior to Tobin. Ford, he wrote, was "by all odds the better man. He controls his men & Tobin is controlled by his. I would rather have Ford with 50 men than Tobin with all his men."

Heintzelman's diary of his tour in Texas is filled with unfavorable comments on the Rangers. He found that he could not "get the Rangers to do anything effective in the way of scouting" and concluded at one point that "We would undoubtedly have done better without the Rangers." Another time he wrote, "They are doing no service & only bring disgrace upon the country." He detested the "excesses of the Rangers"—their "indiscriminate robbing and plundering of the Ranches of the Frontier which is a disgrace to the Ranger Service." Heintzelman deplored the Rangers' tendency to wage war against the general population. On December 16, he noted, "On our way down the Rangers set fire to a number of houses. I saved some, but the most were burned. On Cortinas's rancho there was a heavy fence [that] made an excellent cover for the enemy. I had that burned down but strictly forbade burning anything without my express order. This is setting a very bad example to Cortinas & the Rangers were burning all—friends and foes."

Sometimes Tobin and his men were a worse threat to local Texas ranchers than Cortina was. Supplies from the ranch of F. M. Campbell, near Brownsville, were requisitioned by both Cortina and Tobin. Tobin's men used his fences and pens for firewood and accidentally burned one of his horses. They butchered his hogs and goats and ate fifty barrels of sweet potatoes. Campbell later filed a claim for damages: "I estimate the value of the property taken by Cortinas as fully two hundred dollars, and the value of property destroyed by Tobin's command at fully one thousand dollars."

On December 19 Tobin's men hanged a "well-dressed," innocent Mexican citizen, a crime that much angered Heintzelman. Heintzelman called Tobin in to rebuke him for failing to control his followers. There were other such hangings that Heintzelman may well not have known about. Long years after the Cortina War was over, Dock Burris of Tobin's company told of several Mexicans being summarily executed: "Another Mexican who was captured at the fight of Rancho Davis stepped into the Great Beyond from the back of Captain Tumlinson's saddle horse, and a fourth one was hanged from a large root that projected from a bluff bank out over the waters of the Rio Grande. Each one of these men richly deserved the fate that befell him, for there was not a crime of which one or the other had not been guilty."

About the only thing any Ranger did that Heintzelman liked occurred on Christmas Day, 1859, at a camp about eight miles beyond Edinburg, when a Ranger gave him an armadillo for dinner and it was "very good."

Despite problems with the Rangers, Heintzelman carried out his mission with dispatch and efficiency. Two days after the armadillo Christmas dinner, he attacked Cortina's forces at Rio Grande City, about a hundred miles north of Brownsville, and won a decisive victory. "We made a great march and surprised them," he wrote in his diary. "Near 50 miles & a fight is pretty good business. I hope now the matter is ended." By Heintzelman's reckoning Cortina lost sixty men, probably a conservative estimate, and a host of guns, ammunition, provisions, and carts. Some of Cortina's men drowned trying to cross the river. The matter wasn't ended yet, though, and neither was the lawlessness of the Rangers. A few days after the Rio Grande City victory, Heintzelman reported that the "Rangers are shooting all the dogs & killing all the chickens, not only in town but in the neighboring ranches."

The defeat of Cortina at Rio Grande City lifted everybody's spirits on the American side. One of Heintzelman's officers, Capt. Arthur Tracy Lee, penned a jaunty lyric celebrating the major's feat. He called it "The Rout of the Black Cortina: A Legend of the 'Rio Bravo del Norte'":

The Heintzelman, five hundred strong,
Fresh from the land of doodle dandy;
With Texas Rangers, five miles long,
Came sweeping up the Rio Grande.

As Heintzelman marched south back to Brownsville, Cortina and his forces retreated into Mexico, remaining there for a month until surfacing at La Bolsa, an extreme horseshoe bend where the river almost doubled back on itself, about thirty-five miles west of Brownsville. Here steamboats were vulnerable to attack, and on February 4, 1860, Cortina launched an attempt to capture the *Ranchero,* the M. Kenedy and Co. sternwheeler whose cannon had been used against him by the Brownsville Tigers and which had been recaptured and reinstalled on the boat. The *Ranchero* was also carrying cargo, including payrolls, worth over a quarter of a million dollars. Rip Ford's Rangers crossed the river and attacked Cortina's forces from the south (Mexican) bank. As the shooting raged, according to Rip Ford, a woman on board the *Ranchero* asked, "Is that the Mexicans shouting?"

"No, madam," a man replied, "it is Texians. Mexican lungs cannot produce such a sound as that vengeful war cry."

The Rangers' steady, accurate fire forced Cortina's men to withdraw. Cortina himself tried to halt them and, in Ford's vivid account, played the part of a valiant hero: "One shot struck the cantle of his saddle, one cut out a lock of hair from his head, a third cut his bridle rein, a fourth passed through his horse's ear, and a fifth struck his belt. He galloped off unhurt."

Heintzelman was in bed in Brownsville late that night, reading, when he received news of the attack on the boat. This second defeat ended the Cortina War, though a little time had to pass before Heintzelman could be sure. On February 11 he wrote, "I heard yesterday that Cortinas was going on the road. His diluted followers must see that there is no hope for him or them, on this frontier." Heintzelman remained in Brownsville, writing reports and keeping an eye on the Rangers, whose units were eager to sack Mexican towns. Heintzelman gave orders for them to stay on this side of the river, and soon the Ranger companies began to disband, leaving the area. On February 29, 1860, Heintzelman sent word to his superiors: "The Cortinas war is over." Even so, the Rangers who remained were still a problem. In April false rumors of Cortina's return percolated through the little town, and Heintzelman blamed them on the Rangers, who "circulate them to keep up the disturbances on the frontier" (April 23, 1860). In fact, Cortina and his men were holed up in the Burgos Mountains for over a year, waiting.

Heintzelman stayed in Brownsville through the spring. On February 26 he "went to the Presbyterian Church, with Mr. Gillam & heard Mr. Chamberlin [Chamberlain]." His view of Reverend Chamberlain echoed Helen Chapman's: "He is a good man, but not much of a preacher. He is a missionary and gets but $500." How Heintzelman knew this last fact would be interesting to know. On April 15 he again attended "the Presbyterian Church & heard Mr. Chamberlin preach." This time his companion was Col. Robert E. Lee, who had been made commander of the military department of Texas. Lee arrived in South Texas, which he knew well from his days there in 1856, with a clear mandate: "I have come with full power to put down the outlaws and will do it if it takes all the soldiers on the frontier." Lee, incidentally, on his journey in March from San Antonio to Brownsville, had also noted the devastation wrought by Cortina and the Rangers: "Nearly all the ranches on the road have been burned—those spared by Cortinas burned by the Rangers." Lee and Heintzelman became friends. On April 30 they again went to Mr. Chamberlain's church, and on May 6 they both "called upon Captain King & his wife. She is a daughter of parson Chamberlin. Captain King had a boat on the river during the war & owns boats here now. All the officers here then know him." The next day, Heintzelman and Lee attended a "devotion party" for Mr. Chamberlain.

On Heintzelman's return to San Antonio from Brownsville, he once again stopped by King's rancho. In his diary for May 12, 1860, he observed, "King's rancho is on a rise & is quite a comfortable place." With him was Colonel Lee, who, family legend has it, had advised the captain, years before, to build the house on just that rise. Lee liked what he saw now and noted in his Memorandom Book for May 12: "At 7 miles reached San Gertrudis—Captain King's ranch— A beautiful place on a knoll in a mesquite plain, new house . . ."

Heintzelman and Lee kept up their friendship after the Cortina War, and when they had both left Texas and returned to Washington, Heintzelman visited Lee at his Arlington mansion, two weeks after

Lincoln's inauguration, in March 1861. A new war pitting the one against the other was a month away, but most of their conversation that day dealt with Texas and the Cortina War.

Although defeated and driven into Mexico, Cortina was still defiant. Cortina did return, in 1861, taking advantage of cover provided by the Civil War. By that time Heintzelman had already been wounded at First Bull Run and Lee had pledged his sacred honor to the cause of the Confederacy. It would be left to others to deal with Cortina.

Cortina would go back to Mexico, but he would not go away. Into the 1870s Cortina's appropriation of livestock along the border rankled Texas ranchers; more Texas Rangers were brought in to try to finish him off once and for all, and still he survived. All he was doing, he said, was getting back "Grandma's" cattle. Twice he served as governor of Tamaulipas. It wasn't until the Mexican government arrested Cortina in 1875 that he was permanently retired from the Texas border. But he outlived many of his old adversaries in Texas. He died in 1894, outliving Richard King by nine years. A *corrido* marked his passing: "The Americans made merry, they got drunk in the saloons,/ out of joy over the death of the famed General Cortinas."

Earlier Texas journalists and historians have traditionally painted Cortina as nothing more than a Mexican bandit, a rogue, an illiterate rabble-rouser who represented lawlessness plain and simple. But this view is quite one-sided. All one has to do to see his position is to consider the geography of the border. What had once belonged to his family was now falling into the hands of strangers, interlopers. What had once been a river was now a boundary, which meant, on the northern bank, the occupation of lands that were being gradually but surely converted from traditional Tejano ownership to new Anglo ownership. The means employed were usually intimidation, technicalities, and tireless maneuverings by shrewd lawyers. The Tejanos felt powerless, dispossessed. To them it was the Yankees who were the outlaws. Rip Ford understood Cortina's appeal to Mexicans as well as anybody did. Ford wrote: "One of Cortina's projects, set forth in some of his proclamations, was the reconquest of Texas. This had been for years a dream in which many Mexicans had fondly indulged. . . . many of his countrymen were led to believe him to be the instrument, in the hands of the Almighty, destined to chastise the insolent North

Americans and restore Texas to the Mexican Union." Ford, incidentally, was one of those who was not content with the new border either. He wanted to push American claims all the way to the mountains in northern Mexico. But the river prevailed.

Had Cortina succeeded in kicking out the Americanos, he would have gone down in history, in Mexican history, anyway, as a great hero. As it is, he remains one of the authentic Tejano political heroes along the border. From the Mexican standpoint, that is; from the American, he remains vilified or forgotten.

CHAPTER 6

His Majesty
King Cotton

In December 1860, Richard King moved his family permanently to Santa Gertrudis to concentrate on ranching. The next year the Civil War turned everything upside down, except King's business.

It made him even richer.

During the war years, Richard King was extraordinarily busy. He had his hand in just about every means there was to make money from his location at Rancho Santa Gertrudis. Most of the money he made had something to do with his friend and partner in Brownsville, Charles Stillman. King appears to have operated as a kind of unofficial agent or silent partner with Stillman in a number of economic activities stemming from their joint pastoral undertakings. There is a fascinating batch of letters from King to Stillman that have survived (preserved in the Stillman Collection in the hospitable archives of the Houghton Library, Harvard University). In them King talks about projects they shared in common.

For instance, there was money to be made in salt, and there were salt deposits on Stillman's Laureles Rancho, which fronted on the Gulf of Mexico. A letter to Stillman from King on March 16, 1862, went into some detail regarding the management practices of W. S. Gregory, Stillman's manager at Laureles. Under Gregory, 31,000 bushels of salt had been gathered by August 1861, but the venture lasted only four months, with low profits. In spring 1862, Cornelius Stillman, Charles's brother, took over the salt operations, and the profits were solid until the end of the war. King also gathered salt near his rancho and shipped it as back freight in the wagons of cotton rolling south. King writes of problems concerning Gregory:

After a good deal of humbuging I made Gregory settle six hundred and forty dollars of our interest he says in the salt business I was satisfied one half of the value of the house ought to go to you. He contended not he contended not I knew it was built out of the stock at the ranch and of course one half was yours. I said you and him would settle it You attend to this before he leaves Brownsville . . . I sent 10 men down to get out salt I will go down in a few days and see what is wanted We will have to send a little money to get things for the lake.

There were always cattle, of course, and always trouble for the cattle raiser in that dry country. King to Stillman, February 7, 1862: "The cattle is a little thin and bitter water down in the rincon and no pens." He concluded, "This is wrote in haste." Again to Stillman, March 16, 1862: "I have a good man with the stock if it does not rain in twenty days I will drive all of them in the Agua Dulce." And this P.S. to a letter of October 18, 1863:

S. Fred came up from the ranch this evening informs me the watter is all gone up above so at the pens and the cattle must be moved from there at once. They must go up to our Ranch at the Pereta the Agua dulce where I have John Walker There are at that place plenty of watter and prey write what shall be done in this matter at once as it is important to act in this matter at once.

In a letter to King in 1862, Stillman himself spoke as a rancher: "All is vanity except cows and mares. A blockader cannot prevent them from having calves and colts." Stillman's reference to blockaders would have caught King's eye. The Union blockade of all Southern ports was designed to shut down the South's principal source of wealth, cotton, and Stillman and King together were going to make a fortune out of circumventing the blockade.

As for sheep, enter the shade of Major Chapman. King to Stillman, February 9, 1863:

I had made a contract with Bryden for the sheep on shares also for our own on the same terms that he had with Major

Chapman in his last contract, one third, he paying all expenses which I thought best. I have not mentioned this to any person. The contract is in my name as I infered from your previous letter that you wanted me to keep them. If you wish it, I will see Bryden and see if he will give them up.

PS: I put my fine full breed Merino Bucks with them. . . . There was not a buck with the sheep when I bought them.

And from the sheep came wool. More on Chapman's flock—King to Stillman, July 14, 1863:

The wool is all baled and in fine order, belonging to the Chapman Flock. Mr. Bryden wishes to sell to you his third of the wool. It is in square bales and in a good house at Banquete. . . . It is a better lot of wool that has been shorn from the flock in any of the previous years. . . . Let me hear from you on this matter as soon as you can as Mr. Bryden wishes to go to the Rio Grande to lay in or fit out for his ranch . . .

Sheep raising is a story largely overlooked in the history of that region. In 1867 King sold 25,000 pounds of wool. By 1873 he was one of the top five wool producers in Nueces County.

Salt, cattle, and sheep were sources of moneymaking, but in those years cotton was the ticket. Not raising it, though, shipping it. Thus King wrote to Stillman on October 18, 1862: "There are so many damed secessionests traveling now across You can not tell who to believe, but what I state is true. I could trade a good deal of goods here for cotton if you and Kenedy would assist me." Another letter from Rancho Santa Gertrudis on April 15, 1862, gave details of how the operation worked at King's end:

The Col [a man named Fortune] has about one hundred bales of cotton on the road from the Brasos River for Brownsville from his plantation. He wants you to advance him one thousand doll in Confederate money to pay his taxes as his cotton will not get to Brownsville in time to realize from it to pay his taxes and you can pay yourself out of the cotton when it arrives at Brownsville any interest on the amount he will also pay you. I will guarantee the delivery of the cotton to you if you advance on this.

Texas's distance from the heart of the Confederacy was something of an advantage, as no Sherman ever marched through Texas laying waste to every standing structure and blade of grass. More than that, the uniqueness of Texas geography, with its shared international boundary of the Rio Grande and a usable port at Brazos Santiago, made South Texas absolutely crucial to the South's economy. That economy could be summed up in one word: cotton. Cotton anchored the plantation system, and cotton was the one crop produced in the South that was critical to the economic needs of industrialized nations such as the northern United States, England, and France.

The new Confederate government formed in Richmond and headed by Jefferson Davis knew the value of cotton but miscalculated how best to manage this great and indispensable resource. What the Confederates intended to do was hold cotton off the market and thereby squeeze England into coming into the war on their side. That didn't happen, though England's mill workers certainly felt the effects of declining cotton shipments. In 1862, only eighteen of the eighty-four factories in the district of Blackburn, in northwest England, were working full time. In Lancashire high rates of starvation resulted from loss of jobs based on the unavailability of cotton. Four million people in England's textile mills depended upon cotton for their livelihood; over a half-million in France did likewise.

In April 1861, that first spring of the war, the North announced a blockade of all Southern ports from which cotton could be shipped or military supplies received. By this means the North hoped to strangle the Southern economy and severely cripple its capacity to make war. The blockade proved effective except for one port, Brazos Santiago. Here the problem for the North was, again, the peculiar nature of the geography and history of the area. The Treaty of Guadalupe Hidalgo, which ended the Mexican War in 1848, had established the Rio Grande as an international waterway, "free and common to the vessels and citizens of both countries." Moreover, Union naval ships could not enter the river at its mouth and ascend because of the shallowness of the water and an intervening sandbar. The Confederates also had cannon positioned near the mouth to discourage any that tried.

Charles Stillman, the wily founder of Brownsville and a businessman extraordinaire, grasped the possibilities for shipping contraband cotton with his usual acumen. He formed a new company, Kenedy, Stillman & King, organized specifically to handle the flow of cotton from the interior to the sea. Although born in the North, Stillman had been on the border for a long time, long enough to be known as Santiago, and he loved the South. When war broke out in 1861, he wrote his wife: "I still love our whole country, though I feel that the Northern people are the most unworthy portion. My sympathy is with the South. In fact, I never desire to go north again." He stayed in Texas until he was forced to leave in 1865, when both sides wanted to try him for treason. Stillman was already rich, a millionaire, when the war began; by war's end he was even richer, and he brought along with him his friends Mifflin Kenedy and Richard King, among others.

At the outset Stillman recognized the need for covert action. In August 1861, he told a friend that the entire Texas crop of cotton for that year could be shipped on the river "with Mexican permits, and under the British Flag." He jauntily wrote to his agent in New York: "We must all turn Turks or Japanese, and carry some of their rags at the Mast-head." In the first year of the war Stillman and his associates used British registry to provide cover for their shipments, but when the *Portsmouth,* a U.S. naval blockader, arrived at the mouth of the Rio Grande in February 1862, new measures had to be taken. Stillman met with Rip Ford, commander of Confederate troops in the area, and other interested parties and conceived a plan to foil the blockader. A group asked the captain of the *Portsmouth* if he was blockading Mexico, and when he said no, Mexico was neutral, Stillman and his associates changed the registry of all steamboats owned by M. Kenedy and Co. to Mexican registry. Now the boats of Kenedy and King flew under Mexican flags. The system worked beautifully; there was nothing the Yankees could do. Stillman advised an associate in New York to send a ship carrying goods to Brownsville, where it could be registered under the Mexican flag: "I will sell her to some Mexican friend and we will adopt the Turkey Buzzard now that the Eagle has her wings clipt."

The federals understood the problem perfectly, too. In September 1862, a U.S. naval commander, H. French, sent back reports outlining the difficulties. He noted that there were twenty ships near the mouth of the Rio Grande, each being loaded with cotton. They flew flags of Spanish, English, Bremen, Danish, and Prussian registry, and every day Mexican steamers and lighters ferried bales of cotton to the waiting vessels. There was absolutely nothing he could do to disrupt such international trade. The secretary of the navy, Gideon Welles, wrote Secretary of State William H. Seward in May 1863: "An effective naval blockade of the Rio Grande, which is a neutral highway for Mexico and ourselves, is impracticable."

Off Brazos Santiago ships from many nations awaited the loading of the cotton bales. The ships bobbed at anchor about three miles out in the Gulf. In March 1863, 180 to 200 ships were reported off the coast waiting to be loaded with cotton or to unload their cargoes of goods, military supplies, and sundry items for shipment to the interior. Getting the cotton onboard could be very time-consuming, however. It sometimes took over a month to convey the cotton in lighters from storage on land to the ships. In winter it was worse. Capt. George G. Randolph, in January 1863, reported thirty vessels at anchor awaiting the loading of some 10,000 bales of cotton. Randolph said it sometimes took two to three months to complete the loading of a ship. Low water was a problem, choppy water another. No matter how much time and difficulty were involved, the profits made the wait worth the time spent at the mouth of the river. One merchant sold a quantity of goods in early 1863 for $139,000 that had cost him $36,000. American naval ships were ineffective in stopping the flow of contraband. The Lincoln government did not want to offend other nations, and the presence of ships from England, France, Germany, Switzerland, and "Mexico" rendered the United States impotent to do anything about the shipping. By November 1863, 150,000 bales of cotton had been shipped out of Matamoros. By the end of the war, this number had more than doubled.

Although Mexico was officially neutral during the war, close ties between prominent Mexicans and Texans along the border meant that arrangements of mutual convenience were always possible. Sailing under fake flags and using the names of such friends as Santiago Yturria, José Morell, and Jeremiah Galvan, Stillman's ships carried cotton out of the Confederacy and brought in salt, munitions, and other supplies. Details of a transaction in late 1863 are typical. Stillman, adopting the name of business associate José Morell, sent 530 bales of cotton to New York that sold for $177,511.51. Deducting the cost of the cotton and all other shipping expenses, Stillman would have cleared a profit of about $15,000, or a return of at least 17 percent. The demand for cotton amounted to a frenzy on both sides of the border. José Morell wrote Stillman from Monterrey early in 1864: "Yesterday a lot of Rebs & a lot of Yanks left. Some went up & some went down. Glory be to the Father. They all seem to be after the same object, His Majesty King Cotton."

Although the Yankees were not fooled, they were powerless to stop the commerce. A Union officer declared Matamoros "but another name for Brownsville" and spoke directly of Charles Stillman's part in the elaborate and profitable subterfuge: "It may be that all this correspondence and trading with and consigning cargoes to so notorious a partisan of the rebels as Charles Stillman is perfectly legitimate, honorable, and eminently patriotic, but it still somewhere conflicts with my preconceived ideas of what should be regarded by every loyal citizen and honest man as illegal, dishonorable, and traitorous to the last degree . . ."

Kenedy, Stillman & King located their headquarters in Matamoros. King oversaw the collection and delivery of the cotton from the interior to Brownsville, whereupon Kenedy took over and got the bales across the river to Matamoros; from there he and Stillman sold the cotton and had it conveyed to the mouth of the Rio Grande on M. Kenedy and Co. steamships. General Bee called them "the patriotic contractors, Kenedy, Stillman & King," and they kept the supplies rolling. John Warren Hunter, a teamster who drove cotton to Brownsville, described how things worked along the border. The Mexican customs officials, he wrote, were "human—very human—and were not always immune against the lure of Confederate gold." With bribes in hand, cases of Enfield rifles were labeled "hollow ware," gunpowder was given the name of "bean flour," and percussion caps became "canned goods."

Once again Kenedy, Stillman & King were practicing the form of capitalism they liked best: a monopoly. Only this time they had a double monopoly: on the overland shipment of cotton and on the familiar water route from Roma, Rio Grande City, and Brownsville to the Gulf.

While Stillman and Kenedy labored on the border, King worked tirelessly at his rancho, overseeing every wagon that rolled through it. Early in the war the strategic value of King's rancho was officially recognized. The Military Board of Texas declared in March 1862 that King Ranch would serve as a collection point for Confederate cotton. Here cotton from East Texas, Arkansas, Louisiana, and Missouri would be received, stored, and shipped to Brownsville. The cotton road ran from Alleyton, a small village and railroad terminus located on the east bank of the Colorado River in the southeastern part of the state, to Goliad, and from there to King's rancho and on to Roma, Rio Grande City, or Brownsville. Eventually everything went through Brownsville/Matamoros to the smugglers' village of Bagdad, a few miles from the mouth of the river, on the Mexican side, and from thence to the nations of the world.

Teamster John Warren Hunter noted: "All roads from every cotton section of the state in the direction of Brownsville converged at King's Ranch. . . . and during the spring, summer, and fall seasons, this long stretch of 125 miles became a broad thoroughfare along which continuously moved two vast unending trains of wagons; the one outward bound with cotton, the other homeward bound with merchandise and army supplies." The trains sometimes took months to reach their destination. One that left Pittsburg in east Texas on September 1, 1862, didn't reach Brownsville until July 22 of the next year.

Kenedy, Stillman & King made money from everybody: the Confederate government, individual contractors and shippers, and anybody else who had something to offer in the lucrative business of transporting cotton, the lifeblood of the Confederacy.

On April 28, 1863, the firm signed a contract with the Confederate government to supply and outfit its troops on the border. The government would finance the supplies by delivering 500 bales of cotton to Kenedy, Stillman & King for a period of six months. In the Confederacy cotton was as good as gold.

In 1863 Brownsville was the greatest shipping point in the South and, for a time, the most important city in Texas. Matamoros enjoyed even greater prosperity, going from an obscure little border town to a booming city of 30,000 by the end of the war. An observer writing in early 1865 summed up its importance: "Matamoros is to the rebellion west of the Mississippi what New York is to the United States—its great commercial and financial center, feeding and clothing the rebellion, arming and equipping, furnishing it materials of war and a specie basis of circulation that has almost displaced Confederate paper . . ."

By July 1864, Stillman had invested $432,004 in securities, profits from the rich concourse of goods flowing in and out of the entrepôt at Brownsville/Matamoros. By the end of the war, he had plucked a cool million out of what the Mexicans called *Los Algodones,* the cotton boom.

The fall of Brownsville to Union troops in November 1864 did not dampen Stillman's activities; instead, he went on as before. Even during the first months of the occupation Stillman managed to transport almost a thousand bales of cotton to New York. One shipment, in March 1864, led to a congressional investigation, but the congressmen, although totally convinced of Stillman's involvement, couldn't pin anything on him. Not only did he survive congressional scrutiny, he turned a nice profit on the shipment. In Brownsville the federals seized his property, including his ranch north of Brownsville, but unknowingly placed them under the administration of an old Stillman friend, George W. Brackenridge. Like Stillman, Brackenridge was a flexible businessman. Earlier in the war he had operated a cotton firm and sold cotton to Stillman. But then he had gone over to the Unionist side and was now working for the U.S. Treasury Department—a case of the fox guarding Stillman's henhouse. The profits Brackenridge made from his association with Stillman became the seed money for the San Antonio National Bank, founded by Brackenridge.

Stillman himself also took the Oath of Loyalty to the Union—a tactic for survival rather than an act of principle. When the federals withdrew from Brownsville in the summer of 1864, he regained his property. But that summer he also suffered a debilitating stroke, leaving an arm paralyzed. Early in 1865, before the Confederacy collapsed, he left his beloved border for good and returned to New York, but he did so in typical Stillman fashion, stealthily, by sailing first to England and then to New York on a transport ship that did not have to list his name on the passenger list. He rejoined his family and later that year received a pardon for anti-Unionist activities from President Andrew Johnson.

Stillman invested heavily in the National City Bank of New York, from profits dredged out of the faraway little towns of Brownsville and

Matamoros. His son James, born in the house on Elizabeth Street in 1850, eventually became president of National City Bank in 1891 and enjoyed great success. In Texas alone he held interests in sixteen banks and, with his powerful friends, controlled railroads and land development companies in Texas and Mexico. Money made in South Texas eventually reached around the globe.

Richard King seemed to thrive in the wartime atmosphere. He oversaw all aspects of shipping cotton from his rancho and its vicinity, looking after teamsters and other visitors, outfitting men with whatever they needed, and managing the livestock operations on his properties. He had also to keep a sharp eye out for cattle thieves, raiders, and Yankee troops, who by 1863 had begun to probe the Wild Horse Desert. There was danger everywhere. His family needed to be protected, and his wife was pregnant with their fifth child.

All the activity surrounding the rancho at Santa Gertrudis enhanced King's influence and reputation with each visitor who passed that way. One such was a plucky British officer, Lt. Col. Arthur J. L. Fremantle of the Coldstream Guards, who made a famous three-month tour of the Confederate states in the spring and summer of 1863. Fremantle, who eventually fetched up at the Battle of Gettysburg in Pennsylvania in the summer of 1863, landed at Brazos Santiago in April of that year. After spending some time in Brownsville he, two drunken muleskinners, and a "little Jew" labored over the sands of the Wild Horse Desert, headed toward San Antonio. The most colorful of the muleskinners, a staunch Confederate sympathizer named Sargent, would say to a recalcitrant animal, "I wish you was Uncle Abe, I'd make you move, you G—d d—n son of a ——."

As they neared King's rancho, six days out of Brownsville, Fremantle recorded in his diary for April 20: "We toiled on till 11:30 A.M., at which hour we reached '*King's Ranch.*' Which for several days I had heard spoken of as a sort of Elysium, marking as it does the termination of the sands, and the commencement of comparative civilization." Colonel Fremantle pronounced the house a "comfortable, well-furnished wooden building." The Kings, however, were not there, as they had gone to Brownsville. But Mrs. Bee, the wife of the general with whom Fremantle had visited on the border, was. Fremantle enjoyed his brief visit with this "nice lively little woman, a red-hot Southerner."

When Fremantle and his party rode away later that day, what he saw was testimony to King's progress toward building a major ranching operation: "We now entered a boundless and most fertile prairie, upon which, as far as the eye could reach, cattle were feeding. Bulls and cows, horses and mares, came to stare at us as we passed. They all seemed sleek and in good condition, yet they get nothing but what they can pick up on the prairie."

The livestock in the fields, his house, his family—these were what King stood to lose in the Civil War; these were what he pledged himself to protect.

Later that year, on December 23, 1863, the war came to King's rancho. That morning, at first light, a force of about eighty federal and Mexican troops, under the command of Capt. James Speed, rode up to the headquarters at King's rancho, shouting and firing into the main house. Among the people inside were Henrietta King and her four young children, Nettie, seven, Ella, five, Richard Jr., three, and Alice, one. A word about the baby, Alice: Born on the rancho on April 29, 1862, Alice Gertrudis King, whose very name bespoke her rootedness in that place, would grow up to be the most important offspring of Richard and Henrietta King in the sense that it was her marriage to a Kleberg that would cement the dynasty that would last more than a century.

The day of the raid, Henrietta King was pregnant with their fifth child. Others present in the household were her father, old Hiram Chamberlain, who had been brought to the rancho for safety from the turbulence and chaos of Brownsville, where the war raged; Francisco Alvarado, a faithful Kineño whom Captain King especially valued for his services to the Kings; and possibly others. The little community totaled approximately 120 in all, including about forty Mexican vaqueros and Anglo ranchhands, at least two slaves, and a handful of Anglo ex–Texas Ranger types, gunmen essentially, hired to protect the holdings from Mexican bandits and Yankee troops. There was even a small detachment of Confederate cavalry stationed at the rancho, though they were absent that day, as was Captain King himself.

Hiram Chamberlain provided the best eyewitness account of the episode. Writing in his capacity as chaplain of the 3rd Texas Voluntary Infantry, he related the events to Lt. Col. E. F. Gray of the 34th Texas Infantry, in a letter that was printed in the Houston *Tri-Weekly*

Telegraph, on February 1, 1864. According to Chamberlain, the people in the house offered no resistance, but the house was plundered anyway, the ladies' trunks and clothes spilled out, all the horses and mules stolen, and the "negroes" set free, though they refused to act upon their freedom. He also reported that one "Mexican" in the house was killed. The Yankees took several prisoners, including Anglos and Mexicans, and one lieutenant repeatedly ordered Chamberlain to mount up, as well, but Chamberlain replied, "You don't want me, an old man of 67 and a member of the Gospel." Finally, another officer told Chamberlain "to tell Captain King, that if one bale of cotton were removed or burned, he would hold him responsible with his life." Here was the principal reason the Yankees had Tara-ized King's rancho: It was cotton—and Captain King's role in the contraband game.

The Yankees didn't leave until two days later, whereupon Henrietta King and her family, in her father's words, departed "that once pleasant home" on a "journey to a place of safety." Chamberlain concluded that for the time being he knew "of no better plan to pursue than to remain as a sort of protector of my daughter, Mrs. King, until I receive the orders of the officers commanding."

The "Mexican" whom he mentioned as having been killed was Francisco Alvarado. Far more than a servant, Alvarado had been with Richard King since the inception of the rancho and was considered so reliable and valuable that the captain himself had asked him to move into the main house while he was away.

Chamberlain also mentioned in his report the "absence of Captain King and all military force." Much has been made of this absence, and previous chroniclers have sought to find some excuse for the captain's being away when his family was in such peril. But Captain King had not in fact stayed away or gone into hiding out of some fear or some desire for self-preservation, though it is certainly true that if he had been there, he would probably have been hanged on the spot. King was not negligent regarding his family's safety, nor was he absent for any base motive. Where he was and what he was doing are clear from a cache of letters that cover the period from November 1863 through January 1864, and shed an enormous amount of light on King's thinking and his activities as a Confederate during this period.

On November 2, 1863, Major General Nathaniel P. Banks landed a force of 6,000 Union soldiers at Brazos Santiago and set out toward

Fort Brown, where a much smaller contingent of Confederates, 1,200, was in camp. Their commander was General Hamilton Bee, a friend of Richard King's whose wife in fact was at King's rancho in October and November. Following orders, Bee did not put up a fight. Instead he ordered that the artillery guns be rolled off a high bank into the river. The townspeople were alarmed at the sight, even more so when they saw men with torches, Confederates, setting fire to all the cotton bales stacked in the cotton yard awaiting shipment to the coast.

Next, Fort Brown was put to the torch, creating a general panic. The citizens of Brownsville tried to flee with their valuables across the river, and at the ferry landing fire spread generally when the magazine at the fort exploded, showering the area with flaming pieces of wood and debris. Two city blocks of Brownsville were badly damaged by fire, and much of the city was sacked and looted by border riffraff. Some citizens asked the old Texas nemesis General Cortina for help, but he replied, "This is your fight, not mine," and remained in Matamoros.

General Bee not only destroyed all the cotton in Brownsville, he and his men burned all the cotton they found on their retreat toward King's rancho. In doing so, they were destroying the dreams and hopes of fellow Southerners. The teamster John Hunter remembered a sad occurrence from this time. Visiting at King's rancho a few weeks before the fall of Brownsville, he had encountered a "neighborhood" train of twenty-five wagons that had struggled down to South Texas from Arkansas. The wagons carried cotton that represented the collective labor of families hit hard by the exigencies of war. The wagons were driven by "old white haired men, young boys and a few trusted negro uncles." Dressed in tatters, they were as poor as Job's goat and had in their keeping "the product of the sweat and unremitting toil of tender women and little children."

The day after Brownsville fell, Hunter spotted the remnants of the Arkansas cotton wagons on Jackass Prairie, about four miles from Brownsville. They had gotten that close, only to have General Bee's men, against all pleadings, set fire to their cotton. Hunter could not forget the "pathetic incident." The air smelled of burning cotton, smoke rose from the burning bales, and the forlorn "old men were sitting around as if in a stupor, while the boys wandered aimlessly about, silent, morose, as if trying to comprehend the enormity of the calamity that had engulfed them in general ruin."

With the Unionists in control of Brownsville and the cotton market in disarray, King was busy in November and December trying to protect his family and property. On November 12, a few days after the Brownsville debacle, King wrote to Capt. E. P. Turner, assistant adjutant general and office manager for Major General John B. Magruder, who commanded the Confederate District of Texas.

King, who was perfectly capable of writing a good letter, though perhaps lacking in the niceties of grammar and spelling, relied upon Russell Holbein to handle his correspondence. Holbein, an Englishman, had formerly worked for Henry Lawrence Kinney, the colorful founder of Corpus Christi. King hired him in 1863 as secretary and bookkeeper, services Holbein performed the rest of King's life. Rip Ford recognized Holbein's value to King, calling him a "trusted clerk, undeviating friend, and tried advisor." Holbein was another example of one of King's great strengths—the good judgment to hire men who possessed knowledge and expertise that he did not. Throughout his career on the river and on the ranch, King acquired excellent help from men with special ability, whether they were lawyers or vaqueros or gunmen or, in the case of Holbein, adept in the king's English. Holbein certainly gave King's communications the imprimatur of correct usage, though I actually prefer the directness and vernacular vigor of the ones from King's own hand, written to Stillman.

The letter of November 12 ended with a plea for help from the Confederate army. "We hope to God," wrote King/Holbein, that "this section of Country is not to be abandoned without a struggle or at least without giving the people notice that it is to be entirely abandoned, so that we can at least send our families to a place of safety. We have certainly done our part towards the Government, and look to it for a share of protection in common with the East." By "East" King meant East Texas, which General Magruder seemed more worried about because of Unionist activity in Louisiana. King and his friends strongly disagreed with Magruder's recent reversal of his earlier policy of holding "the Rio Grande at all hazards" in favor of concentrating on the defense of East Texas. The letter closed with a very strong utterance of King's sense of his region's predicament: "We think from 2 to 3,000 Cavalry can protect this section against any thing the enemy can bring—if we cannot get this number, let us have 500 good determined Texans, from whom a good account will be given, and this Country saved from utter destruction—do not abandon us for God sake!"

But help of that magnitude was not forthcoming; in fact, no help at all was on the way.

A month later the situation had worsened considerably. On December 13, King's letter to Captain Turner carried a greater sense of personal urgency. Pointing to the "Confusion created by the occupation of the Lower Rio Grande by the enemy," King described his concern for his family: "As to myself, I am difficult to be moved, but must confess, in common with the multitude, I became somewhat alarmed, and began to consider about moving my family into the interior for safety; and applying the torch to my domicile." Instead, he said, he would wait it out: "So myself and my family are still here, and intend remaining until we see or hear something to warrant our breaking up."

He pointed out that if had he left with the first "Stampede"—a slighting reference to the mass exodus from Brownsville—everything on the rancho would have been lost, and he pledged once more that he had "nothing but what the Government can have, if required." King's patriotism—to the Confederacy—was a constant thread in these letters.

He also stressed that he hoped the enemy would be taught that "the territory between the Rio Grande and Nueces, *is not* 'Public property and free to all' as *he* asserts it to be." King was referring to official Yankee policy as articulated by General N. J. T. Dana, Union commander: "I wish to kill, burn, and destroy all the Rebels own that cannot be taken and secured." To carry out these intentions, General Dana put border riffraff, thieves, and murderers on the payroll. Their mission: to terrorize the cotton trains rolling south.

King asked again for help, specifically for "a few Mounted Companies" that would patrol west of the Nueces River, throughout the Wild Horse Desert, and he suggested these companies be in the command of Rip Ford, his old friend from the Cortina War days, or Matt Nolan, like Ford a stalwart fighter who at age twelve had served as a bugler in the Mexican War, then later as a Texas Ranger, and later still as sheriff of Nueces County. (In 1864 Nolan was gunned down in front of his home in Corpus Christi by two Unionist brothers.)

King also informed Captain Turner of his own efforts to protect himself and his family and ranching operations. During his layover at King's rancho, General Bee had commissioned J. J. Richardson, who worked for King, to organize a company of "Partisan Rangers." The company, in which King served as a private, had forty members, and as King pointed out, they possessed "a thorough knowledge of every trail, water-hole and hiding place." No doubt they did. Their foes were, King wrote, "hordes of Mexican Bandits and Texas Renegades, that are now swarming on the Rio Grande," and, of course, "the common enemy," namely, Yankees.

King promised that his Ranger company's relations with "trusty Mexicans on this and the other side of the Rio Grande" would ensure the collection of accurate information. But he also asked that General Magruder officially sanction the formation of the Partisan Rangers. That way, in case of capture, the members of the Rangers would be "recognized as prisoners of war, and not as an armed mob!" Otherwise they would be subject to summary execution.

The next letter, sent over a month later, on January 20, 1864, filled in King's activities before the raid on the rancho and afterward. Addressed to Col. A. G. Dickinson, a staff officer to General Magruder and commandant of the San Antonio garrison, it was written from the field, where King and his Rangers were encamped at Puerta del Agua Dulce, a big parcel of land (26,131 acres) about twenty-six miles south of San Patricio, which King had purchased in 1857. (King enclosed this letter to Captain Turner in Houston.) Before the raid, King said, he and a company of fourteen Rangers under the command of J. J. Richardson had ridden from the rancho in pursuit of a band of robbers who had driven off some of King's cattle.

King and company rode all the way to Rio Grande City and searched the river northward looking for both cattle and Yankees. They didn't find any Yankees, but "reached the Rio Grande, above Roma," King wrote, "just in time to see my stolen stock on the opposite bank of the Rio Grande; which was mortifying in the extreme." The angry Rangers crossed the river to Mier, the old Mexican city that dated from the 1740s, and told the authorities that any repetition of such actions would result in retaliation. They were informed that 400 Yankees were in the area but never saw any. King went on to point out the need for state troops to patrol the border, and that thousands of horses and cattle had already been stolen and driven into Mexico—

a constant theme from the time of Cortina onward. Still, the Partisan Rangers acted as a deterrent. According to Matt Nolan, writing to Rip Ford in March 1864, Richardson's company of Rangers was "very effective; it is notorious that their presence, activity and vigilance have held the enemy in check, intimidated their advance from penetrating far into our settlements, and have prevented marauding parties from entirely sweeping this section of all stock and moveable property."

It was while the Rangers were on the sortie to the Rio Grande that the Yankees raided King's rancho. King's account obviously incorporated details he would have heard from his father-in-law and wife: "During my absence, a party attacked my Rancho, consisting of about 80 men, one half whites, the remainder Mexicans, fired several shots into the house, killed one man, broke open trunks, and took what they wanted. Stole quite a number of my best animals, all my wife's carriage horses, and made a free gift to my Negroes of all that was left." He also put in a jibe at the Yankees: "They were in a dreadful hurry, and were worse frightened than the ladies in the house." The day after the raid, a detachment of troops came to the rancho and burned all the cotton on hand, about eighty bales.

Back on his home ground of Santa Gertrudis in January, King was trying to gather his horse stock, but he didn't know, he said, "where to drive them, as there is no grass east of the Nueces." In a letter to Rip Ford on January 30, 1864, King noted the grim conditions: "The grass is as bad as it gets here. We Western people are, in fact, in a starving condition." Everybody was complaining about the terrible drought of 1863–64. Major L. M. Rogers gave a fuller picture of the drought in a letter to Ford in February 1864: "You cannot imagine how desolate, barren, and desert-like this country is; not a spear of grass, nor a green shrub, with nothing but moving clouds of sand to be seen on these once green prairies." Ford observed hundreds of domestic animal carcasses shriveling in the dust around dry water holes. Moving cavalry through such country was, he wrote, "an undertaking of great moment."

Weather aside, the main thrust of King's letter to Colonel Dickinson was to protest against false reports circulating as to King's loyalty to the Confederacy and to assert once more King's unwavering commitment to the Confederate cause. Specifically, the false charge, which

King vehemently denied, was that he had taken the Oath of Loyalty to the U.S. government. Said King, "The Commanding General, as well as the entire Army from Richmond to the Rio Grande, know that all I possessed was at the service of the Government." By way of illustration of his loyalty, he pointed out that "When Gen. Bee and Col. Duff passed my Rancho, on their retreat from Brownsville, I tendered them, in writing, my entire stock of horses and mules for the use of the Government, and turned them over, all the horses and mules I could succeed in gathering with the few hands I then had; this looks like my taking the Oath of Allegiance to the Yankee Government!" King also asserted that his partner, Capt. M. Kenedy, stood equally firmly for the Confederacy: "I am satisfied he has not taken the Yankee Oath, and that he never will."

King's indignation led him to further vigorous defense of his own actions. "I have lived twenty eight years of my life in the Confederacy, and intend to live therein, the balance of my days," he wrote. He also asserted that he had "given more to the government, than all the people between the San Antonio and Rio Grande rivers; and still continue to do so." Although he felt himself much abused, he remained confident: "I am broad between the shoulders, and think I can survive the pressure."

Those who said bad things against King were in all likelihood opposed to the speculation in cotton engaged in by him and his friends and business associates, Mifflin Kenedy and Charlie Stillman. One Unionist in Brownsville, Gilbert D. Kingsbury, charged that King was "a slave to Gold!"

In another letter also dated January 20, 1864, from "In Camp, Puerta del Agua Dulce," and likewise addressed to Col. A. G. Dickinson in San Antonio, King again refuted charges of disloyalty and again summarized the ravages of war visited upon his rancho. "On returning to my Rancho," he wrote, "I found it entirely abandoned, in fact a complete wreck; and having no place that I could call my home, being busily engaged in gathering my horse stock (which is scattered to the four winds) to, prevent the same from falling into the hands of the enemy and Mexican robbers." Near the end of this letter, King once more eloquently affirmed his commitment to the South: "All my property has been made in the South by the sweat of my brow, and I intend by the same means to protect and enjoy it therein."

There was also an economic urgency underlying his appeals. The government cotton contract with King and his friends had been canceled under the cloud of suspicion. In February 1864, the charges against King were dismissed, his loyalty reaffirmed, and the contract started up again. The river of cotton flowed south as before.

King insisted that he had not taken the Oath of Loyalty to the Lincoln government, nor had his partner, Mifflin Kenedy. Nor, he believed, had Charles Stillman, but in this he was mistaken, for Stillman had sworn the oath in December 1863. This made no difference in his relations with King and Kenedy, and all three continued to profit from the cotton boom.

In February 1864, the Kings' fifth child was born. They named him Robert E. Lee King.

CHAPTER 7

Ricardo King, Owner of the Hacienda Gertrudis

One day in November 1875, Richard King looked up from whatever he was doing at that moment on the rancho at Santa Gertrudis to see a small herd of longhorns being driven toward his property. They bore his brand; they were his cattle, all right, but he was surprised to see them.

The boys driving them, for they were boys, were Texas Rangers, and they were mighty glad to be back at King Ranch with something to show for their efforts. King came forward to greet them and hear their story. It was a good one. They had ridden into Mexico and fought Mexican bandits on their home ground and the upshot of it was, they'd retrieved these thirty-five of the captain's stolen longhorns and here they were. King couldn't have been happier. This was the first time in all his life as a rancher that any of his numerous stock had been recovered from Mexico.

During the Civil War, from the north bank of the river, he had observed his cattle on the other side, in Mexico, plain as day—and had been powerless to do anything about it. "Mortifying in the extreme," he said. It galled him, but there it was. He knew that other of his cattle had been stolen and driven across the river, and once there, they were gone. But now this band of daring boys had done it; they had brought back some of his stock. A celebration was in order, and King arranged food and drink for the young Rangers and decreed that the right horn of each steer should be sawed off and the cattle turned loose

in the fenced pasture, there to graze out their days like pensioned soldiers returning from a war, which in effect they were. Thereafter they
were called the *viejos,* the old ones, and everybody accorded them
their proper due and respect.

The return of King's cattle, though few in number, marked a special moment of personal triumph for him in the bandit war of the
1870s, an undeclared, bloody, and chaotic period of violence and
fear, a time when all of South Texas threatened to burn out of control.

While the rest of the nation stacked its rifles following the close of
the Civil War, in much of Texas, guns stayed at the ready. The Indian
wars heated up, and in South Texas from 1865 through the 1870s,
losses of cattle and life kept an area about the size of Arkansas in constant turmoil. That old nemesis of Texas ranchers, Juan Cortina, had
much to do with the launching of countless raids against cattle ranchers in a region reaching all the way from the Rio Grande below
Brownsville as far north as Laredo, and northeast to the Nueces River,
which ran north of King Ranch and emptied into the bay of Corpus
Christi. This formidable stretch of desolate hardpan and brush-
covered grasslands acquired a new name in the 1870s: the Nueces
Strip. By whatever name it was dangerous, violent, heartbreak
country.

The sheer amount of cattle theft in the 1870s was staggering and
completely in the open. Everybody knew about it, and yet nobody
seemed to be able to put a stop to it. In 1872 the U.S. Congress
appointed a three-member fact-finding commission to visit south
Texas and report back to Congress. Commissioners Thomas P. Robb,
F. J. Mead, and Richard H. Savage collected sworn testimony from
Mexican-Americans and Anglos that, individually and together, presented an array of powerful evidence. Typical summaries read: "Justo
Lopez has seen stolen cattle crossed into Mexico from Texas, by
thieves, weekly, since 1865"; "Antonio Tigerina testifies that the stealing of Texas cattle by Mexicans existed in 1865, continued in 1866,
augmented till 1868, and since then continues very grievous. In 1870,
'71, '72, he has seen many stolen herds from Texas on the Mexican
side. On one occasion he followed fifteen or sixteen armed Mexican
cattle-thieves, who were driving off four hundred cattle to Las Cuevas
ranch, where they crossed them into Mexico"; and "W. D. Thomas
saw a captain in the Mexican army driving along a road on the

Mexican side of the river a herd of four hundred stolen cattle. The captain said: 'The *gringos* are raising cows for me.'"

One section of their report listed "casual losses of horses and cattle by theft" during the recent past and going all the way back to the 1850s. José D. Garcia, for example, of Santa Rosalio ranch in Cameron County, near Brownsville, made the following claim: "Cattle and increase, 1852 to 1872, less stock on hand, 13,066 cattle, at $10; and 20 yoke oxen stolen, at $50 a yoke," for a total loss of $131,660. Catherine Wallace, from San Diego, Duval County, put in a claim of $77,000, based on "Loss, by theft, of 1800 cattle, from August 20, 1866, to 1872, at $10. Loss, by theft, of 200 horses, in same time, at $40." She calculated her "increase loss" at 3,500 cattle and 400 horses. Some claims came from remote areas of the Nueces Strip. Martha A. Rabb, from Banquete, near Corpus Christi, cited the loss of 20,000 head of cattle since August 20, 1866. There were claims from Adolphus Glaevecke and Cornelius Stillman, prominent, long-standing residents of the Brownsville area. Mifflin Kenedy, Brownsville, entered a claim of $250,000 based on the "Attack on steamer Ranchero, and damages claimed for interruption of business, &c," from the Cortina War of 1859. Kenedy also listed "3,135 cattle, 18 saddle horses, merchandise stolen from store, and for hides"—all the work of Cortina's raiders in 1859. That total came to $670,700. Richard King lodged two claims. The first, under R. King & Co., Brownsville, listed "108,336 cattle and 3,328 horses stolen between 1866 and November 11, 1869," the amount, a staggering $2,480,160. Under Richard King, Santa Gertrudis, Nueces County, the numbers were smaller but still significant: "Losses between November, 1869, and 1872, after deducting present stock sales, including increase, 33,827 cattle, at $10; Losses of horses, same calculation, 978, at $60," for a net loss of $396,950.

Some, perhaps all, of the dollar claims of losses were inflated. Certainly the total was huge: $27,859,363.97 worth of losses attributed to Mexico. Then as now, the federal government was looked upon as a cash cow, and probably, without saying so, the claimants added in their worry, time, anxiety, and the general headaches of having their holdings depleted yearly by the actions of raiders from Mexico.

Astoundingly, the commissioners themselves got a firsthand glimpse of the kind of robbery that was so rampant along the border. One morning on a trip up the Rio Grande they were eyewitnesses to

cattle theft. In their official report they included a brief section headed
"FACTS OBSERVED BY THE UNITED STATES COMMISSIONERS."
The facts were these: On September 6, 1872, the steamer *San Juan* (a
new Kenedy/King boat) was ascending the Rio Grande with the U.S.
commissioners on board. When they passed Las Cuevas, "a notorious
rendezvous of cattle-thieves," damned if they didn't see actual thieves
at work early that morning, crossing cattle over to the Mexican side.
Some of the thieves were naked in order to help swim the cattle across;
some, on horseback, hid back in the brush as the steamer approached.
It appeared that as many as fifty cattle had already been escorted to the
other side. The commissioners noted, too, that within fifteen miles of
this spot on the river was a company of mounted U.S. infantry. The
brazenness of the thieves was obvious. Mifflin Kenedy was one of
three Brownsville citizens who also witnessed the theft that morning.

In Mexico, of course, things took on a different cast. An article in
La Revista Universal of Mexico City published in 1869 addressed the
persecution of Mexicans in Texas and mentioned by name Rip Ford
and Richard King. The article accused the two Texans of organizing
companies of Rangers bent on inflicting upon Mexicans "their hunger
and thirst of justice for the frequent crimes of cattle stealing committed on the frontier, attributed maliciously to Mexicans." Their methods, the article concluded, were no different from those of Apaches.
These were strong words, and there were rebuttals in the Brownsville
newspaper *Ranchero* and in the *San Antonio Express*.

A long report by the Mexican government, published in 1875,
would make a similar case against Texas and Richard King.

Sensitive to the charges against Mexico in the U.S. congressional
commission report of 1872, the Mexican government sent its own
Comisíon Pesquisadora de la Frontera del Norte to the border in
1873. The results were published in an English translation in 1875,
*Reports of the Committee of Investigation Sent in 1873 by the Mexi-
can Government to the Frontier of Texas*. The two countries separated
by the narrow river agreed upon very little except that cattle and
horses were being stolen. The Mexican report pointed to Texans as the
principal thieves, just as the Americans pointed to Mexicans. The
Mexican report showed just how deep and long-standing the grievances stemming from the Mexican War were.

Much of the Mexican report consists of denunciations of Texan immorality. Texas is portrayed as a place of "grossest immorality" where there are "great centers of corruption and unprecedented immorality." Mexico, in contrast, is presented as much more law-abiding, the commissioners asserting that "the moral condition of our frontier is far superior to that of Texas." The report's description of "the district north of Rio Bravo to Nueces"—the Wild Horse Desert, the Nueces Strip—is just as lurid as any found in Texan documents of the period: "It was the refuge for criminals flying from justice in Mexico; adventurers from the United States, who sought a fortune, unscrupulous of the means of procuring it; and vagrants from all parts of the State of Texas, hoping, in the shadow of existing disorganization and lawlessness, to escape punishment for their crimes."

After establishing the historical and geographical dimensions of lawlessness, crime, and immorality on the Texas side of the Rio Bravo, the report cites a few specific instances. One pertains to the most powerful man in Brownsville during the early days, Charles Stillman. Back in 1850, the report avers, a robbery occurred at Stillman's store in Brownsville and Stillman organized a force of Americans to find and punish the thief. They rode to a nearby ranch seeking information and tied up and whipped all of the people there. Someone said it was Juan Chapa Guerra who had stolen the goods. This Guerra lived across the river in Ranchito, Mexico. Stillman at once ordered his men to go to Mexico and bring Guerra back to him, whereupon the man was whipped and then killed. Only later was it learned that the wrong man had been killed; it was Juan Chapa Garcia, not Guerra, who was guilty of robbery. Stillman was so powerful that Guerra's family could find no lawyer willing to act against him. The report concludes that "this simple proceeding is enough to show the condition of things on the Texas frontier. This murder was never punished." (Nor would this episode appear in any biographical accounts of Charles Stillman's life.)

Moving forward to the contemporary scene, the 1870s, the report concentrated not on cattle theft, as the Americans did, but on horse theft. According to the Mexican view, it was horses, not cattle, that were most frequently stolen. And the horses were stolen in Mexico and sold in Texas. Ergo, the thieves were Texans or Texas Mexicans. The Mexican report, for example, cites an instance in May 1872 when sixty-six animals, horses, mares, mules, and colts were stolen from a rancho in Matamoros and traced by their owner, Leonides Guerra, far to the north, where the stolen animals were in the possession of Thomas Marsden, sheriff of the county of Beeville, Texas. Marsden had bought the animals for $11 a head, which was a fraction of the average cost of a horse and the best evidence, the Mexicans believed, that he had knowingly purchased stolen property.

The Mexican report also named names of suspected Anglo thieves. One was Thadeus Rhodes, county judge of Cameron County (of which Brownsville is the county seat). Rhodes was charged in 1858 with possession of stolen stock but was eventually cleared. He later presided over numerous sheriff's auctions at which Tejano land-holdings were purchased by Anglos. Another prominent local Brownsville citizen named in the report was Adolphus Glaevecke, the old foe of Juan Cortina. Glaevecke is cited as "one of those who have most actively engaged in horse stealing in Mexico, ever since the Rio Bravo has been the dividing line between the two nations." The report goes on to offer details of Glaevecke's horse-stealing operation, including his property holdings and the men who worked for him. Among these were Jean Vela, who was executed for horse theft. (Vela, incidentally, was the stepson of Mifflin Kenedy.) Tomás Vasquez was another "famous horse thief" mentioned in connection with Glaevecke, and Tomás Vasquez is important because he also worked for none other than Richard King.

The Mexican report summed up its view of the matter of horse thievery in this way: "A no less general rule may be formed that Texas is the place that receives, and has always received, the benefit of the robberies committed in Mexico; there without the slightest scruple, the dealers in horses receive the stolen goods, purchasing the animals at reduced rates."

As for the question of cattle theft, which formed the heart of charges made by Americans against Mexico, the Mexican report defended Mexico on several grounds. One, the Mexicans attributed the decimation of cattle in Texas to drought conditions in 1872–73 and cited accounts in Texas newspapers attesting to the deaths of "horned cattle" and horses and the disappearance of "native pas-turage." Two, the Mexicans pointed to the lack of reproduction among drought-devastated cattle. And three, the Mexicans cited the "constant removal of cattle to Kansas and other places for consumption." All of these reasons, the report stated, "will serve to explain the decrease perceived in the cattle in Texas, if such has really occurred, without recurring to so extraordinary a cause as that of robberies, committed by gangs of thieves in Mexico."

A second line of defense in the report challenged the figures of losses put forward by Anglo ranchers. The report scoffs at the ability of ranchers to be so certain of the number of cattle lost to theft: "Some have done it with such precision they have not overlooked the most trifling fractions." Among these are "Richard King & Co. [which] make their direct losses between 1866 and 1869 amount to one hundred and eight thousand three hundred and thirty-six head."

The report also mounted a thorough defense of Juan Cortina. The report goes over Cortina's role in the events of 1859 and forward to the present (1873) but essentially absolves him of operating a ring of cattle thieves, contrary to what all the Texans believed to be the case. At one point the report sarcastically ridicules the widespread charges made against him: "Not a cow was stolen in Texas, but General Cortina's hand was discovered in it. When a fact really occurred, it was disguised under the darkest colors, and when there were no facts, these were invented."

Among Anglos, no name in the report receives more extensive commentary than that of Richard or Ricardo King (both forms of his first name are used). His first appearance in the report is preceded by a general characterization of the class of ranchers of which he is representative: "In the Nueces region, there is certain class [sic] of property owners, Americans by birth and nationality, who being influential on account of the wealth they have amassed, are completely unrestrained, because there are no laws or authorities in the county, or in the bordering counties, to restrain them who with absolute impunity commit the greatest depredations, and who unscrupulously use their position to increase their wealth." Getting down to cases, the report compares American branding practices unfavorably with those of Mexicans. Mexicans are accustomed to branding every six months, but Americans brand any old time it suits them. The result, the report says, is theft, and the report gives an account of one such thief: "Generally the American stock owners of the Nueces have no fixed period for branding their animals. There are some, for instance Richard King, owner of the hacienda Gertrudis (Nueces), who has a large retinue of people in his service. (King's people sometimes number as many as sixty men.)" The report then describes the practice of ranchers whose cowboys entered pastures not their own and branded calves not their own. The result is that "Very often these herds leave the place and return to their old pastures, and hence it is that young cattle bearing the brand of Richard King, or some other stock owner, have been seen following cows belonging to different owners." The report also pointed to an article in the Brownsville *Sentinel* (February 11, 1873) that stated that "some men of the Nueces county not far from here came and collected all the calves they could find and branded them for the benefit of those whom they serve. If this business continues nothing will be left to our stock raisers but their corrals and wells."

The Mexican report elsewhere portrayed King as having colluded with other Anglos in legal actions against Mexican thieves. One such case occurred in 1868 when King, along with Mifflin Kenedy, Adolphus Glaevecke, and Dominick Lively gave testimony to a grand jury in Cameron County concerning losses and injuries on their property "which they impute exclusively to robbers living and organized on Mexican soil." The problem, according to the Mexican report, is that King et al. knew that two Americans, Patrick Quinn and Peter Marnill, were in fact among the thieves, but ignored their actions and blamed everything on Mexicans. Not only that, Kenedy and King inflated their losses to millions of dollars. The report accuses them directly of perjury before the grand jury.

Charges against King are restated again and again as he is accused of outright theft and condemned for his general lack of morality: "One of the proprietors who has distinguished himself most in these depredations is Ricardo King, owner of the estate Santa Gertrudis, county of Nueces." The report identified Tomás Vasquez (named elsewhere as one of Glaevecke's men) as one of King's chiefs instrumental in "robberies of horses in Mexico and of cattle in Texas." The report could hardly be stronger in its denunciation: "Ricardo King has a large band who ran constantly in all directions of the country marking calves, though they did not belong to him. It is impossible to admit that the people forming that party possessed any sentiments of morality. The laws of Texas offer no energetic remedies for this evil, and are insufficient."

In another attack on King, the Mexican report also objected to what they regarded as the "moralized language reigning among the stock raisers on the Nueces," who used the name of "orejano" to justify theft. Though, in a curious lapse, the text does not translate "orejano," the word means "unbranded or ownerless." In other words, that which the Nueces cattlemen called unbranded were actually somebody else's cattle. A Mexican's, the report would have us believe.

The report seems incensed at King because he "presents himself as one of the victims of robbery." The criticism is about as strong as anything said against Cortina: "Richard King has in his service a large band; he makes use of it for depredating upon other people's cattle by seizing all of the unbranded calves . . . These depredations are continuous, because King's band is almost always uninterruptedly in movement." The report then continues by claiming that King and fellow Texans, a hundred strong, would gather together and voice their grievances and rehearse their losses, usually exaggerating the total, King claiming that his losses were in the millions. They would then seek further support from relatives and employees and, in the name of reparations, denounce Mexico and its authorities for not stopping cattle thievery when in fact, some of them, the Texans, were stealing cattle as well.

From the Mexican viewpoint, Richard/Ricardo King held the same level of importance as Cortina did in the minds of Texans. Like Cortina, King was all powerful and well connected and controlled a large band of ruthless men ready to do his bidding, whether legal or not. From the repeated representations of King in the report, it seems obvious that the Mexicans regarded him as the biggest man in the Nueces Strip.

In sum, the Mexican report presented a diametrically opposite view from that of the Texans, not unlike the accounts one reads today of Palestinian-Israeli conflicts regarding land, borders, and beliefs. The Mexican report concluded, "Our frontier is tranquil, while in that of Texas exists increasing disorder, and the cattle stealing, under the form of claiming cattle, has assumed extraordinary proportions." Texas, the report insisted, was a place of wholesale corruption and the sole cause "of the demoralization on our frontier." The Texans couldn't have put it any better, except they would have attributed all of the disorder, theft, and demoralization to Mexicans, crossing the river and raiding in the north.

Another U.S. congressional commission, in 1875, gathered still more information and data regarding the situation in South Texas. On May 22, 1875, Charles Best, a steamboat captain, testified that cattle theft from Texas to Mexico was so common that he had ceased to pay much attention to it. On just about every trip on the river, he saw cattle crossing or signs of same. He blamed the lack of American action on the "colored soldiers" at Fort Brown who consorted with Mexican women acting as spies for Mexican bandits. He also said that after making a report of some stolen cattle that he had run into with his boat and drowned, he was later fired upon and warned never to make such a report again, and he did not.

It would seem that Richard King's rancho, 125 hard miles from Brownsville, was remote from danger, but that was not the case. The raiders were bold, mounted on good horses (some stolen from King's stock), and bent on carrying the war all the way to the Nueces River, the old boundary line. Everything from there to the Rio Grande they considered belonged to them. The Mexican War might be officially over these nearly thirty years, but it wasn't over in their minds. They meant to take back the countryside.

A Mexican who had resided in Texas since 1846, Jesus Sandoval, explained the situation in his deposition of May 3, 1875. He lived at Estero Grande, fifteen miles above Brownsville, and was well acquainted with the way cattle theft was handled on the Mexican side of the border: "I know many cattle, stolen from the people of Texas, have been sold in Matamoros, because I have seen them and knew the brands . . . I have seen cattle sold in Matamoros . . . having the brands of Capt. Richard King, Clarke, Wright, Rabbi, and many others, both of Americans and naturalized citizens of the United States. . . . I know that the raiding parties were composed of citizens of Mexico, with few exceptions."

He also understood the deeper political motives of the raiders: "The Mexicans say they will drive the Americans and the American-ized Mexicans out of this country or kill them. They claim the country and all the property." He ended on an eloquent personal note: "For seven months I have not slept in my house; I have slept in the chaparral—and have been a solitary sentinel over my own person." This man, Jesus Sandoval, is the same Jesus Sandoval (sometimes spelled Sandobal) who played such a crucial—and controversial—role in the coming campaign against the raiders.

Richard King, of course, was fully informed of all that was going on. The Nueces Strip was King Ranch country on its northeastern boundary, and King Ranch played a vital role in the taming of the wild land. Cattle theft had been a constant problem since the day King first brought livestock to the acres of the Santa Gertrudis. King absolutely hated to have his cattle disappear into Mexico, and the Mexican raiders absolutely loved it. The old scars of dispossession had never healed along the border and northward into the Nueces Strip, and the desire for both profit and payback proved a durable motive for theft and worse.

As the most visible landowner in the Nueces Strip, Richard King was an inviting target. No man could travel through that country without being heavily armed. King himself was ambushed more than once as he rode in his ambulance (wagon) from his rancho to Brownsville or Corpus Christi or San Antonio. Often he carried large sums of money, another strong inducement to attack him and his armed entourage. The man who killed Captain King would be famous in all the land.

King himself testified, in August 1872, about such an attack. Ironically, he was on his way to appear before the Robb-Savage commission in Brownsville when it happened. On July 31, King left Corpus Christi accompanied by his driver, George Evans, and a stranger named Franz Specht who had asked and received permission to ride with King to Brownsville. At a point about six miles east of King's rancho, around eight o'clock in the evening, a hail of bullets was fired into the wagon, killing Specht. Although it was dark, King believed that the assailants were eight or ten Mexicans. He had seen some Mexicans earlier, crossing the road. "I have been obliged for a number of years," he said, "to keep quite a number of men, for my protection, at my expense, around my ranch; and in traveling I am obliged to have an escort of those men. Citizens of this frontier are obliged to travel armed always in self-defense." Although the governor of Texas offered a reward for information about the murderers of Franz Specht, none was ever brought forward. South Texas in those days was a place of sudden death.

King was always well armed and prepared to shoot if he had to. When a reporter asked him in 1875 why he still carried an old double-barreled shotgun instead of a new repeating Winchester rifle, King replied, "Because I'm a businessman, not a sportsman." The answer—

direct, pragmatic, humorous, tough—was vintage King. He deliberately projected an image of toughness, for any sign of weakness could be fatal. He told one acquaintance, "I have to make 'em think I'm a man-eater. If I don't they'll kill me." He kept a close eye on every animal he owned, on every man who approached King Ranch, friend or foe.

There were three ways to make money illegally from cattle: to steal them and drive them across the Rio Grande to sell in Mexico or out-lets like Cuba, with which Cortina, for example, is known to have had contracts for beef in the 1870s; to kill and skin the cattle on the spot and sell the hides, either in Texas or in Mexico; or to brand or alter the brands of cattle belonging to somebody else and claim them as your own. The killing and skinning of cattle was called hide-peeling, and in the 1870s this was one of the quickest means of converting cows into cash. The resultant "war" over the practice became known as the "Peelers' War." Alberto Garza, an outlaw from Mexico, conducted widespread hide-peeling activities in Nueces County in 1873. In April of that year, his gang sent word to the citizens of San Diego, in Nue-ces County, that they had in their possession six hundred hides for sale. Anglos also engaged in hide-peeling. There were impromptu slaughterhouses built all around the Corpus Christi region, and a brisk business ensued in hide and tallow production. People on either side didn't much care where the cattle came from or to whom they belonged. It was open-range country, for the most part (though Cap-tains King and Kenedy had already begun to enclose their lands), and the cattle, branded or not, were there for the taking.

Violence by both camps, Anglo and Mexican, kept the countryside in a state of upheaval. The Texan press fanned the flames with accounts like the following, which refers to the murder of a Mr. William Mor-dock in 1872, as reported in the newspaper *Nueces Valley*: "The fiends in human shape who committed the act left the unfortunate man lying on his face with the arms bound and with bed clothes and cultivating harrow thrown upon his body. He was literally roasted alive in his own house which these devils incarnate set afire." The account generically identified the perpetrators as "prowling Mexicans."

Steps both lawful and unlawful were taken by Anglo ranchers to defend their properties. On April 20, 1874, for example, Mifflin Kenedy sent a letter to a man who had moved onto a piece of land "known as the Burros," located on the tract of the Concepción

Carricitos in Cameron County. "The land where you are building your Ranch belongs to me," Kenedy stated, "and has been in my possession some twelve years—I am also informed you are bringing or have sheep now at that point." Pointing out that "this is not a friendly act," Kenedy asked the man to remove his sheep and that if that were not done, Kenedy would take "all legal means" to see that it was.

In the absence of law, men took advantage of the lawless conditions. "Minute" men posses were formed on the spot and sent off to avenge this man's death or that man's burned-out ranch. Miscarriages of justice were as common as drought conditions. In 1874 Nueces County and other counties near the Nueces line escalated into repeated outbreaks of violence, theft, and murder. It is hard to say which side, Mexican or Anglo, produced the most lawless actions. What does seem apparent, however, is that the general lawlessness provided cover for Anglo campaigns against legitimate, landholding Tejanos—tactics that led to the transfer of landholdings from Tejano to Anglo.

A raid by armed Mexicans on Penescal Ranch about sixty miles south of Corpus Christi produced sustained, systematic retaliation by Texans. The raid took place on May 15, 1874, when Mexicans attacked the ranch and killed four men. The murder of one of them, John Morton, particularly aroused the ire of Anglos. One of the Texans who set out to punish any and all Mexicans for the Penescal Ranch raid was J. B. (Red) John Dunn. In his memoir, *Perilous Trails of Texas,* Dunn recounts the circumstances of Morton's murder: "From the position in which he was found it is believed that he interceded on bended knees for his life." Despite these pleadings, Morton was shot six times. Dunn and one of his brothers organized a small ad hoc posse and rode in search of any "strange Mexicans" they could find. One night they captured two Mexicans and interrogated them. They suspended the first, Hypolita Tapia, from a tall mesquite tree where they "let him kick a few chunks out of the horizon, after which he stated that he was ready to divulge everything." A vaquero and sheepherder born in Texas, Tapia told of how one Thomas Basquez had been behind the raid and had convinced Tapia to raise a company of men to rob the ranch store at Penescal. "Thomas Basquez" appears to be Tomás Vasquez, who worked as a gunslinger for Richard King. Vasquez's name pops up in the Mexican government report but does not appear in Tom Lea's *The King Ranch* or in Walter P. Webb's *The Texas Rangers*. Nor is J. B. Dunn's account mentioned in these standard, widely celebrated histories. Vasquez, who was also apparently a member of the Corpus Christi police force, is part of the sub rosa and largely undocumented history of King Ranch during the ultraviolent years of the 1870s. Today, even for those who might be admitted to the King Ranch archives at the Henrietta Memorial Center in Kingsville, the decade of the 1870s is closed to all researchers. Are there account books that show Vasquez on the payroll or reveal other potentially damaging information?

Convinced that they had found two of the men responsible for the raid on Penescal Ranch, Dunn and his men turned them over to the sheriff in Corpus Christi. Both men were later hanged, and nothing was ever done to connect Basquez/Vasquez with the crime.

In the Mexican-American community in South Texas, folk memory, part of an oral tradition, whispers darkly of stolen lands and lost inheritances. Following the raids by Anglos at La Atravesada, El Penascal, Corral de Piedra, and El Mesquite, one woman, a Mrs. Tiejerina, remained on her land, and José Maria Morales, who worked for her and had some sheep and horses on her pasture, remembered what happened next. Captain Kenedy "didn't have water in his pasture and Mrs. Tiejerina had a big lake in hers. He fenced in all of the lake to his property. The lake went dry in three months and never filled again. That's what he always fought for—water—he didn't have any." Kenedy then bought José Morales's livestock and José went to work as a vaquero on Kenedy's rancho.

Faustino Morales, interviewed in 1969, remembers what the elders said when he was a child: "There were many small ranches belonging to Mexicans, but then the Americans came in and drove the Mexicans out and took over the ranches . . . after that they fenced the ranches—it was the English [i.e., Americans], they fenced some land that wasn't theirs." In South Texas all Texas Rangers were thought to be "*rinches de la Kineña*," that is, rangers of the King Ranch. Such memories are not evidence, of course, but their persistence, even to this day, is an accepted tradition.

There is a great divide in South Texas on the issue of land ownership. Historian Armando Alonzo puts it this way: "A lot of Mexican-American families seem to have a pretty strong belief, a collective memory of land loss." But speaking from the Anglo perspective, Tobin Armstrong of Armstrong Ranch, a very old ranch south of King Ranch, says, "It sounds like revisionist history. When [the land grants] were litigated, it all fell into place. It was an orderly procedure."

In the 1870s, however, the process was often not orderly at all. The best-known outbreak of violence followed by extreme retaliatory mob action occurred in Refugio County, along the San Antonio River, northeast of the Nueces River. Here, on June 8, 1874, Thad Swift and his wife, who lived in the vicinity of the old Refugio Mission, were murdered. John Young, a local cowboy, described his feelings upon witnessing the victims: "What I saw when I arrived at the Swift ranch . . . changed me from a simple-hearted country boy to a hard-nerved man boiling for revenge. There on the ground just outside the house were the bodies of Thad Swift and his wife cut to pieces." Mexicans who had worked for the Swifts were immediately suspected, and armed posses set out to punish anybody they thought was guilty. It was Young himself who told the sheriff that he, Young, believed a "bad Mexican named Marcelo Moyer" to be guilty. Moyer had been at the Swift ranch the day before, according to Young. The posse, including Young, rode thirty-five miles north to Goliad County where Moyer lived. The posse slaughtered Moyer, his brother, and their father. In the meantime two other Mexicans suspected of having been at the Swift ranch were seized by a mob and hanged in back of the Swift house, their bodies displayed as a warning for over a week. Young joined a band of Regulators led by Coon Dunman whose "avowed purpose . . . was to make every Mexican who could not give an account of himself either leave the country or take his chances of kicking at Texas soil with nothing to stand on." No Mexican in Refugio County or thereabouts was safe. As the fury of the Anglos raged, there was even thought of killing every Mexican who lived in Goliad, but the actions of one man, George Saunders, disrupted that bloody plan.

There are those who believe that the reaction to the Swift murders was tied in with something beyond sheer anger and a desire for revenge. Racism was a part of it, but the opportunity to scare Mexicans, Tejanos, off the land was another. Once the Mexicans fled, as many of them did, their lands could be transferred to Anglo ownership. By this means, the process of dispossession of Tejano landholdings, going back to Mexican land grants of the 1830s and earlier, could be speeded up. A gun was quicker than the law. Hobart Huson, in his monumental two-volume history of Refugio County, describes a mass exodus of Tejanos following the outbreaks of vigilantism and violence in the wake of the Swift murders: "The roads were lined with ox-carts and wagons headed west." According to this view, the murders became the pretext for disinheriting a people.

News of the Swift murders percolated throughout the Nueces Strip, and indignation about their deaths found its way into the congressional reports. Although no strict accounting of the number of deaths on either side of the undeclared war has ever been brought forward, the number was certainly multiplied by fear, prejudice, and rumor, so that the climate of violence had the whole countryside on edge, frightened, desperate.

Certainly the level of racial distrust and hatred was quite high on both sides. General Steele of the U.S. Army noted the deep animosity existing between Texans and Mexicans. "There is a considerable element in the country bordering on the Nueces that think the killing of a Mexican no crime," Steele observed. The Mexican thieves, he added, "think the killing of a Texan something to be proud of." One Mexican raider told a Texas rancher, in 1874: "*Los de Tejas para mi no valen nada, ye me hace muy poco esto*": "Those of Texas mean nothing to me, to me it means very little," that is, whether he killed one of them or not. An American consul in Brownsville, in 1878, remarked on the disparity of justice that he observed in South Texas: ". . . when it is known that a Mexican has been hung or killed in the neighborhood of Brownsville, or along the frontier, there is seldom any fuss made about it; while on the contrary, if a white man happens to be despoiled in any way, there is generally a great fuss made about it by those not of Mexican origin."

The Nuecestown Raid of March 26, 1875, set off another round of bloody reprisals. Nuecestown was a small community, consisting mainly of a store owned by the Noakes family, located about thirteen miles from Corpus Christi. The raiders first stole horses from one ranch and rode them bareback to another site, a scant nine miles from Corpus Christi. Here they stole more goods before going to Frank's store on Juan Sais's ranch, where they stole everything of value, including clothing. They remained for a while, robbing such people as came onto the property and killing one Mexican who refused to join them. They finally left, taking several hostages with them, including women. Driving the hostages before them, they made their way to Noakes's store, well known in the area. Noakes resisted, gunfire ensued, and one Anglo at the store was killed, though Noakes himself escaped through an underground tunnel. The raiders burned the buildings, and the heat was so great that the calves in the pen were roasted. The prisoners were released and the raiders, about thirty-five in all, headed south where, shortly afterward, a small posse tried to overtake them. There was more gunfire, and the posse had to withdraw.

The Nuecestown Raid scared the daylights out of Corpus Christi, and companies of Rangers or vigilantes were instantaneously formed to avenge the attack. At La Parra, about sixty miles south of Corpus Christi, a store was burned and a number of men killed. Those killed may or may not have been raiders. Many of the Texans made no distinctions as to guilt or not, and the law, well, the law was whatever you wanted it to be.

"Red" Dunn went on several raids against Mexicans thought to be involved in depredations against Anglo ranch owners. He and his brothers and friends joined Capt. T. Hines Clark's company and headed for the "lower country" south of King Ranch. Here were located several large Mexican (Tejano) ranches, among them La Travisado, La Mesa, La Prieta, Mesquite, and others. According to Dunn, "All these ranches harbored large groups of men whose sole occupation was killing cattle belonging to American stock men. . . . At most of these ranches were large buildings packed full of dried hides in addition to pits dug in the sand that were also filled with dry hides."

In the "Sand," a bleak, desertlike terrain often mentioned in the travel memoirs of that era, they "found the whole country covered with the carcasses of cattle that had been killed for their hides." After several gunfights with Mexican raiders, they rode back north over the same ground "but could not find a soul." In Dunn's account, some grim humor masks what really happened: "Everyone of the ranches was deserted. Some pyromaniac must have been following us, for every time we passed through a ranch it mysteriously caught on fire."

In another passage he owns up more directly to the burning of ranch properties. At one place the company came upon an ancient Mexican woman grieving over the grave of her son, killed by Mexicans.

She urged the men to "kill everyone of them that we could find, saying that they were all thieves and murderers." The men were moved to pity, and after collecting food and water for her, they "watched her 'jacal' until the others had finished burning and moved on."

The smoke rising from the destroyed ranchos could be seen as far north as King Ranch, as Dunn recalls. When he and his men rode up to King Ranch at dawn, they saw "someone walking back and forth in front of it and when we got closer we saw that it was Captain King. 'What is the matter boys' he greeted us, 'has a volcano broken loose?'" Dunn and company explained that a lot of houses had caught fire and burned up but added that the buildings with hides in them had not. King said to them, "There are plenty of teams and wagons here, hitch them up, go and get the hides and sell them keeping the money." When they said they didn't want to fool with the hides, he replied, "Well, go back and burn them"—which they did.

This bit of scorched-earth policy is confirmed by the recollections of another Texas raider who recalled the episode long afterward, in 1929: "They got a dose they never forgot. Five Mexican ranches 'caught fire.' . . . We burned all but the hide house. . . ." When they saw Captain King the next morning, he asked if there had been a volcano (same as in Dunn's account) and told them, "There's teams; go and get the hides and sell them and put the money in your pockets." They did the same as Dunn says; they burned the hides. King's parting words were: "Don't leave them for the Mexicans."

Other contemporary reports by Anglo law officers spoke of widespread miscarriages of justice. The adjutant-general of Texas, responsible for advising the governor on military matters, concluded that "parties of Americans living near the Nueces have banded together with the object of stopping the killing of cattle for their hides, but have themselves committed the greater crimes of murder and arson."

N. A. Jennings, a Ranger who wrote a book about his experiences, described the situation: "Large parties of mounted and well-armed men, residents of Nueces County, were riding over the country, committing the most brutal outrages, murdering peaceable Mexican farmers and stockmen who had lived all of their lives in Texas. These murderers called themselves vigilance committees and pretended that they were acting in the cause of law and order."

The raiders who burned jacales and hides and killed Tejano rancheros, unloosing terror upon the countryside, were later disbanded but were never held accountable for their deeds. The women and children of the burned, abandoned ranchos fled to the border, to the *villas del norte,* the old towns built by the Spanish in the eighteenth century. Eventually, most of those properties that were sacked and burned by the raiders became part of two large ranching operations, those of Mifflin Kenedy and Richard King. The vaqueros who survived went to work for King, Kenedy, and other Anglo ranchers. By such means the Americanization of Nueces County and lands south of King Ranch continued.

As flames literally lit up the countryside of the Nueces Strip, calls for help from the state government became insistent. Citizens in South Texas believed, and rightly so, that the few federals stationed at the old posts from Fort Brown west to Laredo were largely powerless to do anything. In fairness, the federal troops were bound by constraints that hampered their effectiveness. They could not, for example, use force to gain information from suspects. But someone was on the way who was willing to use whatever methods it took to suppress the raiders. He would leave his mark on South Texas. His name was Leander H. McNelly.

CHAPTER 8

A Second Alamo

After the turmoil following the Nuecestown raid and the attack on La Parra in spring 1875, John McClure, sheriff of Nueces County, wired Austin for help:

> IS CAPT MCNELLY COMING. WE ARE IN TROUBLE. FIVE RANCHES BURNED BY DISGUISED MEN NEAR LAPARRA LAST WEEK. ANSWER.

He was. He was on the way. Captain McNelly, who had the demeanor of a Methodist preacher and the heart of a fighting cock, was coming to save South Texas.

Leander H. McNelly had arrived in Texas from Virginia in 1860, when he was a mere youth of sixteen. The next year he joined the Confederate Army and for the rest of the war fought in campaigns in Louisiana, New Mexico, and Texas. He won distinction and promotion for his "daring gallantry," and after the war he took up farming near Burton, a tiny community between Austin and Houston. It was just a shirttail cotton farm, but McNelly liked to describe himself as a planter—one of his few affectations. During Reconstruction he served for a year as a captain in the discredited state police, a law enforcement agency much despised by many Texans because of black officers and charges of corruption among its officials. McNelly was the only one to emerge with his reputation intact.

In 1874 duty called again. The Texas Rangers, which had been dissolved following the close of the Civil War, were reconstituted for two reasons: to protect citizens from Indian attacks in West Texas and to bring order to South Texas, where the bandit war raged. McNelly drew the South Texas assignment. By this time he was a dying man. He was fragile, rail thin, and pale, made so by tuberculosis, a deadly killer

Leander H. McNelly, Texas
Ranger Captain who led the
fight against Cortina's bandits in
South Texas in 1875–76.

in those days, but despite his physical condition, McNelly set about
signing up recruits for a Ranger company. Hard-case men and boys
were eager to follow McNelly. There was something about him that
made men obey. He had the stern manner of a father whose word was
law. He possessed a relentless will, he had courage to spare, and he
was always at the front of his men when they were going into battle.
Ranger N. A. Jennings described him as "a very quiet, reserved,
sedate sort of a man, but he always had a pleasant word for those
under him and was greatly loved by all the men."

In a short time McNelly had forty-two men in the saddle, and they
rode south, where things were worsening rapidly. When McNelly
arrived in Corpus Christi that April of 1875, he found conditions grim
indeed. On the way into the town, the Rangers saw the body of a Mexican hanging from a big pecan tree. The citizens of Corpus Christi were
huddled in their homes, fearing attacks from raiders. Fresh in their
minds were the assaults on Nuecestown.

But McNelly did not act the way local citizens expected him to. He
was not nearly as partisan as they had anticipated. He wired headquarters in Austin: "The acts committed by Americans in this section

are horrible to relate. Many ranches have been plundered and burned and the people murdered or driven away; one of these parties confessed to me in Corpus Christi as having killed eleven (11) men, on their last raid." Though he did not say so, these vigilante raids were doubtless the ones on Penescal and other ranches south of King Ranch, in what is today Kenedy County.

McNelly's first actions surprised and angered some locals. He ordered all armed parties to disband. This included "minute" companies organized to protect ranchers and citizens in the area. From now on, there would be only one duly authorized law enforcement unit in the region, and that would be McNelly's Frontier Battalion. There were tense encounters with Anglo partisans, but each time they gave in to McNelly's steely manner. He also issued a special order in the Corpus Christi paper stating that he intended to crack down on "all such bands" and that any "armed bands of men acting without authority of law" would be arrested. He meant to put a stop to the "recent outrages" no matter who had committed them, Mexicans or Texans. The local press said he was acting like an "emperor."

Mostly, McNelly seems not to have given a damn what anybody thought. He knew his job and headed southwest, where the bandits were. He had one strong clue to go on. The Mexican raiders had stolen a number of new saddles from Noakes's store. Anybody caught with one of them in his possession was a thief and would be dealt with accordingly, McNelly told his men.

One of his recruits, George Durham, left a stirring account of his time as a McNelly Ranger. Durham was just eighteen, "a big hunk of farm boy," when he left his native Georgia and came to Texas in the spring of 1875. "The way we heard it," he wrote, "this was a fairyland where beeves by the thousands ran loose and belonged to anybody with a rope and a branding iron and able to hold his own." Instead of becoming a rich cattleman, Durham became a McNelly Ranger, or a Little McNelly, as the men in the captain's company liked to style themselves. He had heard about Captain McNelly from his father, who rated him ahead of General Lee because unlike Lee, who made his plans first, McNelly "made his plans like a chickenhawk, after he had located his target and was coming in for the kill."

The first time George Durham laid eyes on McNelly, he couldn't believe that this "little runt of a feller" was the famed warrior his father had told him about, but it was. Though the boy had never fired a shot at a man, McNelly signed him on. The pay was $33 a month in state scrip, and the Ranger had to furnish his horse and gun; the state would provide the ammunition. What lay ahead was the prospect of high adventure and possibly death—strong elixirs for a southern farm boy who had missed out on the Civil War.

The landscape they rode through might have been something out of Sir Thomas Malory. The bodies of two Mexicans, hanged days earlier by unknown parties, dangled from an embankment. McNelly drove his men along muddy trails where they had to walk, pushing the horses forward. Their destination was King Ranch, famous in the land.

On the way they passed through Banquete, the last organized "town" in the region. There was no other from there to the border. Banquete had once been a Mexican settlement where *bailles* (dances) were held. Now it was a ghost town with one inhabitant, W6 Wright as he was called. "One of him was enough—more population than most places," opined Durham. W6 took his name from the brand he had devised for such cattle as he could burn a brand on. A "talky old booger," he questioned Captain McNelly as to whether he was going into the "lower country." The captain said, "Maybe." W6 wanted to bet him that not all of the forty-two Rangers would go with him and that not twenty would come out, but the captain wasn't a betting man.

From Banquete, they moved south, down the old Taylor Trail where the army of 1846 had ridden on the way to fight Mexico. Their next stop was King's rancho at Santa Gertrudis, which seemed to Durham like a town, with more than a hundred people installed there. The main ranch house had a high steeple, seventy-five feet or so, from which two lookouts could see whoever was approaching. Captain King himself rode out to the edge of the buildings to greet the Rangers. To Durham, King and McNelly bore a strong resemblance. Neither man "wasn't too much to look at the first time." In fact, Durham thought, King "was a dead-ringer for Captain McNelly at a short distance. Each of them hefted around 130 or 135, stood about five and a half feet, had brown hair and beards. Neither of them looked like a storybook captain of anything. But they were. Both of them."

Durham was very impressed with King Ranch, as were all who have left accounts of their visits there. To Durham, the ranch house "was more like an army arsenal inside. In one big room there were eighty stands of Henry repeating rifles and maybe a hundred boxes of shells."

They stabled their horses, and King, looking them over, marveled at their sorry condition. "How in the world did you get this far on those nags?" he asked McNelly, who said, in typical McNelly fashion, "The main fact is—we're here."

King's hospitality included the best beef stew Durham had ever eaten ("greased his chin with," he said), washed down with cups of steaming hot coffee. They all ate in a large hall, where four tables could serve maybe a hundred. Young Durham kept drinking the coffee because he found that every time he emptied his cup, a young girl kept refilling it. It seemed to Durham that "somebody had dumped over the lilac water," she smelled so good. Later he found out her name from a ranch hand. She was Caroline Chamberlain, a niece of Captain King's wife. He instantly began to dream of leaving McNelly, going to work for Captain King, and marrying Caroline. "Only a country boy could have had such crazy ideas," he remembered.

The next morning, Durham woke up to find his fellow Rangers selecting new horses from King's herd. King came up to Durham and asked him why he'd joined up with Captain McNelly. Durham told him, and King looked at Durham's shabby, worn-out old farm saddle and told a vaquero to get him a good saddle and a rifle scabbard. Then he gave him a fine sorrel gelding, and the farm boy was mounted in a style he could never have imagined. Durham noticed that Caroline was in the corrals, too, as at home there as she was in the kitchen. He realized that if he quit Captain McNelly, there was no way King would hire him. So he stuck with McNelly and figured he'd let the future take care of itself.

Everybody had a new horse except McNelly, and he had his eye on a big bay named Segal. He allowed to King as how that horse was worth $500 and that the state of Texas would never permit such an outlay for a mount. King told him it was his to keep: "I'd rather give him to you than have those bandits come and take him. Most of those rascals are mounted on my stock, and I at least want to do as good by you, Captain."

Fed, rested, and outfitted by King, McNelly's Rangers were "forted and ready for anything." They said their goodbyes and headed south.

Once deep into outlaw country, McNelly filled his men in on their mission. He made a little speech: "There are only two kinds of people for us—outlaws and law-abiding." He told them to treat the law-abiding with respect and to arrest the outlaws. All prisoners, he said, would be "put under the old Spanish law—*la ley de fuga*—which means the prisoner is to be killed on the spot if a rescue is attempted." The entire history of the Rangers in South Texas can be summed up in the rationale of *la ley de fuga* (law of the fugitive), a tactic easily abused and easily covered up in official reports: Prisoner killed trying to escape. Ranger historian Walter P. Webb defends *la ley de fuga* in his famous book, *The Texas Rangers*.

As they rode still deeper into bandit country, McNelly added two men to the company. One was a tough, seasoned scout from Brownsville named J. S. Rock, or Old Rock as he was called. Rock knew all about the doings of Mexican thieves on the border. During his tenure as deputy inspector of the customs house in Brownsville, Rock had reported on hides he had observed in Mexican hands that bore "brands representing nearly every stock-raiser in Western Texas." During a period from August 15, 1871, to August 19, 1872, when he testified before the commission, Rock recorded nearly five hundred stolen hides representing fifty different stock raisers. The majority belonged to "Richard King, of Rancho Santa Gertrudis, Nueces County."

The other new member of McNelly's company was one of the strangest, scariest men then living in the Nueces Strip, Jesus Sandoval (sometimes listed as Sandobal). Sandoval was one of the men who had testified so powerfully before the Robb commission. The Rangers mangled his name to Casoose, spelled variously. To Durham, Casoose "looked like a crazy man." The story was that he had been made so distraught by the loss of his wife and child to bandits that he had become monomaniacal in his pursuit of revenge. In his book *A Texas Ranger*, N. A. Jennings devoted pages of highly romanticized narrative describing Sandoval's appearance, unending grief, and relentless vengeance against Mexican bandits. In any event, all agreed that Casoose hated the bandits and used extreme methods in the war against them.

Ever deeper into the lower country they rode, armed, wary, gathering information, seeking contact with bandits. Eventually they made camp at Rancho las Rucias, an old hacienda dating from the Spanish era. Durham saw in it a symbol of the whole region: "But it now showed the wear and tear of the rowdy border life. It was only about ten miles back from the Rio Grande and seemed to belong to anybody who was man enough to hold it." While there, McNelly received some intelligence information from a daring bit of spying performed by George Hall, a sergeant whom McNelly had sent to the mouth of the river, McNelly said, "in the character of a spy."

What Hall witnessed gives a good picture of Mexican cattle-stealing operations. On about June 1, 1875, a Spanish steamer appeared on the coast near the mouth of the river, its purpose to receive a cargo of cattle to be sent to Cuba. Shortly after the steamer landed, General Cortina himself appeared at Bagdad, the smuggler's town famous from the cotton-running days of the Civil War. Cortina was there to oversee the loading of the cattle to fill a contract he had made with the Cuban government. With him were an armed bodyguard of about a hundred or so men. The contract called for five hundred cattle, but there were only about half that amount there. (The rest were presumably on the way from Texas.) Hall got onboard an American lighter carrying the cattle out to the Spanish steamer and counted sixteen American brands among the cattle. Cortina himself later confirmed his presence in Bagdad at that time, noting in one of his pronunciamientos, written from house arrest just outside of Mexico City on August 20, 1875, that "It is true that days before my arrest I was in Bagdad, at the mouth of the river of the heroic Matamoros, delivering a herd of 429 cattle of different brands to be taken to Havana."

News of the Cuban contract fired up McNelly; he knew cattle were being moved, he could be certain of it. But then, in that period, cattle were nearly always being shuffled south from the ranches and prairies, headed for the river. The deputy customs house collector at Edinburg, on May 13, 1875, wrote a congressional committee: "I do not think there is a week that passes that there is not from one to three hundred head of cattle stolen and carried across the Rio Grande River." During the spring and summer of 1875 Cortina was shipping an estimated five thousand cattle every month. Some were killed for their hides, some were butchered for meat to feed Cortina's men, and some were sold to markets like those in Cuba. McNelly himself estimated that as late as November 1875, 1,800 to 2,000 head of cattle were stolen in that month.

On the basis of recent intelligence and his best guess, McNelly sent a patrol under the command of Old Rock to the river to try to catch what McNelly believed to be a significant movement of cattle by outlaws. They rode all one night, Durham in the group, and arrived at La Bolsa (The Pocket), the big, fordable bend in the river west of Brownsville, an hour too late. From the north bank of the Rio Grande they could see, as the morning fog lifted, the last of the cattle being gathered on the south bank, in Mexico. With their big Sharps rifles it would have been easy to pick off the bandits, but they were forbidden to fire. That was a foreign country over there; they didn't want to set off an international incident. On the Mexican side, one of the bandits blew them a kiss; another thumbed his nose and fired his pistol.

Timely, accurate information was the absolute key to any success in the campaign against the bandits. In his own testimony before Congress in Washington, D.C., on January 24, 1876, McNelly spoke in detail of the problems he had faced in trying to locate bandits: "The country is filled with numbers of armed Mexicans; and it is a most common sight to see four or five or six men, well armed and mounted, whose business no one knows." McNelly would ask them questions and receive vague answers. If he took them to a ranch they said they belonged to, "the servants of the ranch generally, without hesitation, verify their statement; in many instances, from friendship; most frequently from fear." Finding out what was true was one of the toughest jobs facing him in South Texas. Essentially he was fighting a kind of guerrilla war in enemy territory where it was hard to tell who was the enemy and who was not.

McNelly's testimony also revealed a keen understanding of the problems faced by Mexican ranchers in Texas—and consequently of the problems McNelly had in trying to gather reliable information: "The Mexican owners of ranches on this side of the river, those who are citizens of Texas, are, almost to a man, as much opposed to this system of raiding as the American citizens of Texas are. Many of them have not nerve enough to take an active, decided stand against it either by giving information or by personal assistance."

Those who did provide information faced swift retaliation from the bandits, who would send out the word that a certain rancher was to be targeted; often that rancher would be killed. McNelly also pointed to the difficulties posed by the complexity of kinship ties between Mexicans on the Texan side of the river and those just across the river in Mexico. He spoke of people who lived in the United States but whose citizenship was Mexican: "They are their kinsfolk, their cousins, uncles, and brothers—for it seems to me as if all the Mexicans on both sides of the river are relatives."

Lest McNelly be convicted of racism by today's standards, consider the rest of his testimony, in which he expressed his admiration for Mexican owners of ranches. He said they were the only ones he could trust: "I do not know of any Mexican who owns a ranch on this side of the river and who lives in Texas whom I do not consider to be a good citizen. I believe they are all good citizens." Mexican ranchers wanted the same thing as McNelly—law and order. He understood, too, why so few of them took an active role in helping him with his mission. They were in constant danger, in constant threat of bloody reprisals. In a remarkable bit of testimony, he told the hearing, "I am willing to take a good many chances, but I certainly would not live on a stock-ranch west of the Nueces River, at any point from the mouth of the Devil's River to the mouth of the Rio Grande. I think that the risk is too great—so great that scarcely any compensation would pay for it." He went on, "My position in command of a company of troops I do not consider half so hazardous as that of those men living on ranches."

Given such a climate of fear, the gathering of accurate information called for tactics that were themselves outside the law—or so thought McNelly and most of his men. The man who got the information that McNelly needed was Jesus Sandoval, Casoose. The method he used was torture, pure and simple. McNelly knew about Casoose's methods and overlooked them. Most of the Rangers did, too, although Durham admitted that he did not like *la ley de fuga* or Casoose's ruthless practices.

One who wholeheartedly agreed with McNelly's strategy was William Callicott, who, as an old man, described the torturer's techniques in some detail. Callicott spelled Jesus "Casuse." When a suspect was brought in, Casuse conducted the interrogation. If Casuse knew the suspect to be a citizen or if under questioning he proved to be one, then he was allowed to go on his way. But if he were judged to be a spy or a bandit, Casuse set to work with his rope. He would find a suitable tree and haul the bandit up and down on a limb, strangling him, then questioning him, until he got what he wanted. According to Callicott, "As far as we knew this treatment always brought out the truth." Once Captain McNelly had all the information he wanted, the man was turned over to Casuse for good, who then made a hangman's noose, drew it over the man's head, tossed it over a limb, then placed the man on a horse and drove the horse out from under the man, breaking the victim's neck. "Captain McNelly didn't like this kind of killing," Callicott reported, "but Casuse did. He said if we turned a spy loose he would spread the news among the bandits and we would never catch them. We caught several spies on that scout before we overhauled the bandits with the cattle, and Casuse dealt with all of them alike, showing no partiality—he always made them a present of six feet of rope."

S. N. Hardy, a McNelly Ranger, told J. Frank Dobie many years later a story about what he saw Sandoval do once, when they were camped on the Rio Grande. Hardy came upon Sandoval in the process of hanging a Mexican, after which Sandoval "dismounted and showed me another Mexican whose throat had been cut to the neck bone. He then explained that these two victims were the last of the gang who had burned his home and ruined his wife and daughter." Hardy concluded, "I did not say anything about the matter to Captain McNelly until months later. Lots of things happened on the Rio Grande that never got into the ranger reports." Hardy's statement could be expanded to fit the entire period of the 1870s in South Texas, from the Nueces to the Rio Bravo.

Jesus Sandoval's methods were also detailed in the writings of T. C. Robinson, a lieutenant in McNelly's company. Robinson's story has its own interest. He was a young man from Virginia who came to Texas in the 1870s, forced by a feud with a neighbor to leave his native state. The cause of the feud was the neighbor's teenage sister. Once in Texas Robinson knocked around as a would-be cowboy and sometime author—he possessed a first-class literary education and sprinkled all of his writings with allusions and quotations, many from one of his favorite authors, Lord Byron. During his years in Texas he published twenty-three pieces—poems and articles—in Austin newspapers. One of them, in 1874, was a "pome" signed Shortfellow. All of the publications appeared under the pseudonym Pidge. On October 1, 1874, T. C. "Pidge" Robinson became a McNelly Ranger.

From the field Pidge sent several long "letters" datelined "Rio Grande Frontier." These were published in the Austin *Daily State Gazette* and offer, along with newspaper accounts and McNelly's reports, some of the best, certainly most contemporaneous versions of the activities of McNelly's Rangers. In one letter (September 20, 1875), Pidge wrote of Jesus Sandoval as a "trump—a perfect Chesterfield in politeness; he puts us to shame by the elegance of his manners . . . and he is *so* kind and *so* considerate that it is almost a pleasure to be hanged by such a nice gentleman."

One man interrogated was an American. Although he claimed he was a gambler, he had in his possession a new saddle that had been stolen in the raid on Nuecestown. He claimed he'd won the saddle in a poker game, but in Casuse's hands he told a different story. Casuse knocked him down with a pistol, tied him up, and set to strangling the truth out of him with a rope. After repeated applications of this technique, the man told of about fifty raiders headed for the Rio Grande, driving around three hundred cattle stolen from as far north as La Parra, south of King Ranch. Once the information was obtained, Captain McNelly turned him over to Casuse for final safekeeping, with the usual results. George Durham remembered, "I reckoned Old Casoose had him a prisoner camp off to himself. We didn't have any prisoners. When I found out later it just about turned my stomach." McNelly believed the information was accurate and acted accordingly.

Another suspected bandit, or bandit ally, captured before the big fight at Palo Alto was placed in Callicott's keeping. Callicott fed the man plenty of jerked beef and coffee and gave him cigarettes, and the man seemed to enjoy himself. Then, as it grew dark, McNelly and some other men came over to take the prisoner off his hands. The captain asked if the prisoner had had plenty to eat, and Callicott said "he had all he could digest on six feet of rope." (Callicott accepted Casuse's methods without any of the qualms felt by Durham.)

.The prisoner was led away, and old Casuse brought over his old paint horse, a sure sign of what was to come next. Casuse and the prisoner disappeared from view, and a short time later Casuse returned, saying "He all right—he come backy no more."

Although, according to Callicott, the captain "could stand death in any other form better than hanging," he went along with Casuse's ruthless methods. McNelly felt he could get accurate information in no other manner. General Edward Ord, commander of U.S. forces in Texas, testified to Congress on the effectiveness of McNelly as compared to that of U.S. troops: "Captain McNelly had a big advantage over the U.S. troops mainly because he employed means of getting information from prisoners that was denied the military. His prisoners would talk. Ours wouldn't."

One of the men who was hanged had reported that seventeen Mexicans and one white man were in possession of a herd of cattle numbering about 150 and that they were cutting cross-country between where McNelly was and the border, headed for a point upriver from Brownsville where the cattle would be swum across the river. The next morning, June 12, at first light, McNelly led his men south, seeking to cut the trail of the bandits pushing the herd toward the border. The hanged man's information proved to be good as gold, and McNelly's Rangers caught sight of the raiders near the Palo Alto prairie, where General Taylor had fought the Mexicans in the first battle of the Mexican War. This would be the Second Battle of Palo Alto, and it, too, would be a decisive win for the Americans.

The Rangers gave chase, with McNelly's blooded, expensive King Ranch horse, Segal, way out in front. The Rangers rode hard and arrived at last at a *resaca*, a small shallow lake. The bandits had decided to make a stand on a little island in the middle of the resaca. As the Rangers grouped around the captain, McNelly noticed the presence of L. B. "Berry" Smith, the youngest member of the Rangers. At this point Smith's father, D. R. "Dad" Smith, appealed to the captain to let his son sit out the impending fight, owing to how much the boy's mother would grieve if their only son were lost. The captain agreed, but upon hearing the boy's own appeal that he wanted to fight, gave his approval, and Berry Smith lined up with the rest of the company. McNelly made a short speech. According to Durham, he told the men, "This won't be a standoff or a dogfall. We'll either win completely, or we'll lose completely." And he gave directions: each Ranger was to follow the captain in a skirmish line, five paces apart, and no one was to fire until the captain did.

The resaca was a quarter-mile wide, and they waded into the water, the horses splashing, moving forward, the Rangers with their big old Sharps rifles at the ready. A Sharps could bring down a buffalo at a thousand yards, and although you only got one shot before having to reload, the captain preferred them to the newfangled Winchester repeating rifles. He expected his men to make their shots count. About halfway across, the Rangers began to take fire from the bandits. The captain, out front on Segal, continued to press forward, and his men followed. Several horses were hit, and still McNelly held his fire. Durham's horse gave out and he jumped off and walked, following McNelly. Now the Georgia farm boy was really scared, and he prayed he wouldn't turn back from fear.

Thirty yards away from the bandits, McNelly opened fire with his pistol. Durham spotted a target and years later described the scene in vivid detail. When the man left cover and headed for a horse at the rear, Durham saw a big beaver hat and a white scar running down the man's cheek: "I got that scar in my sight and dropped the hammer. Both hat and head seemed to explode." This was a big moment in the boy's life: "I had made my first shot in combat and I hit my target. I had brought down the prize—that scar faced dude who had quirted down Martha Noakes. Right then I quit being a scared country boy. I was a man. A Ranger. A little McNelly."

Now the rout was on. In one instance McNelly himself had a close call. He tracked down a bandit hiding in a thicket and went forward to finish him off. The bandit was out of ammunition, and the captain, with one ball left in his pistol, pretended to be out as well. Callicott tells what happened: "The Mexican drew his Bowie knife and with a grin on his face, started toward Captain McNelly, saying as he came, 'Me gotta you now, me gotta you.' The Captain leveled his pistol and placed the last shot he had between the bandit's teeth as if he had put it there with his fingers." In the case of one stricken bandit who requested a chaplain, McNelly drew a small testament from his pocket and read words over the dying man. As a fighting man, McNelly was much impressed with the tenacity and bravery of the Mexicans. He made note of their courage in a report he sent back to headquarters in Austin soon after the fight: "I have never seen men fight with such desperation. Many of them, after being shot from their horses and severely wounded three or four times, would rise on their elbows and empty their pistols at us with their dying breath. After they broke cover it was a succession of fights, man to man, for five or six miles across the prairie."

The remaining Mexicans fled, and the Rangers raced after them. Durham, who had lost his own horse, mounted one of the outlaws'. "He was a good one," Durham noted. "He had a Running W burned on his left hip, and any animal with that brand was good. That was Captain King's brand."

In all, over a dozen bandits were slain in the headlong fight at Palo Alto. One Ranger was killed, Berry Smith, whose father had tried to keep him out of the fight. Dead at seventeen, Smith remains the youngest Ranger to die in the long history of the Rangers.

News of the gunfight and its outcome spread like wildfire along both sides of the river. McNelly's next action, some thought, was like pouring kerosene on the conflagration. On the way to Brownsville, a short distance away, about ten miles, McNelly conferred with James Browne, sheriff of Cameron County, and ordered him to send a patrol out to Palo Alto, collect the bodies of the fallen bandits, and bring them back to Brownsville. With a small detachment, the captain rode into Brownsville and set up headquarters at Miller's Hotel, a longtime popular establishment in the city. Captain King used to drink there back in the steamboating days.

Once the bodies were brought into town, McNelly issued orders for the corpses to be stacked in the main plaza beside a fountain and an invitation for anyone seeking to claim them to do so. He meant to arrest anybody who did, but as Durham, who was on guard duty that night, said, "Nobody came to try and get one, and none of the dead bandits tried to leave." McNelly's decision cannot be so easily charged to arrogance or racism on his part. It was a message, brutal, yes, but a tactic in a war with no quarter given.

The next day, the fallen Ranger Berry Smith received a military funeral. Col. Rip Ford, who always seemed to be around when important things happened along the border, was one of the marshals. The pomp and pageantry of young Smith's sendoff further stirred resentment against the Rangers among the Mexican community on both sides of the river. The angry mood was not lost on McNelly, who wrote of his concerns in his official report to Austin: "The Mexicans on the other side of the river are very much infuriated and threaten to kill ten Americans for each of their Bravos. And then on this side the Mexican residents of Brownsville—that is, the majority, the 'canaille' or lower class—are public in their denunciation of the killing and the

attention given my dead soldier seems to have exasperated them beyond measure." Not only that, but there were rumors that Cortina was
capable of mustering twelve to fifteen hundred men, many times the
number of ineffectual U.S. troops stationed at Fort Brown. McNelly's
lack of faith in the black soldiers at Fort Brown was widely shared by
other whites, who believed, rightly or wrongly, that the black troopers
kept company with Mexican women, who in turn gave information of
impending military movements to Cortina's agents.

Even as McNelly savored the triumph at Palo Alto, his health was
growing increasingly bad. He experienced a fit of violent coughing
during the funeral service for Berry Smith. Still he pressed on. From
their base in Brownsville, McNelly's men frequently crossed the river
into Matamoros. Their purpose, according to N. A. Jennings, was
twofold: "To have fun, and to carry out a set policy of terrorizing the
Mexicans at every opportunity." Captain McNelly, Jennings maintained, "assumed that the more we were feared, the easier would be
our work of subduing the Mexican raiders, so it was tacitly understood that we were to gain a reputation as fire-eating, quarrelsome
dare-devils as quickly as possible, and to let no opportunity go unim-
proved to assert ourselves and override the 'Greasers.'"

His men also patrolled the brush country up and down the Rio
Grande, with McNelly continuing to gather information from a net-
work of paid informants, spies, who kept him apprised of the bandits'
movements. Pidge Robinson gives the best account of what the daily
scouting patrols were like. He reports that "scouting duty is very
arduous" and tells of a tipoff that a party of raiders were going to be
in a certain place "on a certain day, *certain,*" but they weren't. Pidge
and the Rangers "laid in the hot sun two days without food, and getting water by stealth, at night, from a well fives miles distant; at last
word was received from our Mexican scout that they were near by,
forty strong." The captain made a speech, and the Rangers set out in
columns of four. Eventually they spotted, distantly, a party of "Aztec
Arabs" riding back and forth. "Capt. M—s face," Pidge wrote, "is
flushed with the joy of battle; all is ready; and we look for the bugle
notes to ring short and sharp in the charge." But then the Rangers realized that "the Forty Thieves are discovered to be a party of Capt.
King's *vaqueros.*" Pidge feigns disappointment, in typical Pidge fashion. The other interesting fact about this incident is the wide-ranging

movements of Captain King's men. Here they were, far from King Ranch, and obviously well known, as the mention of Captain King's name requires no further identification by author Pidge.

In the wake of McNelly's success at Palo Alto, reprisals from Cortina were widely expected among the Anglo community. The Galveston *Daily News* so reported right after the battle: "Gen. Cortina is incensed at the killing of his cattle thieves. The Mexican papers say the raiders were assassinated while asleep. Capt. McNelly says if they were asleep he don't want to find any of them awake. Cortina swears he will have revenge."

More help for South Texas was on the way. On June 22, Lieutenant James W. Guyon, a "dry goods drummer" who lived in Washington County, assembled twenty-five men in a volunteer militia company and headed south to the camp at Santa Maria to reinforce McNelly's Rangers. On the way, Guyon and his men passed through the "miserable muddy village" of Banquete and then on to King Ranch, where, on July 9, they were received with King's usual hospitality. Guyon's account is another record of King's memorable presence and generosity: "Capt. King [was] a gentleman of the highest standard. He came forward and made us every proffer of assistance, furnishing us with food for ourselves and horses." He gave Guyon a good saddle horse and additional horses to replace the jaded, worn-out ones ridden there by the Rangers. The captain's layout was impressive, too: "86,000 acres of land under one fence for pasture grounds. . . . His residence is located upon a high hill, commanding a view of the surrounding country for miles around us." When Guyon's command rode away from King Ranch, they gave the captain three cheers.

On the way to join McNelly in Brownsville, they experienced the Wild Horse Desert in all its characteristic harshness: sand, no water, good grass, and "the constant bombardment of rattle snakes by the entire company, as their dead carcasses left in our wake will testify." On July 14 they reached Brownsville, where a reporter described them as "splendid looking scalp hunters." McNelly was glad to have some capable new men, but he told them straightaway of his rules: no gambling, no cursing, no drunkenness. Five men decided they'd best move on, and were promptly taken off the roster.

While McNelly's men went about gathering more information on bandit activities and sending out patrols, Cortina's days on the border were coming to an end. Under intense diplomatic pressure from the United States, Mexican authorities arrested Cortina in early July and transported him to prison at Santiago Tlatelolco, near Mexico City. The Texas government, of course, was elated at his removal but at the same time fearful he might effect a return. Cortina, after all, had proved to be an incredibly durable figure, surviving all the turmoil and intrigue of Mexican politics and creating havoc among cattle ranchers in Texas for going on three decades.

Despite the big success of Palo Alto and the display of bodies on the plaza in Brownsville, raiding from Mexico did not let up. Reports kept coming in of stolen stock. Cornelius Stillman, Charles's brother, of Santa Rosa ranch, about sixty miles northwest of Brownsville, testified on June 24, 1875, as to his experience following McNelly's victory over the bandits: "After Captain McNelly's fight . . . I thought I could live at my ranch." But he could not because of threats received from "a citizen of Mexican origin," who said that "the Mexicans were determined to kill Americans to revenge the defeat inflicted by Captain McNelly." Stillman decided to leave his "ranch and property at the mercy of the marauders" and to remain in Brownsville "until it was safe to return."

And so it went all that summer and fall, up and down the Rio Grande.

In August McNelly got wind of a big raid emanating from Las Cuevas, a ranch on the Mexican side known by just about everybody in South Texas. Mexican raiders had been taking cattle across the river to Las Cuevas since before the first Cortina war, in the 1850s, and government commissions in the 1870s gathered numerous accounts of stolen cattle being crossed there. The Las Cuevas crossing, in fact, was where the Robb commissioners themselves observed Texas cattle being moved to Mexico in broad daylight in 1872.

Through the late summer and into the fall of 1875, McNelly's men continued to pursue bandits along the river, but without any notable success. McNelly himself was often absent from camp because of failing health, administrative duties, and, perhaps, the concocting of a bold plan to take the fight directly to the bandits, in their home country in Mexico. One says "perhaps" because the story is complex, tangled, and suppositional, but the eventual actions themselves were perfectly clear. McNelly became increasingly vexed at the protection afforded Mexican raiders by their home country. All the raiders had to do was swim the Rio Grande and they were safe as burghers. McNelly later expressed his frustration and irritation in testimony before Congress: "I have followed fifty herds of cattle to the bank of the Rio Grande, and I would see the stock on the opposite bank. The Mexicans dare me to cross the river and take them. They would say, 'Here are the cattle, come across and take them if you dare.'"

Which is what McNelly eventually decided to do: accept the dare, cross the river, and invade Mexico. In another statement made to a congressional committee, McNelly explained the premise for such a strategy: "I believe that if orders were issued to our military authorities to pursue these bands to the other bank of the river, and punish them so severely that the pay they got for crossing a herd of cattle would not compensate them for the risk they run in making the raid, it would be the most effectual and rapid way of breaking this thing up, without subjecting any innocent parties to harm."

An opportunity came in November when, on the eighteenth, McNelly ordered his men to ride to Las Cuevas as fast as they could; cattle were being crossed. Pidge Robinson wrote a long letter from CAMP TEXAS RANGERS at Laguna de los Calabaso (January 15, 1876) detailing his impressions of the invasion of Mexico. According to Pidge, they rode fifty-five miles in six hours, each man carrying a hundred rounds of ammunition. At one point they came upon a not-unfamiliar sight in that country: ". . . swung to the tree in full view of the road, was a hideous object waving in the night breeze, fearful to look upon." One of the Rangers, "who had music in his soul, and a little mescal in his canteen," sang, "He sleeps his last sleep, he has stole his last cattle./ No sound can awake him to plunder again."

McNelly was already there, waiting for the Rangers to join his detachment. The captain was much put out with Pidge when he reported that the men had not brought any provisions but only cartridges. Every time Captain McNelly asked about bread or salt or coffee, all Pidge could answer was cartridges, to the point where the captain said if he mentioned the word "cartridges" one more time, he'd have him arrested and confined to the Texas side of the river, a prospect that led Pidge to a "mental prayer that he *would* put me in arrest."

McNelly was also in touch with elements of the U.S. Army stationed at Fort Brown. Captain James F. Randlett of the 8th U.S. Cavalry had two hundred troops just across from Las Cuevas, with two

Gatling guns. Although Captain Randlett's orders forebade him from crossing the river, McNelly was under no such compunction. His blood up, he sent telegrams to Austin reporting on his decision. On November 19 he wrote, "I commence crossing at one oclock tonight. Have thirty one men will try & recover our cattle. The U.S. troops promise to cover my return."

Just as he had done before the engagement at Palo Alto, McNelly made a speech to his men. The best rendering is Callicott's inimitable backwoods vernacular: "Boys, you have follered me as far as I can ask you to do unless you or willing to go with me . . . it is like goen into the Jaws of deth with only 26 men in a forren cuntry wher we hav no Right accorden to law but as I hav went this far I am Goen to the finish with it . . . Some of us may get back or part of us or mabey all of us or mabey non of us will get back and if any of you doent want to go over with me Step a Side I doent want you unless you or willin to go as a vallentier. . . . under Stand thire is no Surrender in this we ask no canters [quarter] nor give any If any or you doent want to go Step a Side." Who wouldn't want to cross the river after a speech like that?

Pidge Robinson was at his most eloquent, echoing a well-known hymn in his description of the crossing: "In single file and leading the horses, we gathered at the beautiful, beautiful river and in silence commenced the embarkation; on each side of the crossing crouched the men, gun in hand, to protect the passage of the first boat."

The boat, a crude dugout, leaked, and one man had to bail water. McNelly, Jesus Sandoval, and Tom Sullivan, an interpreter, were the first to cross. McNelly told Pidge Robinson to remain behind and cross in the last boatload, and that while he was waiting, he might "improve what few shining hours remained to me by leaving directions as to what disposition should be made of my personal effects. He seemed to take a malicious delight in causing me to feel as badly as possible." Pidge's will didn't take long; he simply directed that all his effects be placed in a cartridge box and forwarded to Fort Brown. In the meantime, the river proved so difficult to cross that all but five horses had to be left on the Texas side. This meant that now the invasion would be on foot!

Twenty-six men and five horses, with the whole of Mexico awaiting them, they set out before dawn to attack Las Cuevas, which they believed to be no more than a mile distant. Pidge's description is best:

"We laid upon our arms till the dawn of day, and then marched to Las Cuevas, said to be one mile distant; after we had walked about three, we concluded there must be a mistake somewhere, or that the town was marching too."

There was a mistake, and the ranch they came to, the ranch they opened fire on, was Las Ancharvas or Cachattus—the names differ, but in any event McNelly gave orders to fire at everybody they saw except old men, women, and children. He gave Jesus Sandoval pride of place, for, as Callicott said, it was "the first chance old casuse had to Breeth mexican air or to hav a chance to giv a yell in over 20 years." Running through the gates, the Rangers shot down men at their daily tasks of cutting wood for breakfast, and, in Callicott's words, "wher ever we Saw one we Killed him till we Killed all we saw." They saw an old woman making tortillas who never stopped what she was doing but just kept on pulling tortillas amid the gunfire and death. Then McNelly realized, from the lack of opposition and the small number of men at the ranch, that this was some ranch other than Las Cuevas. They had attacked the wrong target.

So they headed toward Las Cuevas, which was fully alerted now by the sound of the gunfire at the wrong ranch. Neither McNelly, incidentally, nor any other of his Rangers ever expressed any regrets about the men killed at the first ranch. They believed that all the Mexican vaqueros hereabouts were raiders, cattle thieves. In front of the heavily gated Las Cuevas, which was also defended by artillery pieces, the Rangers saw arrayed before them hundreds of men on horseback. Pidge Robinson said he "caught a glimpse of a column of cavalry, in sets of fours, which seemed to me to stretch to Matamoros."

When firing commenced, McNelly led his men on retreat back to the edge of the river. They passed the quiet ranch where the dead men lay and no women or children could now be seen. Repeated attacks that day failed to repulse the Rangers, and some forty U.S. troops under Captain Randlett's command crossed the river to help. One of the Gatling guns also fired at the Mexicans from the U.S. side, leading Pidge Robinson to memorialize that event in his funniest prose: "On the Texas side were some of the Eighth Cavalry, and a Gatling gun, and just here I would like to remark that if there is an inanimate object in this whole world for which I have a pure and unadulterated veneration, respect and love, that object is a Gatling gun; if Mr. Gatling has a daughter I would marry her to-morrow, if she would have me, for the sake of her father—and the gun."

The Mexicans launched attacks at them throughout the day. General Juan Flores Salinas, a well-known *Cortinista* who had been engineering raids on Texas cattle for years, led one of the assaults. McNelly ordered a counterattack on the charging Mexican forces, and Salinas was shot down, as Callicott put it, "with his pistol in his hand with 2 needle gun Bullits through his body Killen him ded." Considered a hero of Mexican resistance against Anglo incursion on the border, Salinas is remembered today with a monument and a plaque that reads in part, "*Murió por su patria el 19 de Noviembre 1875*" (Died for his country on November 19, 1875).

McNelly sent several telegrams explaining his actions. One of them read: "I am in temporary earthworks and have refused to leave until the cattle are returned. The Mexicans in my front are about four hundred. What shall I do?"

On the next day, the twentieth, McNelly and his men were still precariously perched close to the river on the Mexican side. Seeing more Mexican forces forming lines to attack, McNelly ordered the digging of a forty-foot-long trench. Pidge Robinson called it a "beautiful little fort, but it was terrible hard ground to dig." One of the men said that Texas "never looked so charming to me before" and that "I will wager six months pay against a *tamale* that there is more love for Texas, more pure admiration for the State in this little band of Rangers than in all the rest of the citizens combined." Pidge wanted to know who was in charge of the Gatling gun and hoped to hear its bullets whizzing into Mexico, but aimed high enough so they wouldn't hit him and the boys. Seeing what they were up against, a handful of men facing a massed array of Mexican troops, Pidge was reminded of another such moment in Texas history: "We are going up the Great Spout now; a second Alamo, but not half so romantic in name; just fancy being killed at the *Rincón de Cucharras;* in plain English, the spoon corner."

McNelly, meantime, was determined to stick until he accomplished what he had come for, to recover the herd of stolen cattle, and he resisted all entreaties to do otherwise. Several meetings between McNelly and Mexican authorities produced an understanding. McNelly and his men would return to Texas, and the stolen cattle would be handed over the next day, fifteen miles upriver at Rio

Grande City. By now Washington was intensely interested in McNelly's presence in Mexico. Secretary of War William W. Belknap ordered federal troops not to assist or support McNelly in any manner, a directive that infuriated McNelly when he learned of it.

At Rio Grande City on the twenty-first, the Rangers waited from ten that morning, when the cattle were supposed to be delivered, until four, when they were told that the cattle had to be inspected first. The Texans considered this new impediment ridiculous. Pidge Robinson reasoned, "They went over without any permit and it was *surmised* that they might return in the same manner." The Galveston *Daily News* account (December 12, 1875) mocked the position put forward by the Mexican authorities: "The bovine captives seemed to wonder why it was that, crossed to one shore without a permit, they could not be recrossed without one, considering, also, that they were returning to their lawful owners." McNelly's response was typical McNelly: direct, aggressive, no-nonsense. He instantly put his men on a ferry and crossed the river once again. Once on the Mexican side, he talked and then he acted. In Callicott's words, he "told tom to tell him a Son of a bitch if he dident cross them cattle in less than 5 minutes he would Kill the last one of them." Pidge Robinson added some sound effects in his account: "The ominous 'kerchack' of the carbine levers as the long, murderous looking cartridges were chambered home, satisfied them as to the permit and the cattle were allowed to cross over without one; such is the power of Sharp on International law."

The total recovered was sixty-five, delivered into McNelly's hands and driven to near Brownsville, where a little over half of them belonging to Richard King were separated out and the rest left to drift back to their home ranges.

McNelly had risked his life and the lives of his Rangers, he had acted illegally in invading a sovereign nation and shooting down some of its citizens, and he had done all of this for sixty-five cattle. In the eyes of Texans like Richard King, McNelly was a great hero, and the battle at Las Cuevas something to be remembered and honored.

On the border, while McNelly was publicly fêted for his high deeds of daring in a foreign land, things continued pretty much the same. Texas cattle continued to flow south across the river. In December 1875, for example, a month after Las Cuevas, cattle were reported disappearing at the following rates and places during November, the month of the Las Cuevas standoff: Edinburg, 350 head; Roma, 180; Ringgold, 150; Brownsville, 435; Los Grullos, 300; and Las Cuevas, 300, making a total of 1,715 cattle. In Monterrey, it was reported, a contract for 18,000 cattle had been agreed upon, and Texas ranchers could expect more theft because the Nueces Strip was still the best source for good cattle.

Still, at King Ranch, the thirty-five head of stolen cattle returned by McNelly's Rangers meant a great deal. Four Rangers volunteered to drive the little herd home, including Durham and Callicott. Callicott reported that King had read reports of the "second Alamo" and had been busy raising a hundred men to go to McNelly's rescue. According to Callicott, King said, "Out of the many thousand hed I hav had Stolen and driven to mexico this 35 hed or all I have ever got back." These cattle, he said, would neither be killed for beef or sold, and would instead be permitted to live out the "the ballence of thire days in Piece."

King invited the Rangers to sleep in the house that night, but as they were dirty from the range and used to living outdoors, they chose to sleep under the stars. They were, however, brought to the ranch house to meet the captain's two daughters, Nettie and Ella, who were home from having recently completed school in Kentucky. The girls sent the Rangers two big pound cakes, "Compliments of the 2 Miss Kings to the McNelly Rangers." Later the captain showed his appreciation by giving $500 to McNelly's company of Rangers. The Galveston *Daily News* (December 13, 1875) noted, "It is a source of satisfaction to the soldiers to know that the people, whom they serve, have among them such princely characters."

McNelly's health was going downhill, and the last time Durham saw him, at the Menger Hotel in San Antonio, the captain looked the "same color as the bed sheets." Still a commanding presence, he told the boys to go buy some good clothes and make a good appearance in town. McNelly himself was mustered out of the Rangers in January 1877, a result of new political conditions in state government, and went back to his cotton farm near Burton, officially underappreciated but a hero in South Texas, to the men who rode with him, and to men like Richard King.

When McNelly died, in September 1877, he was buried in a country cemetery a few miles from Burton, and a short time later, in

January 1878, a tall, obelisk-type monument was erected beside his grave. The man who paid for the stone memorial, at a cost of $3,000, was Richard King. Although the state of Texas did not honor McNelly, King did.

And the other young Rangers who wrote of their days with the captain? Pidge Robinson went back to Virginia to see his sweetheart. On April 4, 1876, armed with the navy Colt he had been provided by the state of Texas and a small derringer, he got into a gunfight with his sweetheart's brother in what newspapers miscalled a duel. Pidge, who had faced all those dangers on the Rio Grande, died from his wounds. The state of Texas deducted the value of the navy Colt, $16.50, from his discharge pay.

William Callicott lived to be an old man and wrote his story down in that remarkable English that violated every law except vividness, and was interviewed by historian Walter Prescott Webb.

R. G. Dunn, though not one of McNelly's men, but in a way one of King's, lived to a ripe old age, as well, and in 1930 he and his brother Matt happened to be riding through that country when they came in sight of King Ranch. It was the first time Dunn had laid eyes on it since 1875. They decided to stop and were invited to visit with Robert J. Kleberg, who was ill and confined to his bed. Kleberg welcomed the two brothers, and, Dunn remembered, "We talked over the old times when the captain was alive in the troublesome days of the '70s."

And George Durham? The Georgia farm boy who had become a man under Captain McNelly's leadership said he would always be a little McNelly till the day he died.

Lee Hall replaced McNelly, and though Durham judged him all right, he was not McNelly, and when the size of the company was reduced, Durham drifted south, headed for the Santa Gertrudis. He put on his best clothes and "rode in," he said, "like I might be looking the place over figuring on buying it." Captain King came out from his office and thought he recognized Durham as one of McNelly's Rangers. King asked him what he was looking for, and Durham spoke right up: "A job." King asked him if he had ever worked stock, and Durham said no, all he knew how to do was chop cotton and use a sidearm. King hired him on the spot for $60 a month and assigned him to the Laureles division, northwest of the Santa

Gertrudis. Many a time he drove Captain King on trips to Corpus
Christi, Brownsville, and San Antonio. Then he got promoted to
caporal—straw boss—on the Santa Gertrudis, and in 1882 he fulfilled
the final part of his King Ranch dream by marrying Caroline Chamberlain, the girl he had been smitten with back in 1875. Captain King
made him foreman of El Sauz, sixty-odd miles to the south, and there
he and Caroline resided until her death in 1915. Durham lived on until
1940, long enough to dictate his story to Clyde Wantland for the most
readable of the Texas Ranger memoirs, *Taming the Nueces Strip*. The
only jobs he ever held in his entire life were working for his father
back in Georgia, rangering for Captain McNelly, and managing stock
on King Ranch.

CHAPTER 9

The Great Cattle King of Texas

The Mexican commission's report was certainly right about one thing: Ranchers in Texas were sending cattle north, to a degree unparalleled in the history of Texas or anywhere else. During a fifteen-year period, 1870 to 1885, hundreds of herds were launched to railheads in Kansas and beyond—a torrential, lucrative flood of cattle, the greatest migration of livestock in human history, the transshipment on hoof of upward of ten million beeves to feed a burgeoning nation. The trail drives from King's rancho were part of this vast surge of economic activity, and Richard King's successes in these years made him, in the words of the Galveston *News*, "the great cattle King of Texas."

From the beginning Richard King had conceived of his rancho as a cattle operation—the raising of cattle for market lay at the very heart of his pastoral enterprise. Back at the beginning of Santa Gertrudis, in 1853, King had procured cattle to stock the pastures. He brought cattle from Mexico on that trip he made when he brought back with him the entire village. He continued to build up his herds with each passing year. He sold only steers (castrated animals), keeping cows and bulls for the increase that slowly, steadily expanded the number of stock on the rancho. But in the early days King, like all the Texas ranchers, faced a significant problem: There was no sizable market for cattle. The cattle business on the scale of the years to come simply did not exist.

There was a market for hides and tallow before the Civil War, and makeshift slaughterhouses sprang up in the area around Corpus Christi. As late as 1869, there were four tallow factories in Nueces County. King and Kenedy owned two of them. King disposed of some of his cattle—the culls, the weaker ones—in that fashion. And there were the beginnings of a search for external markets to which cattle could be profitably driven.

In Texas, pre-Civil War drives were made to Louisiana and Missouri in 1842, and after the Gold Rush, to faraway California in 1848. Drives to California were risky but not infrequent in the years before the war. In 1854, the peak year of the treks to California, ten thousand Texas cattle were counted crossing into the state near the ferry at Yuma, Arizona. Drives from Texas were also launched north to cities in the Midwest. One drive of 600 cattle reached Chicago in the fall of 1854. That same year, Texas cattle arrived in St. Louis, where one newspaper reporter noted, "Texas cattle are about the nearest to wild animals of any now driven to market. We have seen some buffaloes that were more civilized." Although midwestern farmers wanted no part of a longhorn invasion and consumers in New York complained about the toughness of the meat, the drives continued all through the years leading up to the war. In 1858 a "fine drove of Texas cattle" passed through Mark Twain's hometown of Hannibal, Missouri, and in that same year, Oliver Loving, one of the best known of the old-time Texas cowmen, partnered with a neighbor to drive a herd to Illinois. In 1859 Loving trailed a herd to Colorado. All in all, the future for Texas cattle looked bright. The *Texas Almanac* of 1857 put it this way: It cost "$25 to raise a cow in Connecticut, $15 in Indiana and $12.50 in Illinois. In Texas it costs to raise a cow about what it costs to raise a chicken."

Richard King may well have sent some cattle to Louisiana in the 1850s; no one knows for sure. But he was certainly interested in developing markets for his growing inventory. Some buyers from Mexico came to his ranch to purchase cattle, and King disposed of culls and barren animals in the hide-and-tallow trade along the coast. He also tried out an experiment in beef preservation, long before refrigeration would transform the widespread transportation and marketing of meat. He held the conviction that a saltwater solution could be injected into the veins of hunks of beef, thus preserving them along the lines of salted meat. But the idea of brine-embalmed cattle did not catch on, and King abandoned the experiment.

When the Civil War broke out, the market for Texas cattle was utterly flattened. In August 1861, President Lincoln cut off all trade with the South, which suited states like Missouri and Kansas just fine because they had already taken steps by passing laws to prohibit Texas cattle from spreading disease among their domestic cattle. Although drovers like Oliver Loving and John Chisum sent herds southeast to Louisiana, Tennessee, and Mississippi, the war effectively put on hold the possibility of developing a larger trade in the North; the promising trends of the 1850s were, for the moment, forgotten. In the meantime, with many ranchers and ranch hands gone off to fight the Yankees, the cattle wandered as they had before, unbranded, unclaimed, while the nation worked out its destiny.

In Texas the cattle were waiting. Northern visitors were amazed at their abundance. A young man named Charles F. Gross, who traveled with a team of surveyors from Shreveport, Louisiana, to Brownsville, Texas, in 1865, recalled that the survey "took us through the heart of the cattle ranges of Texas; and I saw buffaloes, cattle, and wild horses galore." The cattle and horses, he said, "were running wild and waiting for someone to gather them and drive them to the northern market."

When the war was over, those Texans who had been away from their plantations and ranches came riding back to their lands to resume their life's work. Some were not happy with what they found. At Capt. R. H. Williams's ranch west of San Antonio, things were in complete disarray: "I arrived late in the evening, to the great surprise of the Mexicans. I was the last person they expected, or wished, to see. Having no one to look after them, these gentry, after the manner of their kind, had been taking things easy, and everything had been neglected. Calves had been left unbranded and horses allowed to stray away on the prairie. The only wonder was that the Indians hadn't cleared out the lot." Captain Williams was still able, that same year, 1865, to put together a small drive of cattle to Mexico, where he made a profit, and, later in the season, another drive to New Orleans. Cattle were driven to Arkansas, New Mexico, and Louisiana, while other cattlemen waited until the next year before taking to the trail. In 1866 the numbers of cattle trailed north increased dramatically, to between 200,000 and 260,000. That year, too, the Goodnight-Loving Trail was forged from West Texas to Fort Sumner, in eastern New Mexico.

Unlike Captain Williams, Captain King had not gone off to distant states to do battle for the Confederacy; he had fought the war in his own—and highly lucrative—way in South Texas. The first thing he had to do following Lee's surrender at Appomatox was to secure amnesty from the old/new government, the United States of America.

Once again his ubiquitous friend Col. Rip Ford was in a position to help. In the summer of 1865, as Union forces occupied Brownsville, Ford arranged a meeting with Union commander Major General Frederick Steele. Ford and his entourage, composed of Captain Kenedy, Captain King, Major Felix Blucher, Mr. Vance, and others crossed the river from Mexico to meet with Steele on the American side. The former Confederates "attempted no concealment of their adhesion to the Confederacy and their readiness to renew their adhesion to the Constitution of the United States." The general was agreeable and felt that men of such standing, "representative men," should be treated with due regard, as their influence would have a good effect on the general populace. Things went swimmingly, and Steele accepted the offer of King & Kenedy to renew their steamboat services as before. One thing about King & Kenedy: They could get along with governments, United States, Confederate, or again United States, in the interest of commerce and profit. They were good businessmen, and they were survivors of the constant warfare along the border that had been going on now, in one form or another, declared and undeclared, for the past eighteen years, ever since King stepped ashore at Brazos Island.

But achieving amnesty was not automatic for a man of King's standing. Ordinary former Confederates had to swear an oath to support and defend the Constitution and to abide by laws freeing the slaves. But King fell under another clause of the Amnesty Proclamation—the $20,000 clause. Because his net worth was in excess of $20,000, he had to make application for amnesty directly to the president. He did so, swearing that he had always been loyal to the United States. He also made an appeal, on September 15, 1865, to Maj. Gen. Giles S. Smith, the new Brownsville commander of occupation forces. King asked for the return of his house on Elizabeth Street, which he stated was currently being occupied by a tenant installed there by military authority. He stated that the house needed repairs and that he wanted to take possession and speed those repairs forward in order to bring his family back home from their long, wartime-forced sojourn in San Antonio (following the raid of December 1863). Ford's help was crucial in King's being fully reintegrated into his former status as U.S. citizen, and years later a grateful

King anonymously repaid Ford by having a deposit of $250 placed in the old Ranger's bank account each month for two years, during a time of protracted poor health when Ford was unable to pay his rent on the house where he lived in San Antonio.

In 1866 Kenedy and King set about rebuilding their steamboat business on the Rio Grande. One of their partners, Charles Stillman, had of course returned permanently to the East Coast, and another longtime partner, Charles Walworth, had died the year previously, whereupon King and Kenedy had immediately settled with Walworth's widow. For $50,000 cash they paid off her husband's interests in M. Kenedy and Co. and R. King & Co.

The reorganization brought in several new partners, including the county judge of Cameron County, and men Kenedy and King had worked with running the contraband cotton down the river to the markets of the world. The new company was called King, Kenedy & Co., and like its earlier incarnation, its partners loved monopoly and hated competition. Hence they opposed the building of a railroad to Brownsville and did everything they could to prevent it. Along with their lawyer Stephen Powers, they became known in the Reconstruction press in Austin as the "Sesesh Clique." They had enjoyed a monopoly since 1850, and they did not intend to relinquish it.

Also in 1866, King and Kenedy set in motion a plan to dissolve their ranching partnership. They did so on the most amicable of terms, dividing all the stock equally. It took the better part of three years, for they had a lot of stock to round up and sort out. In 1866 they had a total of 94,000 cattle and 5,400 horses; in 1869, the totals were 48,664 cattle and 4,400 horses, with an estimate of 10,000 cattle still loose on the prairie. Yet during the three previous years they had sold only 1,000 cattle and 570 horses. Where were the missing thousands? In Mexico?

By 1870 King was ready to act entirely on his own. After all, he was the richest man in Texas, with assets of $200,000 in real property and $365,000 in personal property. By comparison, Mifflin Kenedy's net worth of $21,000 in real and $139,600 in personal property fell considerably short of his old friend's.

The year before, King had settled on a brand that his cattle and horses would make known everywhere where there were cowboys and ranches. It was the Running W, a wavy W that Mexicans called the "little snake." The *Ere Flecha* was the first brand, going back to the earliest days of the rancho—a capital R with an arrow crossbar. Then the HK in honor of his wife, then an LK design (Lewis, his first partner, and King?), and then a modification of LK with a little *v* at the top to designate the partner who replaced Major Chapman, James Walworth. The HK, LK, and modified LK were all registered in 1859, the Running W in 1869.

By 1870, the problem of markets for Texas beef was solved. No longer, as one historian put it, would ranchers have to worry about how "to link a four-dollar steer to a forty-dollar market."

The solution lay eleven hundred miles away, in Abilene, Kansas, where an energetic, loud-talking, enthusiastic young visionary capitalist named Joseph G. McCoy had hit upon the idea of making the little shiny-new frontier town into a center for collecting and shipping cattle to packinghouses in Chicago. Construction of cattle pens and stockyards was launched in 1867, too late to attract much business that year, but McCoy expected to be ready for the next year. In 1868, Abilene received 75,000 cattle and expected double that the next. Cowboys, cows, and cow towns were about to enter the permanent lexicon of American myth.

The way north became famous, too. Cattle drives northward followed a myriad of routes to reach the main trails: the Shawnee and the Chisholm trails. Both began in deep South Texas, at Brownsville, and ran north toward San Antonio (passing west of King Ranch by not many miles), then to Austin, and then to Waco, where the two separated permanently. The Shawnee, the older trail, proceeded north through Dallas up to the Red River and then through Oklahoma's Indian Territory and on to Sedalia, Missouri, to connect with the Missouri Pacific Railroad. The more famous Chisholm Trial, following its westward divergence at Waco, ran through Fort Worth, across the Red River, though the Indian Territory, and into Kansas and the trail town of Abilene, where the tracks of the Union Pacific were. The trails were like rivers with many smaller tributaries feeding into them, and the current that flowed in them was made up of cattle, a cascading stream of cow meat pouring into the railroad towns, their destination the packing plants and meat-processing centers of Chicago. One result of the cattle drive era was that beef replaced pork as the mainstay of American diets.

What were the cattle themselves like? They were longhorns, and they looked like holy hell on hooves. Everything about the longhorns was long, from tail to legs to the elongated heads that gave them a fierce demeanor, and, of course, there were the sweeping, dangerous horns. An average longhorn weighed in the neighborhood of fifteen hundred pounds, and its horn span from tip to tip ran to four or five feet.

John Washington Lockhart described those he found in the lower Brazos Valley as "trimly made, with legs and feet built for speed. It would take a good horse to outrun one of them. They ran to one color, being black with brown backs and bellies. In time, they became mixed with domestic cattle, and their calves took on mixed colors. When harried or wounded, they were vicious and would fight any living thing. Their sharp horns made them a formidable foe."

The wild, tough, nearly indefatigable longhorns were the best breed there was for the long trail. Their meat might be stringier, the taste a bit gamier, but for trailworthiness, no cow could match the longhorn. Charles Goodnight, the best-known pioneer rancher in the Panhandle area of northwest Texas, drove longhorns and knew their merit: "As trail cattle, their equal never has been known. Their hoofs are superior to those of any other cattle. In stampedes, they hold together better, are easier circled in a run, and rarely split off when you commence to turn the front. No animal of the cow kind will shift and take care of itself under all conditions as will the Longhorns. They can go farther without water and endure more suffering than others."

Longhorns were also immune to a deadly fever that some Texas cattle carried. Texas fever or, variously, Spanish or Mexican fever devastated susceptible cattle, made them run a fever and lose weight, made their breath stink and their urine turn dark and sometimes bloody, made them go glassy-eyed and either lapse into a coma or go crazy. It killed a lot of them. Farmers in Missouri and Kansas feared infection spreading to their cattle, and sometimes desperate measures were employed to prevent such cattle from entering their states. J. M. Daugherty, "Uncle Jim," ran into a passel of trouble the first time he took a herd north. In 1866, near Fort Scott, Kansas, he and his men were overtaken by Jayhawkers (at that time a pejorative term for anti-slavery guerrillas operating out of Kansas, but later embraced by all Kansans as a favorable name). Years later Uncle Jim explained what happened: "The Jayhawkers tried me for driving cattle into their country, which they claimed were infested with ticks which would kill their cattle. I was found guilty without any evidence, they not even having one of my cattle for evidence. Then they began to argue among themselves what to do with me. Some wanted to hang me while others wanted to whip me to death." Fortunately for Daugherty, one Jayhawker took his side and finally convinced the others to turn him loose.

The problem of Texas fever wouldn't be solved until well into the next century, long after the trail drives were ended, and when it was solved, it would be King Ranch that solved it.

Ultimately longhorns would give way to gentle, tamer, more meat-efficient breeds, but Texas wouldn't have been Texas without the nineteenth-century critters that had roamed wild in South Texas since the Spaniards introduced cattle to the New World in the sixteenth century. Herds of longhorns are still maintained, though almost entirely by rich people, weekend ranchers mostly, who seek to connect symbolically with Texas's heroic past by decorating their front pastures with brindled, four-footed Lone Star icons. The easiest way for the average citizen to see a longhorn today is to scan the end zone of a University of Texas football game where the mascot Bevo is featured; then try to imagine a mass of fifteen hundred or so Bevos walking from South Texas to Kansas, a trip of over a thousand miles, loose-herded by twelve to fifteen young men on horseback. Imagine that, and you have the inherent drama of a cattle drive.

In 1869, 150,000 were trailed to Kansas. The drives averaged about a thousand head of cattle, but herds two or three times that size became common. The biggest drive on record occurred in 1869 when a group of disaffected ex-Confederates combined their resources and trailed 15,000 cattle from Texas to California.

But the real market was Kansas, and in 1870 Richard King was poised to send his cattle north. Consider his situation that spring. In February he and Mifflin Kenedy concluded the dissolution of their partnership, having rounded up and sorted out the cattle and other livestock belonging to each. King had approximately 33,000 cattle on his range in the spring of 1870, and going back to the previous year and forward to 1872, he sold 13,500 head of cattle, fetching good prices.

Richard King might have thrilled at the sight of his herds as they left the Santa Gertrudis range on their way north, but in his account books he always referred to the trail drivers as "Kansas Men"—an unromantic phrase for those who performed the dusty, dangerous job of pushing herds of longhorns up the long trail that wound from deep South Texas into the heart of the American imagination. But trail driving was first of all a question of business, of venture capitalism, and Richard King was like a CEO of cattle. He authorized the drives, oversaw the selection of herd bosses and foremen, worked out the terms of the contracts, and kept in close contact, by means of the mails and telegraph, with the progress of the herds.

King always kept a sharp eye out for anybody trying to cheat him. He hired a Kentuckian named Colonel Crump, a big, tough, capable man who had a reputation in South Texas for hating rustlers and showing it. King sent Crump to Kansas, where his job was to oversee incoming herds and cut out any Running W cattle that might have fallen into the hands of other drovers. Sometimes King traveled north himself, going by steamboat to St. Louis and by train to Abilene, to handle details of the sale and to savor the pleasures of being a cattle king in those heady times.

He was a businessman, not a trail driver. From his desk in the office of the commissary on his rancho, he planned the whole thing down to the last centavo. At the same time, he kept close personal tabs on everything having to do with the gathering and marshaling of cattle and personnel there on the ranch as well. He was constantly on the move, looking at grass, at the condition of his livestock, at the watering holes and creeks. He worried, always, about rain and grass and the weather and the conditions along the trail and the prices in Kansas and all the hundred imponderables that made the business of raising and selling cattle a constant throw of the dice. For about fifteen years after the Civil War, the dice were very hot. And then it was over, and a new era, a far less exuberant one, began. But Richard King would not be around for the next phase. His death coincided with the end of the trail drives.

King's Kansas Men took herds to Abilene in 1870, the first boom year of the cattle drive era, when 300,000 beeves were sold, and, in 1871, when over twice that many cattle were driven north. A Wichita merchant observed in July 1871: "The stream of cattle still pours in. Its line is now continuous from the Rio Grande. If the flow continues, the prairies will be inundated with Texas Longhorns before the close of the season. Fully half of the beeves passing here are ready for the butcher."

King sent herds to Kansas in 1872, when the overall total fell by half of the previous year's. Conditions in Kansas were constantly altering to fit trends in marketing, and a preference for better-quality beef than the longhorns provided was affecting prices. Always interested in upgrading the quality of his product, King, looking to the future, bought Durham bulls and cows from Kentucky in 1873 to improve the grade of beef produced on his rancho.

In September 1873 a national panic on the stock market saw, among other things, the collapse of the beef market, but King had already sold his cattle for that season and so escaped any losses. During the worst of the depression in 1874, King could draw upon his diversified holdings in livestock and still do all right. He kept large flocks of sheep, and their wool was a steady earner; the inferior cattle could still be disposed of at his hide-and-tallow works, located about two miles north of the rancho. He also had hogs in the thousands. Anything with a cloven hoof was a potential moneymaker, and King owned an abundance of all forms of marketable animals. King had been right when he had told Mifflin Kenedy, "Land and livestock have a way of increasing in value. Cattle and horses, sheep and goats, will reproduce themselves into value. But boats—they have a way of wrecking, decaying, falling apart, decreasing in value and increasing in cost of operation."

Harbingers of change were much apparent in these years as well. Barbed wire, invented in 1874, was being sold to ranchers in Texas, and it would spell the end of the open range. Before barbed wire, fencing was very expensive, but farseeing ranchers saw the advantages, and some had the wherewithal to pay the cost of wooden fencing. Richard King, for one. He began fencing in 1871 and by 1874 had 70,000 acres of pastureland fenced. Fencing principally meant two things: increased security against theft and better conditions for controlling breeding programs. The wild old days of open-range longhorns were closing fast. The other big change was the steady, inevitable penetration of railroads into Texas. It wouldn't be long before all of Texas was fenced and webbed with tracks.

When the market for beef recovered, it did so in a big way, and

King was ready. He sent herds north in 1875, though in one instance not so far north. A total of 4,737 cattle, divided into four herds of approximately 1,200, left Rancho Santa Gertrudis on March 12. Just two days later, before crossing the Nueces River, the cattle in one herd stampeded, and twenty-seven wound up missing. That was the only mishap with the stock on this relatively short drive, which ended at Denison, in north Texas, thirty miles south of the Red River, in late July. (Denison had recently become a railroad town, competing with the ones in Kansas for the cattle trade.) Richard King kept in close contact by letter and telegraph with his herd bosses, men with whom he had made separate contracts in a sort of profit-sharing strategy unusual at the time, most cattlemen simply paying their trail bosses a flat salary. King went up to Denison himself in early August to handle the final details. His trail bosses made money, and so did King, whose net profit was $50,000. The foremen, cowboys, and vaqueros were paid wages, however, the same as with other ranchers. A cook made $30 a month; cowboys, $25. King's hacendado system applied to the trail just as it did to the rancho.

The trail drive era of the 1870s marked the triumphalist, public phase of Richard King's ascendancy from steamboat roughneck to cattle king. His newfound stature was marked by that usual barometer of success and approbation in American society, press coverage and popular interest. Prior to the 1870s, King's rancho had always impressed visitors—from the famous, like Robert E. Lee, to foreign visitors, like Colonel Fremantle, the British officer. But in the 1870s the rancho began to receive its first real attention from the daily press. In 1874 a reporter from the *Corpus Christi Gazette* wrote a lengthy account of a visit to King's rancho. The reporter stressed the size of the rancho's holdings, including recently acquired acres south of the Santa Gertrudis site. The reporter noted that 65,000 acres were under fence and described the composition of the forty miles of fence in great detail (planks, posts, and wire). Other details included mention of a hundred men "constantly employed in looking after the various interests of the immense hacienda." The stock on the rancho were enumerated as well: 50,000 cattle, 6,000 horse stock, 30,000 head of merino sheep, and 6,000 to 7,000 hogs.

The reporter was most impressed with two things: the appearance of the rancho and the rancho's owner. At the main rancho, "situated on a high hill" between two creeks, stood "a tower or lookout, erected on the top of a large brick warehouse." From there one could admire the countryside for twenty miles around. The reporter also praised the "large and commodious dwelling" of the captain's, the stable, the houses for the vaqueros, and the well-groomed grounds. It all looked like a "well cultivated park, interspersed here and there with beautiful shade trees." What struck the reporter most about King was his "indomitable energy."

But probably the most interesting picture of King and his rancho appears under the thin disguise of fiction, in a novel published in 1894 by Richard Henry Savage titled *For Life and Love: A Story of the Rio Grande*. Savage, one of the three commissioners who visited South Texas in 1872 and again in 1873, spent considerable time at King's rancho, becoming quite conversant, it appears, with the capacity and character of its owner. Savage was himself a man of impressive credentials—a West Point graduate, an army officer, a world traveler, and the author of thirty volumes of prose and poetry.

Savage's novel contains an elaborate account of a visit to "Rancho San Miguel"—obviously, Santa Gertrudis. It is introduced as "at once a camp, a plantation, a fortress, and the abode of a patriarch of flocks and herds." The description of the site itself tallies closely with that in the *Corpus Christi Gazette*: "On a raised plateau, fifty feet above the plain, was a huge masonry square keep, three stories high. And, at some little distance, a great, roomy Southern planter's home rose from bowered gardens, and in the rear an extensive series of offices, with immense stacks of prairie hay, rising unhoused toward the blue skies."

Savage devoted considerable space to describing the interior of the Southern planter's home. Unpretentious in its exterior, the great low plantation house was a very dream of refined luxury. The main hall contained robes and skins and the heads of many "unfamiliar beasts"—elk, panther, wolf, buffalo, bear, a virtual menagerie of hunting trophies. In the rooms were "countless treasures picked up in the Rio Grande Valley—Mexican silverware, ornaments, and pottery; superb embroidery, and knightly saddle-gear; minerals, Aztec relics, rare carvings; Indian spoils in endless profusion, and an extensive collection of weapons, personal ornaments, and masses of old books, religious ornaments, and costly vessels."

Is that what the interior of King's house at Santa Gertrudis looked like? Other than the description in Savage's novel, there is no account anywhere of the interior of King's rancho, of the house's décor—the house that burned to the ground in 1912, all its contents consumed. Perhaps Savage was investing a lot of imaginative capital in this description; it is impossible to know. The acquisitive, colonizing domination of nature, along with a taste for the art of the conquered, is certainly well captured here; it suggests an internalization of King's empire. In any case, Savage's rendering of the castlelike feeling of hospitality and safety extended at "Rancho San Miguel," part of its master's largesse, certainly rings true with other eyewitness accounts of visits to Rancho Santa Gertrudis: "Generals, diplomats, foreigners, army officers, rich traders, explorers, judges, and governors thronged his board, and none failed to admire the simple elegance of the Lady of San Miguel."

Savage also describes the site as a kind of fort where "The alarm-bell at any moment would bring a hundred men, Winchesters in hand, to the bidding of the grim chief of San Miguel." The grim chief is a character named Silas Leavenworth, who is to some degree a dead ringer for Richard King: "As for old Si Leavenworth, he is indeed a strange character. He went to Texas in 1846 as a camp follower of General Taylor and a deck-hand. He is cool, sly, desperate, suspicious in business, and yet hospitable and liberal. He has dozens of active schemes . . . he was a noted Confederate." Other details seem to be drawn from what we know elsewhere of Richard King: "Strange man Si. His tough old body is scarred with bullet and knife wounds, and he is as fearless as a Sioux brave. His education is that of hard experience, and he is a very Machiavelli in cunning. He has the ablest advisers, and has gathered around him, from the Nueces to the Rio Grande, some remarkable adventurers. . . . His wife is an educated woman of exemplary character, a clergyman's daughter."

This stands as the fullest, richest description of King at the height of his powers, in the turbulent 1870s, when he was at once cattle baron and fierce defender of home, hearth, livestock, and land. Savage's thumbnail estimate of Leavenworth/King rings true: "Rude, and wholly wrapped up in his schemes, Silas Leavenworth still was devoted only to the modest woman who has given him the children of his heart."

Lifelong friend Mifflin Kenedy considered King "violently opinionated." He was "a rough old devil," according to one old trail driver, and he enjoyed a good fistfight so much that he kept an Irishman around the rancho to fight with when he felt like letting off some steam. At the same time, he was a person of openhanded generosity. Everybody who came to King's rancho remembered the hospitality extended by King and his wife. An article that appeared in *The World,* a Corpus Christi newspaper, on May 23, 1878, described King as "eccentrically baronial and given to the wildest excesses of semi-barbaric hospitality." The article declared that hospitality was "King's saving clause"—and faulted Kenedy for his lack in this area.

The year 1876, notable for the celebration of the centennial in Philadelphia, the Great Northfield Minnesota Raid of Jesse James's gang, and George Armstrong Custer's downfall at Little Bighorn, proved to be a very good year for Richard King. As Mifflin Kenedy noted in a letter to Stephen Powers in January, King was "busy getting thirty thousand head of cattle on the road to Kansas." In all, twelve herds went waltzing out of the pastures of Rancho Santa Gertrudis for the trip to Kansas. The first King Ranch herd arrived in Ellis, Kansas, in early June, followed in just two days by a second herd.

An interesting picture of King's personality emerges from a letter written by his friend Uriah Lott, who accompanied King on the 1876 trip to Kansas and who, as always, was seeking funds to build a railroad from Corpus Christi to Laredo. In a letter to his wife, Lott remarked, "I have gotten to a full understanding with Captain King. He got up the other night about 2:00 o'clock [A.M.] and sat down by my bed . . . and talked until morning. He told me that he was going to give me the first $20,000 he got out of the cattle to operate with . . . and build the railroad."

Other battalions of the King army of cattle were trailed to Indian agencies in Red Cloud, Nebraska, and Ogallala, Nebraska. A total of 313,248 cattle were driven to market that year, of which just under 10 percent belonged to Richard King.

In 1877 the total number of cattle dropped to 201,159 head. There were many reasons. A freezing winter killed many cattle in northwest Texas. There was more difficulty in getting the cattle through, thanks to increased fencing. But still the drovers rounded up cattle and headed them north. In 1878, the tally bounced back, to 265,649, and the next year was nearly as good, at 250,927 head. Any year that hit a quarter of a million was a good year.

Beyond the prosaic line entries in King's account books, there is not a great deal of firsthand documentation of King Ranch herds on the trail. What little there is, however, is telling. Cattle drives by King Ranch outfits seemed to have a distinctive quality, or so thought John Maltsberger, who at fifteen ran away from his home in Cotulla, Texas, to become a cowboy. Years later he remembered that "the long herds of the King Ranch . . . [were] . . . a pretty sight. The herds of cattle and horses were of a color. The horses were uniform and beautiful. They had long manes and tails, long hair and fetlocks. . . . There would be bay horses with red cattle, black horses and black cattle, brown horses with brown cattle."

Another cowboy, Sam Dunn Houston, was in Nebraska in 1879 when he joined up with an outfit to trail a herd of King Ranch cattle to the Red Cloud Agency in Wyoming, a big herd, four thousand strong. He described how he felt upon entering a town with such cattle: "They were one of the old King herds which had come in by way of Dodge City, Kansas, from the old coast country down in Southern Texas . . . Everybody in town was out to see the big King herd go through. I threw my hat back on my head and I felt as though the whole herd belonged to me." Jeff Connolly, a cowboy from Lockhart, southeast of Austin, remembered some trail-driving work he did for Richard King in 1880: "Drove on the trail for old Captain King of Nueces County in 1880 with a man by the name of Coleman as boss . . . and I helped another brother of this man Coleman drive another herd of the King cattle to Red River. The only white men with the herd were Coleman and myself, the balance of the bunch being Mexicans—he had them do the work and let the white men do the bossing."

In the early 1880s the market remained strong: 394,784 cattle in 1880; in 1881 and 1882, 250,000 each year. The next two years saw 267,000 in 1883 and nearly 300,000 in 1884. Richard King's last herd, a big one, 5,600, was trailed north in 1884. Trail boss Walter Billingsley, who was in charge of that herd, found himself in trouble in Fort Sidney, Nebraska, on the way to Cheyenne, Wyoming. He had to dismiss some cowboys for drunkenness and they wanted their pay, but he didn't have any cash. So he went into town and tried to borrow some money from a local banker, who told him the bank would need some sort of identification. Billingsley, far from home, had none, but he had something just as good. He returned to his outfit and then went back into town and told the banker: "Here is a hundred and fifty saddle horses branded Running W, chuck wagon, mules and most everything that has that brand on it, and the brand is known from the Rio Grande to Canada, and if that is not enough, I have fifty-six hundred steers out there about three miles, all the same brand." He got the loan.

The massive movement of cattle northward accomplished many things for Texas. Profits from the sale of cattle in such numbers helped the state recover from the ravages of the Civil War, tied the state more closely to national aims, and helped reduce some of the still-fierce sectional passions stemming from the war. It is not true, however, as the myth insists, that the cattle industry propelled the Texas economy. Statewide, it was still cotton, not cattle, that generated the most income, and this would be the case for many years to come. The famous football stadium in Dallas, after all, is named the Cotton Bowl, not the Cattle Bowl. Cotton would not be eclipsed until 1950, when oil overtook both of these agrarian economies and a new Texas was born. From 1939 on, oil became a huge part of King Ranch's economic productivity, providing money in amounts that cattle never could. Yet King Ranch had been envisioned as a cattle ranch, a pastoral livelihood, and so it would continue.

From the 1860s through the end of the nineteenth century, cattle was the game in South Texas, and one of the men who was master of that game was Richard King. The cattle drive era extended the sweep of his influence and enlarged his legend. It also made him a great deal of money. All the years of struggle on King Ranch seemed worth it when the accounts were settled and the gold was in the safe.

CHAPTER 10

Cause No. 1279

After a tumultuous decade of raids by Mexican bandits and counter-raids by King's Rangers, the gathering and driving of longhorns to Kansas railheads, and the fencing of miles and miles of property, Richard King faced a stiff legal challenge at the tail end of the 1870s. Helen Chapman, the widow of his old partner and friend Major W. W. Chapman from back in the 1850s, filed a lawsuit against King in 1879. It had been brewing for over a decade. In *Helen B. Chapman v. Richard King,* Cause No. 1279, Mrs. Chapman claimed ownership of one half of the Rincón de Santa Gertrudis grant, the long, peninsular-shaped piece of land, consisting of 15,500 acres, that stretches from near the present-day headquarters of King Ranch through the center of Kingsville and part of the Kingsville Naval Air Station.

This event was definitely more than a nuisance to King. At that time he was busy shipping cattle to Kansas and he was, as always, adding new land to his holdings. One such acquisition was from Miguel Gutiérrez, who in 1878 conveyed for "valuable considerations" two thousand acres of land. "Valuable considerations" is not defined. In 1880, King acquired more Gutiérrez land, a good-sized chunk, 17,872 acres, for a song: $240 in back taxes. (Presumably Miguel Gutiérrez had died sometime in the interim.) The next year, King paid a considerably larger sum, $4,000, but for a great deal of land, 25,354 acres, purchased from María Gutiérrez. This made a grand total of 44,226 acres, the entire Gutiérrez Santa Gertrudis tract, for $4,240 and "valuable considerations."

For many reasons, the Chapman suit must have felt to King like a dagger thrust into the heart of the precious original site of his rancho—his first land purchase, made on July 25, 1853. He would have had a strong attachment to this site; the whole family would have.

The acquisition of the Rincón seemed vexed from the beginning. The short-lived partnership with Gideon K. (Legs) Lewis, initiated on November 11, 1853, ended precipitously with Lewis's sudden death in 1855, followed by a second partnership with Major W. W. Chapman, in 1856, that either ended or did not, depending on conflicting interpretations, when Chapman left Texas in 1857. The circumstances surrounding his relationship with Richard King would remain murky, perplexing, and charged with contradictory meanings in the half-light of historical uncertainty that comes down to us today, like a grainy, faded nineteenth-century daguerreotype.

Major Chapman's post-Texas life was brief. After being transferred back east in 1857, he was posted at Fort Schuyler in New York in 1858, and the next year at Fort Monroe, Virginia. Here, at Old Point Comfort, Virginia, he died by his own hand on September 28, 1859. Following the major's death, Helen Chapman remained in the east during the Civil War. Both the major and his widow were ardent Unionists, and one of their favorite books, which they read excitedly before leaving Texas, was *Uncle Tom's Cabin*. They would have not found it easy to live in Confederate Texas during the war.

Helen Chapman in particular was a staunch abolitionist, as perfectly reflected in a letter from a friend of both William Chapman and his brother Robert, who lived in Austin in the 1850s. The friend wrote to William, "Your brother owns two carriages horses etc. And half a dozen negroes or 'niggers,' but this 'entre no[u]s' I would mention low, in a whisper. He thinks you would not like to hear it or at least Mrs. C. would not. So don't speak it out loud!" William and Helen's son Willie fought for the Union, and after the war moved to Texas and became a herder of sheep in the Corpus Christi area. Helen Chapman visited Texas many times, both to see family and to attend to matters relating to landholdings. Ironically, she died in the heart of the old Confederacy, in Columbia, South Carolina, on December 10, 1881.

From the time he was transferred to Corpus Christi in 1852, Major Chapman was very interested in securing ranching properties. He wrote his wife on September 16, 1852: "Good grazing land can be purchased [nearby] at $1 per acre." In 1853 he purchased two ranching properties, Las Comitas and Palo Alto, and by 1856 had started a rancho on the Santa Gertrudis near the rancho owned by his good friend from Brownsville, Richard King. He called it the New Santa Gertrudis. His investments in land for raising livestock coincided closely with those of King's.

Chapman was an absentee landlord but one who kept a close eye on his holdings. Chapman placed his land under the management of James Bryden, a Scot who pioneered the raising of sheep in Nueces County. Bryden managed stock for Chapman and his widow for many years. The detailed involvement of Chapman in the rancho's operation at Santa Gertrudis can be discerned from entries in his *Account Book and Ledger.* Entries for 1856, for example, included under the notation "Purchased for the Rancho": 115 cows, 88 calves, 3 bulls, and 16 heifers for a total of $2,339.50, plus 1,109 sheep purchased at $2 an animal. The building of a house on the rancho cost $441.57. Another entry for the next year listed items "Sent to the Rancho March 26, 1857": a box of sherry (12 bottles), a box of claret (12), six bottles of brandy and one of whiskey, two boxes of cigars, two camp tables, a buffalo robe, and so on. Clearly, Major Chapman had the money to support the rancho, and he gave his full attention to its operation.

On April 25, 1856, Chapman entered into a partnership with Richard King, receiving from King and his wife, Henrietta King, a warranty deed for a one-quarter undivided interest in the Rincón de Santa Gertrudis property. Later that year, on August 1, Chapman, acting on King's behalf, purchased Gideon Lewis's one-half of the Rincón, put up for auction because Lewis had not left a will. Chapman's share of this purchase was an undivided one-quarter, leaving him in possession of one-half of the Rincón de Santa Getrudis grant, or 7,749 acres. These purchases—and the partnership—were at the center of the legal dispute then and now.

Shortly after the second transaction with King, something happened that would forever cloud the circumstances of their partnership, but nobody is quite sure what it was except that Major Chapman was suddenly faced with the prospect of being reassigned from Corpus Christi to far-distant California, a posting he was ultimately able to avoid. But he did have to leave Texas, and the major's hurried farewell to his ranching operation is a story told long after the fact and

dependent upon the memory of James Bryden, Chapman's representative on the land and, later, a King Ranch foreman, and those of two
very interested parties, Richard and Henrietta King.

In the lawsuit brought by Helen Chapman, Bryden testified that he
became "associated with the Major in the sheep and cattle business,
and during the summer of that year [1856] a Rancho was established
on the Santa Gertrudis Creek about one and a half miles from the present residence of Capt R King whose Rancho was then in charge of and
being conducted by James J. Richardson." Bryden also attested to the
major's involvement: "While our new Rancho was in process of construction the Major paid us frequent visits, and it was during one of
these visits that the conversation . . . took place." The crucial conversation occurred in July, Bryden says, when Chapman came to the rancho and asked Bryden if Mr. Richardson was at home. Bryden replied
that he was, and Chapman asked Bryden to bring Richardson there
because he wished to "see him on business of importance to Capt
King—explaining at the same time the nature of the business he felt so
anxious about." Bryden fetched Richardson, whereupon "The Major
then said to Mr. Richardson. You will see Capt King for me at the earliest possible moment, and inform him that I attended the auction sale
the other day . . . and that I purchased the land belonging to the Lewis
estate, that I regret that I had to pay such an extravagant price owing
to the opposition of Capt Fullerton [rival bidder]. Say to Capt King
that I have established Bryden in the stock business, that I have not the
means to justify me in retaining a half interest and request the Captain
to release me from my obligation therein. Say also that I will write him
shortly on this subject."

In her own sworn testimony of March 22, 1881, Helen Chapman,
"nearly sixty-four years of age," offered a completely different view
of her husband's state of mind and economic circumstances during that
period. "My husband," she stated, "to the best of my knowledge and
belief, never lost interest in his ranche. He inherited horticultural and
other tastes incident to a farm life. He was wearied and harassed by his
official duties in the Quartermaster's Department of the Army and
always looked forward to resigning his commission in the Army and
returning to Texas. He received quarterly reports from his agent James
Bryden to the last. It seems incredible that while all this was going on
and no desire expressed or effort made to sell this rapidly increasing

stock he should deliberately make arrangements to part with all the land he had been so anxious to secure."

In answer to another interrogatory, Helen Chapman insisted that her husband's demeanor did not fit the description supplied by Bryden. According to Mrs. Chapman, "In the latter part of the year 1856, his financial condition was, to the best of my knowledge and belief, perfectly good, he was not embarrassed by want of ready money, just before he left Texas. He did not inform me of any want of ready money, and I have not only *no knowledge but no suspicion of such a condition.*"

Another time she stated the matter with equal firmness: "My husband Major WW Chapman was always in the habit of talking and advising with me about his business affairs; second, he had a very strong desire to own all the land necessary for the successful conduct of a ranche, and was very anxious in furtherance of this desire to make a purchase from the estate of GK Lewis, and expressed great satisfaction when the purchase had been consummated. From that moment to the time of his death, he never intimated to me orally or by letter that he was dissatisfied with the purchase or anxious to be released therefrom."

Tangentially, at least one of the major's friends regarded him as a rancher as late as May 1859, four months before the major's death. An old friend from Brownsville then living in San Antonio, N. J. Jarvis, sent Chapman a newspaper article containing a photograph of a Mexican general and rancher, General Usquiza, whose visage reminded Jarvis of the major's, alluding to Chapman's "pursuits of soldier and Ranchero" and joshing him a bit: "I suppose General Usquiza's ranche is somewhat on a larger scale than yours, containing as he says 270 leagues or miles of land in one body with 300,000 head of horned cattle and 60,000 mares."

The Kings, of course, told a different story from that of Helen Chapman. In testimony given on August 2, 1882, Henrietta King recalled receiving a letter from Major Chapman, the very one that Bryden had said the major had promised to write. "The substance of that letter," Mrs. King stated, "was the writer Major W. W. Chapman had been ordered to San Diego, California, that he could no longer retain the lands he and the defendants had been jointly interested in, and wished to be released from any further responsibility for, or connection with said lands. He wished the defendant to assume entire ownership and control of the lands, and thanked him for the use he had had of these. My husband read it in my hearing, I read it myself, and I also heard it read by Capt. James Walworth, who remarked, as I distinctly remember, that it was a very important letter, and ought to be taken care of."

Mrs. King was just as confident about her husband's dealings as Mrs. Chapman was about hers. And Mrs. King was most emphatic on another point, as well: "No consideration was ever paid by Major Chapman to myself or to my husband, for the conveyance referred to—not one cent. Had any such payment been made, I am certain my husband would have mentioned it to me. There was no note given for the payment of the price named in the deed, and no security offered or given for the land to my knowledge, and if either note or security had been given, I should have been likely to know of it."

At the time of the trial, however, the Kings were not able to produce the letter that Walworth had said "ought to be taken care of." In King's pleadings to the court, King's position restated Bryden's account of the verbal message and the promised letter: ". . . that the said Chapman would in a few days write to this defendant to the same effect. That this message was conveyed to this defendant by one J. J. Richardson, since deceased. That a short time afterwards the said W. W. Chapman did so write to this defendant, and his letter to the same effect precisely as his aforesaid verbal message and dated some time prior to the month of March, 1857, was received by defendant and the proposition therein contained as aforesaid, accepted and acted upon by this defendant. That in consequence of said verbal message and letter, this defendant paid and caused to be paid on his individual account the whole of the purchase money for the interest of the said Gideon K. Lewis's estate in the said tract of land as aforesaid, and has ever since openly and notoriously treated and regarded as the pretended joint ownership of the said Chapman with him in the said tract of land, arising from the deeds aforesaid, as wholly closed and ended."

Ah, but the letter. The letter "was seen and its contents noted by James Walworth, since deceased, who was then in the employment of this defendant. That said Walworth especially called defendant's attention to the said letter, and to the importance of preserving the same. That said letter was accordingly carefully filed away, but that during the confusion incident to a hasty removal of his effects from the ranch of defendant, caused by a raid during the late civil war, the said letter was lost, and cannot now be found although diligent search therefore has been continued since the institution of this suit. . . ."

In another part of the pleadings, King explained the long process by which clear title of the Rincón was not secured until 1868, owing to another loss of "original papers" relating to the earlier Spanish ownership of the Rincón. In this instance the documents were lost "while in the hands of the Land Commissioners in Austin." Since 1857, King had heard nothing, he said, regarding any claims from Chapman's heirs. During those years he had paid all legal costs involved in securing perfect title, one free from the dread words "inchoate and imperfect." He had also paid all the taxes, $3,000, receiving in that time not "one dime" from any of Chapman's heirs. His pleadings argued further that too much time had elapsed since 1857 for the suit to have merit. It was, in the language of the pleadings, "a stale demand."

The seeds of that "stale demand" were sown in 1866, when Richard King, setting about the fencing of his lands, caused Mrs. Chapman's sheep to be removed from the property operated by Bryden. "I was surprised that the sheep had been removed but was informed that Capt King would be able to explain it in a personal interview," Helen Chapman recalled during her interrogatories of 1881. The next year, 1867, Captain King and Helen Chapman reached a settlement relating to property confiscated by the Confederacy. But nothing was said or done about the Rincón de Santa Gertrudis. "I knew perfectly well at the time of these settlements that I owned considerable portion of Santa Gertrudas," said Helen Chapman in 1881. "To my knowledge and belief my husband Major WW. Chapman never sold or agreed to sell to Capt King or any other person, any portion of the *land now sued for*," she added.

When Helen Chapman tried to get in touch with Richard King, she had no luck in doing so. As she explained in 1881, "I never had any conversation with Capt King, written or oral in relation to said land, though I made persistent and repeated efforts, to communicate with him directly. He promised on two occasions to call on me, but the first appointment was not kept and a promise to call and see me on his return from Kansas was never performed. To the best of my knowledge and belief I have never at any time seen or conversed with Capt Richard King." The fact that they never met is one of the mysteries of her years in Brownsville and later. She knew Henrietta Chamberlain well, and she knew virtually everybody else in Brownsville. Perhaps King was too much of a roughneck for her taste; they hardly belonged to the same social stratum, though if he did attend Sunday School to court Henrietta, as family legend has it, why did Helen Chapman not take note of him there? Surely a frontier diamond as rough as Richard King would have been worth a paragraph in one of her letters back to Westfield, Massachusetts, but it never happened, they never met.

Perhaps King's failure to meet with her pushed her to take legal action. She was still on excellent terms with James Bryden: "The business relations that existed between James Bryden and myself after my husband's death were those that usually exist between owner and agent. They were interrupted by the war but, so long as our business relations existed, they were friendly." She saw Bryden in Corpus Christi in 1866, and "he did not seem to know anything about the matter in controversy, except the fact that he had been told to remove the sheep. What he then said had no possible influence on me in regard to this subject, and I do not think he sought to influence me."

While on another trip to Corpus Christi to attend the wedding of her daughter Nellie to Ellery Brayton on July 17, 1878, Helen Chapman secured the services of a local law firm, Lackey and Stayton, to sue Richard King. Lackey was based in Cuero, Stayton in Victoria. Soon they would acquire a third partner, a promising young attorney living in Corpus Christi who had taken his degree in law from the University of Virginia. His name was Robert J. Kleberg. It would be Kleberg who would represent Helen Chapman's interests and those of her grandchildren in the years following her death in 1881 until the final settlement in 1883. Helen Chapman would never meet Kleberg, either, no more than she would King—these two men who played such a role in her family's history both during her lifetime and afterward.

Shortly after Helen Chapman's death, Robert J. Kleberg wrote to Ellery Brayton, the son-in-law and executor of Mrs. Chapman's estate: "There is a suit pending in the District Court of Nueces County instituted by Mrs. Ella Chapman, now dec'd, against Richard

King involving the title to a tract of land." Kleberg never mentioned that the land was a slice of a huge rancho owned by the best-known rancher in Texas. It seems odd, though, that Brayton, who married Helen Chapman's daughter and might be expected to have had conversations with his mother-in-law about land and legal matters, never seems to have known anything about Richard King or the location of the contested tract of land.

What Kleberg wanted, he wrote Brayton, was permission to continue the lawsuit, and authorization was granted. When the suit was resolved in April 1883, the court found in favor of Helen Chapman's estate—meaning that one-half of the Rincón de Santa Gertrudis belonged to the grandchildren of Helen Chapman. This was a huge victory and a thorough vindication of the claims made by Helen Chapman on behalf of her deceased husband. The principal basis for the finding on behalf of Helen Chapman was her copy of the deed of April 25, 1856. What Helen Chapman said in her testimony of 1881 proved to be crucial: "The deed given by Richard and Henrietta King was kept with other deeds and titles to real estate and my husband never gave me any reason to suppose that the transaction had been cancelled."

According to the deed, produced in court, Richard and Henrietta King, for the sum of $100, "granted, bargained, sold, and released" to W. W. Chapman "one half of all the right, title and interest in and to a certain tract or grant of land, lying and situated in the County of Nueces, State of Texas, and called 'Rincón de Santa Gertrudis,' and containing within its boundaries three and half sitios, more or less, and [   ] as follows, to wit: commencing at a [   ] about two miles above the old road where it crosses the Arroyo Santa Gertrudis on said Arroyo, thence running due north across the Trananitas Creek to the Arroyo of San Fernando, thence down said Arroyo San Fernando to the junction of the Santa Gertrudis Creek, thence up said Santa Gertrudis Creek to the place of [   ]." The deed was signed and sealed with Richard King's quite distinctive, bold, and confident "R. King," the "R" large and sweeping, and in tinier, neater, perfectly scripted letters, "Henrietta M. King" (M for Morse, her mother's maiden name). It was a deed, all right, and it conveyed the land to "W.W. Chapman and his heirs and assigns forever." Amen, Helen Chapman might have said, had she been around to say it.

But King denied ever having been paid anything by Chapman, declaring in a pleading of November 11, 1880, that he never received payment of $100 for the April 25, 1856, transaction. Though not introduced in the trial, Major Chapman's *Account Book and Ledger* contained these entries for 1856: "Land purchased of Capt. King 100.00" and "1/2 of Lewis interest in Santa Gertrudis 787.50." There were also entries for "recording of deed" and "preliminary survey." The total expenses on that page of the ledger, all having to do with land and King, were $1,000.

No matter. The court's ruling was not carried out in any event. It was, in fact, set aside by the tactics of Robert J. Kleberg, acting on behalf of his other client, who happened to be none other than Richard King. Nobody knew this at the time, but in 1881, following a case in which Richard King had been bested in court by a young Kleberg in court, the rancher had called upon him personally one night and made him an offer he couldn't refuse. King offered to put Kleberg on a retainer of $5,000 per year, and Kleberg accepted. (Tom Lea's revered book is the source for this bit of news, complete with some invented dialogue. Lea does not ponder the implications of dual representation by Kleberg.) This was a lot of money in those days, somewhere in the neighborhood of $65,000 today. Kleberg, on the other hand, was working for the Chapman estate on a fee contingency basis. So from 1881 to the final resolution of Cause No. 1279, *Helen Chapman v. Richard King,* Kleberg was representing simultaneously the interests of his out-of-state client, Helen Chapman, *and* the interests of his unacknowledged in-state client, Richard King. This, one might say, is the J. R. (Ewing) moment in the history of King Ranch.

The other thing that Kleberg did was to discount Chapman's claim to one-half of G. K. Lewis's deed. This meant that instead of being entitled to 7,749 acres (one-half of the Rincón), Chapman's ownership could only be proved for 3,874½ acres (i.e., one-fourth). King maintained that he did not have in his possession or know the whereabouts of the Lewis deed (and Helen Chapman did not find one among her husband's papers), but later, in 1904, the Lewis deed that King claimed to have no knowledge of was filed by James B. Wells, a King Ranch attorney. This deed proved Chapman's ownership to one-half of the Lewis title. One-fourth plus one-fourth equals one-half.

So, after interpreting Chapman's claim as one-half of one-half, that is, one-fourth, Kleberg recommended to his out-of-state client a solution highly advantageous to King. Brayton, Kleberg argued, should accept a cash settlement. Following the April 1883 ruling, Kleberg wrote Brayton in South Carolina, telling him that emergency circumstances required him to accept an offer from Richard King of $5,811.75 to buy the land. The presumed emergency, Kleberg explained, was the necessity of entering the King offer in open court before the end of the term; in the event it was not, the court would not be able to act on the offer until the fall of 1883.

Obviously the suit had already gone on for some time, five years and counting, so what was the real emergency entailed by a few more months of waiting? Brayton in distant South Carolina said as much, but Kleberg was insistent, explaining in a letter on June 22, 1883: "As to the settlement, we have simply to say that it was to the interest of counsel as well as the estate of Chapman to get all we possibly could, as their interests were identical. This we think we succeeded in doing. Our next court convenes in December [1883] & we could not see any advantage of delaying until then when we probably could not have done as well. While the money was not paid at once, the sum is bearing interest. We feel that we have done what was best for our client, Mrs. Chapman, now dead, in this matter & regret that you should not seem satisfied."

If the ruling had been carried out as decreed by the court, the history of King Ranch would have been altered, though probably not drastically. The township of Kingsville could have been laid out on other King Ranch land, and King Ranch would probably, sometime in the future, have tried to buy out the Chapman heirs. Or not. If the Chapmans had held on to the land, they might have prospered from the revenue produced by oil wells found on it; they might have built a town called Chapmanville. *Es posible,* as they say in South Texas.

CHAPTER 11

Quieted in the Possession of His Lands

If there was one thing Richard King loved, it was a good lawyer, and in 1882 he lost a good one when Stephen Powers, his longtime friend, attorney, and politico in Cameron County, died. King moved immediately to put Powers's young partner, James B. Wells, on the payroll. Wells, twenty-eight, was a graduate of the University of Virginia law school, like the other young lawyer, Robert J. Kleberg, whom King had placed on retainer the year before. King made it clear what he expected from Wells: "Young man, the only thing I want to hear from you is when I can move my fences." Kleberg's task, of course, was handling, among other matters, Cause No. 1279.

Richard King, cattle king, enjoyed the perks of power and success. There were numerous trips to St. Louis, where the family always stayed in style at the Southern Hotel and where, for several years, various of the King children attended school. King lavished gifts upon his children, whom he loved and for whom he laid up earthly treasure. He called them his "pets" and believed in spoiling them. "See that none of Papa's pets wants for anything money will buy," he wrote his wife. His own early impoverished beginning was probably a factor in his conviction that his children should have whatever they wanted to make them happy, and at times he probably ran headlong into Henrietta King's rather sterner Presbyterianism. Although Henrietta apparently enjoyed the privileges of having money and clearly relished traveling and staying at first-class hotels, her rock-ribbed New England Protestantism

186

sometimes manifested itself in strange ways. When her husband gave her a gift of expensive diamond earrings, she had a jeweler coat them over with dark paint—in her mind, vanity of vanities wasn't just a biblical quote. Perhaps Richard King at times felt the need to lobby for his children, or so one letter certainly suggests: "Life is short," he wrote his wife, "and why be so mean as not enjoy ourselves now." He seems to have had little use for Presbyterianism's deferral system of rewards in heaven.

All the children received good educations. Nettle and Ella attended Henderson Female Institute, a Presbyterian school, in Danville, Kentucky, and the youngest girl, Alice, also spent a year there. Ella and Alice finished their schooling in St. Louis at Mrs. Cuthbert's Seminary. Richard King II attended Centre College at Danville. He cut quite a figure there, caparisoned with a carriage and a body servant. Later, Robert E. Lee King, the youngest, whom the family called Lee, attended Centre as well, before transferring to a business college in St. Louis.

The two oldest daughters, Nettle and Ella, perhaps didn't marry as well as King would have liked, but there were limits to an indulgent father's say-so in such matters. In 1878 Nettle married a major who worked in the United States Army Quartermaster Department, and Ella, in 1881, married a businessman. In the beginning both couples lived in St. Louis.

Within his family, King's generosity and imperious will were well known, but in the outside world, sometimes the will predominated. There were public displays of King's exuberance and contrariness, too. According to family tradition, such occasions were usually fueled by one drink too many. Once at their favorite place to stay in San Antonio, the Menger Hotel (across the alley from the Alamo), King, possibly impelled by too much whiskey, expressed his anger in a fashion not soon forgotten by family or hotel staff. When a pitcher of water was not brought to his wife with sufficient alacrity, he tossed an empty pitcher from a balcony onto the marbled lobby floor, smashing it to smithereens and saying, "If we can't get any water up here, we don't need a pitcher."

Another time, upon returning from a trip to New Orleans, King joined his family dining at a hotel in Galveston. A guest of Mrs. King's had been served a tough steak, and King set about to get her another one. He spoke to the waiter first, then the headwaiter, and, receiving no relief, swung into action himself. He went to another restaurant across the street and ordered an entire new selection of food for himself and guests, and told the waiters to serve it in the hotel restaurant. When the new food was brought to King's table in the hotel restaurant, the hotel service refused to take away the original plates, whereupon King ripped off the tablecloth, with everything clattering onto the floor, and ordered the waiters to serve the new meal.

Men who knew King man to man knew he liked to drink. E. R. Jensen, who worked as a private ranger for King, liked to tell about the time one of King's trail foremen was reported as being drunk in Dodge City at the end of a drive. King said, "Nothing wrong with that. I've been drinking whiskey for thirty years." Jensen considered King a "kindly man," but knew, like everybody else, about the captain's temper. According to Jensen, when King came out on the gallery with one pants leg in his boot and one out, it was time to clear the area.

The locally famous railroad junket of 1881 was another instance of King's public carrying-on. King, Kenedy, and their mutual friend with the Dickensian name, Uriah Lott, had a great deal to celebrate when the Texas-Mexican Railroad, connecting Corpus Christi and Laredo, 162 miles away, was completed. Lott, a passionate advocate of rail development, had worked for King and Kenedy's steamboat firm, based in Brazos Santiago. When they told him, back in 1867, that Corpus Christi was the new up-and-coming city and that Brownsville was fading, he had moved to Corpus. With Kenedy and King providing money and contacts, he pushed the line through. It bisected the Wild Horse Desert and assured, among other things, the growth of Laredo and the languishing of Brownsville. Thus King and Kenedy, who had made so much money in Brownsville, contributed to its economic decline with the advent of the Tex-Mex Railroad. King and Kenedy rarely, if ever, let sentiment stand in the way of economic possibilities. The one law was change; the second was adaptation. Together, King, Kenedy, and Lott eventually made a profit of just under half a million dollars on the railroad.

With the track completed, it was a time to celebrate, and celebrate they did. Apparently everybody got drunk. A local paper reported that someone "poured three gallons of Rose Bud and twelve quarts of Champagne into the ready brew and the result was a most excellent type of Roman Punch." That someone was most probably Richard King, whose favorite brand was Rose Bud. If King supplied the liquor, South Texas supplied the heat. It was so hot that sugar melted.

A poem by a "Poet Lariat" was written to commemorate the occasion. Titled "The King-Kenedy Excursion to Laredo," it begins: "September twenty-seventh, eighteen eighty one/Will long be remembered for pleasure and fun." After mentioning virtually the entire passenger list by name, the poem concludes: "Long life to Captain King and Kenedy, too,/And Col. Hungerford who put us safely through,/To all of them our lasting thanks are due/For our pleasant trip to Laredo." The train clattering down the tracks had more metrical rhythm than the poem.

Kleberg was on the train, as well, and wrote his sister a vivid account of the proceedings: "On last Tuesday Capts. King & Kenedy, the great stock men, chartered the train and gave a free excursion to many of their friends—on the first passenger train to Laredo." There was much to eat and "over forty baskets of champagne, some two thousand cigars and plenty of other liquors . . . to be drank on the way—the consequence was that quite a number of our leading citizens & Pillars of the church were perfectly exhausted with pleasure by the time they reached Laredo."

Those were the good times.

Spring 1883 was the cruelest season for the Kings.

Lee, nineteen years old, came down with pneumonia while attending college in St. Louis. The family rushed to St. Louis, but by the time they arrived, he had little time to live. He died on March 1 and was buried in St. Louis.

His mother remained in the city for months, too sick with grief to do anything but grieve.

Lee had been the one Richard King was counting on to run the rancho after he was gone, in the right order of things. Lee was perfect for the task: he loved the rancho and the life on horseback; he took an interest in all the elements of ranching; he seemed destined to continue the work his father had begun. As a child he was taken, when he was four, to visit his namesake in Virginia, who was then president of Washington and Lee University. Robert E. Lee King was the future of

King's rancho, and now that future lay dead in a St. Louis cemetery. (Richard King's friend Mifflin Kenedy, who lasted until 1895, lived to see three of his sons die before him. One was killed in a fight over a married woman, one was killed by Bat Masterson, and one was killed by a firing squad in a Mexican prison.)

At fifty-eight Richard King felt himself old—for so others spoke of him—and he was ready to throw in the towel for the first time in his life. He told his wife in a letter, "I am tired of this business, as I at all times have made a mess of everything that I have undertaken . . . and now I want to quit the Rancho business and will do so." He meant to sell it, and there were interested parties. Syndicates were plunging into the cattle business in a big way, investors from Great Britain intrigued with the prospect of cashing in on the cattle boom. Mifflin Kenedy, the year before, had sold his Laureles Rancho—242,000 acres—for $1,100,000 to a Scottish syndicate that became the Texas Land and Cattle Co. King was asking a good deal more, a king's fortune: $6,500,000, one newspaper reported.

When the British agents arrived, in June 1883, King ordered his cattle to be rounded up so that the Brits could see what they were getting. Victor Alvarado, one of the old Kineños, recalled in his "Memoirs" how, following the captain's orders, the vaqueros gathered a herd of around 12,000 beeves. When the captain saw the cattle, he queried the bosses, wanting to know why they'd brought in such a small herd. They said they hadn't had time to gather more, whereupon the captain told them that the next day he wanted a larger roundup. The buyers then asked the captain how many more cattle there were, and the captain said he could produce four or five more roundups of similar size. In Alvarado's words, quoting from Tom Lea in another fabulous document from the King Ranch vault: "Then the buyers looked at one another and said to King that they didn't want to see any more than that one, it was enough to know they couldn't buy even the herd they saw, much less the land, and they left very sad."

In the end King decided against selling, partly because there were no buyers prepared to pay such sums as he demanded and partly because by then he was beginning to resume his usual interest in all matters relating to the rancho as he recovered from the devastating blow of his youngest son's death. The prolonged dry spell of 1882–83 also broke that summer of 1883; there is nothing like rain to brighten a rancher's outlook. Perhaps the settlement with the Chapman estate, engineered by Kleberg and consummated in June 1883, also helped. In July there were nuptials. Richard II married a girl from St. Louis, his wedding present a 40,000-acre tract called Rancho Puerta de Agua Dulce. Richard II followed his own counsel on the Agua Dulce and soon converted many of its acres into farmland to raise cotton. After that summer, King never mentioned selling the rancho again.

The year 1884 marked King's last hurrah as a cattle baron. King Ranch herds were once more pointed north. Kansas was still viable, for one more year, anyway. Walter Billingsley, a King Ranch trail boss, took a large herd to Dodge City and joined up with another herd headed for Montana—the combined herd of 5,600 cattle the largest that had been seen in some time.

King himself attended a national cattlemen's convention in St. Louis that year, the first time the organization had met. The chief goal was to convince Congress to authorize a National Cattle Trail, a kind of grass superhighway that would run from Texas to North Dakota. The cost of such a stretch of land—envisioned as three to six miles wide and over fifteen hundred miles long—was too high for even Congress to stomach. King proposed to the convention that cattlemen form a corporation to do the job themselves and argued that such land would be valuable when the trail drives were over. In retrospect, this whole plan seems to have been a bit grandiose—and worse than that, completely irrelevant. King himself had already begun sending cattle to market down the Tex-Mex line. The future was in railroads, not cattle trails, and railroads were everywhere.

That fall, Kleberg became engaged to the youngest King daughter, Alice, who lived at home with her parents. She had been smitten with Kleberg since the first time she had seen him, three years before, when her father brought him out to the rancho on the night the captain offered to put him on an annual retainer. Things had worked out beautifully for all parties. They had won the Chapman case by converting defeat into victory—the cash payout—and now Kleberg had won Alice. The more King saw of Kleberg, the more he figured that Kleberg was the one to take over when he was gone. As much as King loved lawyers, nothing made more sense than to place his rancho in the hands of one.

As the year 1885 began, Richard King made no plans to send

herds north or anywhere else, for by February he was too ill to do much of anything. Near the end of the month, on February 25, he left Santa Gertrudis for good. His last actions were in character. He told Russell Holbein, his longtime secretary, to write attorney Jim Wells in Brownsville: "Tell him to keep on buying. And tell him, tell him not to let a foot of dear old Santa Gertrudis get away from us."

It must have been painful to leave Rancho Santa Gertrudis, the lands on which he had worked so hard and pinned so many hopes these thirty-odd years. In Tom Lea's rendering, it was the old man's last chance to see his "centaurs."

In San Antonio King and his wife took rooms where they always stayed, at the Menger Hotel. The attending physician delivered bad news: King had stomach cancer and could not live long. He died on April 14, and funeral services were held at the Menger the next day.

King left a will, dated April 2, 1885, drawn up under the supervision of his lawyer and son-in-law-to-be, Robert J. Kleberg. King left everything, the whole shooting match, to Henrietta M. King. Everything meant 614,000 acres, more or less, $564,784 in real estate, and $496,700 in livestock and other property. The total came to $1,061,484 in assets and an estimated $500,000 in debt.

One Texas newspaper eulogy noted of Richard King that "his history is almost a history of this frontier."

CHAPTER 12

The Succession

Unlike Richard King, who came from nowhere, Robert Justus Kleberg belonged to a family so distinguished that it would take many pages to recount their luster. Ten Klebergs were notable enough to have entries in *The New Handbook of Texas,* the state's historical bible.

Robert Justus Kleberg, father of the King Ranch Kleberg line, was born in Herstelle, Westphalia (Germany), in 1803. He received a J.D. degree from the University of Göttingen, married Rosalie von Roeder, and emigrated to Texas in 1834. He would later explain why: "I wished to live under a Republican form of government, with unbounded personal, religious and political liberty, free from the petty tyrannies, the many disadvantages and evils of old countries."

Texas offered him plenty of opportunities for distinction. He fought at the Battle of San Jacinto and was one of the men who guarded Gen. Santa Anna following his capture. After the war he fought Indians and would have fought in the Civil War for the Confederacy, except by then he was too old. A *paterfamilias* who with his wife raised seven children, he was also a citizen devoted to public service, holding such offices as president of the Board of Land Commissioners, justice of the peace, and chief justice. He read Latin and Greek and spoke three modern languages. He died in 1888. Many of his qualities seem to have passed down to the son who bore his identical name, Robert Justus Kleberg. Born in 1853 in De Witt County, Robert Kleberg evinced an early interest in education, attending Concrete College near Wharton, southwest of Houston. He earned a law degree from the University of Virginia and set up practice in Corpus Christi in 1880. The next year, that much-debated year of 1881 in the modern Chapman-King lawsuit, he became one of Richard King's attorneys. In 1885 he was hand-picked by the dying King to manage King Ranch, and in 1886, following a suitable period of respect for the fallen King, he married Alice Gertrudis King.

Kleberg and his new bride spent a two-month-long honeymoon on the East Coast, accompanied by the bride's mother, Henrietta King. Then they returned to the vast acres of Santa Gertrudis, where Kleberg set about learning the busy, all-consuming task of managing the largest ranch in Texas, on the job. Duly appreciative of the pioneer who came before him, Kleberg wrote his correspondence on wonderful rococo stationery bordered at the top with a late photograph of Richard King wearing a thick short black beard in the best Victorian style; a drawing of a herd of longhorns, the Running W brand prominently featured; and, like a heraldic device, the words SANTA GERTRUDES (the old spelling) and Kings Ranche (the old form).

Tradition was one thing, but the present was another, and Kleberg would succeed or not on the basis of how he panned out as a rancher. The Kineños called him *el abogado,* the lawyer, but he didn't act like a lawyer, he acted like a rancher, worrying about the usual array of potential disasters: disease, drought, debt, you name it. Think of a problem and the cattle business had it.

Following the end of the cattle drives in 1885, the market fell to almost nothing, and a terrible drought struck from 1892 to 1894 and hung on; it wouldn't go away. All the watering holes, lakes, and creeks dried up, and the land lay brown and dead under the relentless sun. In the Great Die-Up, as it came to be known, cattle died by the thousands, many of them unable to extract themselves from the mud of dried-up watering holes. The vaqueros carried skinning knives to take the hides of starved-dead cattle.

The drought pushed Kleberg to try to find a solution, to find new sources of water. He had been on the case almost from the day he took over management of the ranch. In February 1889, he commented on the situation in a letter: "Cattle are dying daily. I lost 150 cows in the Mula [pasture] last month on account of bad water. I have been trying to sink a well deep enough to pass the salt water and reach the good water. But while I am down with the well 460 feet in the Mula I have found nothing but water too salty for any use." He believed that if one dug deep enough, deeper than seemed possible, there was good water that could be brought to the surface. More wells were dug, and no water was found. The voice of the cicada trilled in the dry brush. There was dirt and no water.

The difficult conditions faced by those trying to ranch in the Wild Horse Desert were obvious to all who lived there, but an outside perspective is helpful to understand just how harsh that country could be. Richard Harding Davis's *The West from a Car-Window* (1892) gives us just such a picture. Davis, a popular novelist, globetrotting journalist, and dashing New York celebrity, reached for extremes to describe the landscape of the Wild Horse Desert. "This particular country is the back-yard of the world," he wrote, continuing, "It is the country which led General Sheridan to say that if he owned both places, he would rent Texas and live in hell." But Davis wasn't through. "It is the strip of country overwhich we actually went to war with Mexico, and which gave General Sherman the opportunity of making the epigramme, which no one who has not seen the utter desolateness of the land can justly value, that we should go to war with Mexico again, and force her to take it back." Still he went on: "It is a country where there are no roses, but where everything that grows has a thorn."

The one place he found to admire in that terrible country was King Ranch, where he spent enough time to take it all in and explain to his northern audience the awesome scale of the ranch. He used domestic details to make his point: "The ladies who come to call on Mrs. King drive from her front gate, over as good a road as any in Central Park, for ten miles before they arrive at her front door, and the butcher and baker and iceman, if such existed, would have to drive thirty miles from the back gate before they reached her kitchen."

He was also vastly impressed with the organizational complexity of managing such a huge ranch, with its 300 cowboys, 1,200 horses, and 100,000 head of cattle. He describes the process by which Mr. Kleberg would set things in motion when an order came in from a Chicago firm: "The breed of cattle which the firm wants is grazing in a corner of the range fenced in by barb-wire, and marked pale blue for convenience on a beautiful map blocked out in colors, like a patchwork quilt, which hangs in Mr. Kleberg's office." From his office, orders would be issued, and the cattle gathered by a foreman and a small contingent of cowboys.

In the end, Davis came back to the phenomenon of sheer size as he tried once more to convey the ranch's dimensions to readers back east:

"It is rather difficult to imagine one solitary family occupying a territory larger than some of the Eastern States—an area of territory that
would in the East support a State capital, with a Governor and Legislature, and numerous small towns, with competing railroad systems
and rival baseball nines."

What that solitary ranching family needed more than anything
was a reliable source of water, as prolonged seasons of drought
remained the steadiest feature of climate in that arid land.

Kleberg didn't give up. In 1898 he spotted an item in the press
about a new drilling rig made by a company in Nebraska that promised to send a shaft of steel deeper than anyone had before. He sent an
experienced well driller to Nebraska to bring one back to the arid
acres of Santa Gertrudis, and on June 6, 1899, they hit pay dirt,
which was in this case artesian water, at a depth of 532 feet. There is
a photograph of Kleberg and his mother-in-law standing beside the
artesian well. They look as though they have discovered oil; that is
how precious water was to their livelihood as ranchers. By 1900 there
were twenty-two new wells on King Ranch, with more to be drilled.

The importance of the wells is but one of several fascinating details
that appear in a 1903 account of a visit to the ranch made by Francis
William Reitz, former president of the Orange Free State in South
Africa. Reitz and his party rode to the ranch by coach from the town
of Alice, bumping along the prairie. Upon arriving at King Ranch,
which Reitz calls a farm, the first thing they were shown was "a borehole of 1,100 feet where the water spouts from a four-inch pipe emerging above the surface and irrigates a large tract of land." Reitz speaks
of the house, a "genuine Spanish castle," and of the "manager of the
farm, a Mr. Kleberg." After surveying fields of vegetables and pastures
of horned cattle, the party sat down to a table with fifteen courses, "all
from produce grown and made on the farm."

And over dinner they were treated to a fantastic account of how
the farm (ranch) was acquired: "We were told that the land had been
given to the late Captain Richard King, husband of the owner of this
tremendous estate, by the government for services rendered in the war
against the Mexicans. Around the castle six cannon, which he had
taken from the Mexicans, were still mounted. These were being preserved as monuments." Apparently mythmaking proceeded apace
during the rule of the good queen Henrietta.

Kleberg had other successes. If Richard King believed in lawyers, Kleberg the lawyer believed in science. Texas fever, the old bugaboo of the trail drives to Kansas, attacked the new breeds of cattle brought to the ranch to replace the old longhorns. Kleberg studied the problem hard, and he began to notice that the cattle that sickened and died were covered with ticks. During a vacation trip to Maryland in 1889, Kleberg happened to meet the secretary of agriculture, and they talked about Texas fever, among other things. The upshot was that a scientist was sent to King Ranch that year, and after three years of studying the problem on site, he was able to prove that the cattle tick was the culprit that caused Texas fever. On his own, Kleberg devised a method of dipping cattle in a big vat, using a chemical solution to kill the ticks. It worked but was awkward, time-consuming, and expensive. The U.S. Department of Agriculture, in 1906, launched a nationwide campaign to wipe out cattle ticks. It was a slow process, however, and the government-sponsored program, working from north to south, did not reach Santa Gertrudis itself until 1928.

The out-of-control spread of brush was another problem. When Captain King first saw the future pastures of Santa Gertrudis, there was heavy brush along the creeks and there were mottes, clusters of trees, but the predominant feature of the land was miles and miles of grass. In the years of intensive concentration of animals on the pastures, especially horses, which loved to eat mesquite beans only to recast them in a different setting somewhat later, the prolific growth of mesquite trees threatened to smother the pastures in dense thickets of drought-resistant, hardy, and almost impenetrable brush. So Kleberg began a long-term war against it. In the 1890s he hired Mexican day laborers to clear brush; the method was slow, but it was a start. It wasn't until much later, in 1951, that King Ranch acquired new technology that could battle the brush much more effectively, a huge bulldozer that pulled a huge root plow that simultaneously knocked down trees and cut, deep in the ground, their roots. The contraption weighed over fifty tons.

Bad economic conditions helped Kleberg and Mrs. King acquire more land. Small-time ranch owners folded, and the availability of bank credit to bigger Anglo operations was a distinct advantage to the biggest Anglo ranching enterprise of all. King Ranch made thirty-six acquisitions of land, for example, in the Kleberg County area from

1886 to 1903. Most of them averaged around 3,000 acres in size. Seventeen of them were from owners with Hispanic surnames. In the land books in which the transactions were recorded, under the heading of "Considerations," sometimes there are entries other than amounts of cash paid for the land. Of the seventeen Hispanic acquisitions, eight of them bear, instead of amounts of cash payments, the terms "Sufficient," or "Taxes," or "Indefinite." "Taxes" is clear enough, but the other terms are by no means clear. The largest transaction, acquired from Flores Garcia in 1889, was for 53,136 acres. It is marked "Sufficient."

From the other side, such practices looked like something more than shrewd business. A Mexican-American landowner in the Valley, interviewed in the twentieth century, put the matter this way: "This robbing has always been in all countries. A man that could not rob could not be in society. When these people [King] got enough they put up laws against stealing. King took the land and Kleberg settled it." As usual, the Anglo version is different.

Kleberg and Mrs. King were colonizers compared to founder and pioneer Richard King. They acquired land, as he had, but they also sold it, partly to pay debts and partly for other purposes. Leroy Denman Jr., longtime attorney for King Ranch, points out that Kleberg and Mrs. King were interested in "colonizing and town building, subdividing and selling the land to bring 'civilization' to the area." Speaking of all the big landowners just before the turn of the century, he says, "They all wanted to name towns after themselves and get the railroad in and be the one that had colonized this great wild country. So to sell land was not an anathema to any of them." And so Kingsville was founded, in 1904 (and the "lost" Lewis deed recorded there). Captain King's railroad friend Uriah Lott was still around, and he, Kleberg, James B. Wells (King's old attorney), and other prominent citizens in the area formed the St. Louis, Brownsville & Mexico Railway Co. They built a line from Corpus Christi to Brownsville that opened up the valley to a new economic boom, bringing in thousands of new settlers and small farmers.

But the great wild country could still be pretty wild. Just because it was a new century didn't mean that things had changed much in South Texas when it came to the use of Texas Rangers on behalf of King Ranch in cases involving Mexican-Americans. What happened to the de la Cerda family beginning in May 1902 is a case in point, although what happened also depends entirely upon the ethnicity of the tellers. Some points are agreed upon. Ramon de la Cerda ran a small ranch bordering a section of King Ranch in Cameron County. According to Walter P. Webb, foremost chronicler of the Anglo version of Ranger history, cattle were being stolen from King Ranch, and three Rangers, dispatched to prevent same, came upon a "Mexican" branding some calves. Gunfire ensued, and Ramon de la Cerda Jr. was killed, shot by Ranger A. Y. Baker. The killing sparked an uproar in the Mexican-American community, and more incidents of Ranger abuse followed. Several months later, an attempt was made to assassinate Ranger Baker in Brownsville. A King Ranch cowboy was with the Rangers, and one Ranger was killed. Baker was slightly injured. In October, Baker killed Ramon de la Cerda's brother Alfred on Elizabeth Street in the heart of Brownsville. Baker was arrested but quickly released to resume his duties, a $10,000 bond being paid by King Ranch officials and other big ranchers. A grand jury was convened to look into the de la Cerda matter. The grand jury commended the Rangers for their sterling performance of duty, and the judge asked for more Rangers to be sent to the valley. James B. Wells, who had been hired by Richard King back in the 1880s, was still on the King Ranch payroll. He was also the chief political boss in the valley, in which capacity he sent a telegram to the Texas adjutant general shoring up local Democratic support for the "faithful and successful services of Baker and his men." Wells was so highly regarded by King Ranch that the Norias division was named after him (*norias* is Spanish for wells). Wells, it should be said, was also admired by Mexican-Americans along the border. He learned Spanish, converted to Catholicism, and acted as a benign patron for the poor as well as the well-to-do.

A Mexican-American version of the story descends from Concepción Villareal, a domestic servant for the de la Cerda family, who tells a different tale. According to Villareal, when the Rangers suspected the de la Cerdas of cattle theft, the elder de la Cerda invited the Rangers onto his ranch to look about, but the Rangers declined because he was known to carry a gun and was a good shot. An Anglo married to de la Cerda's niece invited Ramon Jr. to a fiesta at a "ranchito" (a small two-/three-man station) on King Ranch property, but it was in fact an ambush. The Rangers had tied some calves to a tree as "evidence," and Ranger Baker killed Ramon Jr. Another King Ranch worker, who happened to be perched on a nearby windmill, reported the fake theft and very real murder to the de la Cerda family. A few nights later the elder de la Cerda was ambushed near his home and killed. Some months later the youngest de la Cerda was shot to death in a Brownsville store where he was trying on gloves. The de la Cerda story has all the elements of a *corrido* decrying the cowardly, bullying, and murderous tactics of the hated *rinches*.

In 1912 the Main House burned down, the handiwork of an arsonist. Henrietta King gave instructions to build a new one where men could feel comfortable wearing boots. It opened for business in 1915 and stands there still.

That year was like old times on the Rio Grande. The Mexican Revolution was in full sway, and the border more porous than ever. Mexican revolutionaries were offered sanctuary in the basement of the principal Catholic church in Brownsville. The violence in Mexico spilled over into Texas and was met by violence, as a new wave of undeclared guerrilla warfare brought the two uneasy peoples into conflict once more.

The inciting factor was the *Plan de San Diego*, a fiery piece of revolutionary rhetoric that helped turned South Texas upside down once more. The radical manifesto, issued on January 6, 1915, supposedly from the little town of San Diego, northeast of King Ranch, was actually written in a jail in Monterrey, Mexico. The *Plan* was clearly based upon real conditions in South Texas. The Preamble dealt directly with issues of civil rights: "In Texas, [whites] have paid their workers with an unjustified race hatred that closes to the Mexican, the Negro, the Asian, the doors of the schools, the hotels, the theaters, of every public place; that segregates them on railroad cars and keeps them out of the meeting places of the 'white-skinned' savages who constitute a superior caste." The *Plan* also took a long historical view dating back to old grievances from the time of the Mexican War, declaring "the liberty of the individuals of the black race and apaches and its independence of Yankee tyranny which has held us in iniquitous slavery since remote times and in the same manner we will proclaim the independence and segregation of the states bordering upon the Mexican Nation which are TEXAS, NEW MEXICO, ARIZONA, COLORADO, AND UPPER CALIFORNIA which were robbed in a most perfidious manner by North America imperialism."

All of this seemed like radical utopian wishful thinking to Anglo residents, but the *Plan* also had some more alarming provisions. It called for the execution, on sight, of all white males over the age of sixteen, and for the liberation of any funds ("loans") that might be possessed by same. The revolution would begin on February 20, 1915. That time came and passed, and nothing happened except the issuance of another manifesto, which this time concentrated on Texas and called for the formation of a "social republic," a redistribution of rural property, and "Modern Schools" that would "be governed by the norm of UNIVERSAL LOVE."

More pronunciamientos followed. Aniceto Pizaña, one of the signers of the *Plan,* issued a handbill attacking "the crimes and outrages perpetrated upon defenseless women, old men and children of our race by the bandits and despicable Rangers who are guarding the shores of the Rio Grande." Any criticism of the Rangers would resonate in South Texas, where "los diablos tejanos" had been, with good reason, feared and hated since the time of the Mexican War. Pizaña was an interesting case. A Tejano who owned his own ranch, Los Tulitos, on the river west of Brownsville, he had long followed anarchist policies enunciated in the California-based radical publication *Regeneración.* When he saw Mexican-Americans in a subjugated role, he was moved to write stinging poetry: "With suffering and pain that grows greater/I say that there are Mexicans/Who hate and despise their own race/In order to lick the feet of the Americans."

In July 1915, the words of the *Plan of San Diego* were put into action. Raiders, *Los Sediciosos* (the seditionists), led by Pizaña and Luis de la Rosa, a Tejano who had been radicalized by the *Plan*'s call for redress of injustices, began attacking targets along the border. About forty in number, the raiders killed several Anglos in scattered locations, burned railroad bridges, disrupted telegraph and telephone lines, and shot at passing trains. Anarchy was loosed upon the region.

The single best-known raid occurred at Norias, the southernmost outpost of King Ranch, a semitropical fiefdom presided over by genial but savvy Caesar Kleberg, a bachelor cousin of Robert J. Kleberg and one of the most beloved figures in the King Ranch pantheon. He wouldn't harm a fly unless it was Mexican raiders. But in any event, Caesar Kleberg wasn't in Norias when the attack occurred. He was in Kingsville taking care of some business.

The ranch house in Norias where Caesar ruled was a large two-story white frame house sitting out in the open, right by the railroad tracks, completely vulnerable to attack. On August 7, de la Rosa's raiding party joined up with a detachment of twenty-five Mexican soldiers. Their target was the King Ranch outpost at Norias. They captured an old Kineño, Manuel Rincones, forcing him to serve as a guide, and on August 8, late in the afternoon, while a party of Rangers were scouting the countryside looking for bandits, the raiders and soldiers came riding at good speed toward the Norias headquarters.

One of the defenders, Marcus Hines, started toward them, thinking they were the Ranger scouting party, when the raiders opened fire. The people at Norias included seven cowboys, a squad of soldiers, a black cook, and several women. In the raid, two civilian fighters and two soldiers defending the ranch house were killed. Manuela Flores Rodriguez, wife of a railroad worker, was killed, probably by a stray bullet. Long years later her son Nicolas remembered that day: "I was working in the field and, when it was almost sunset, I could hear the guns shooting. . . . It was at the house of Caesar, at the big house which they call El Hotel. One of the bandits tried to come into the house, but he first put in the rifle carbine through the door, and everyone got scared and jumped under the bed. When the gunshots died down, we got back to the ranch to find that our mother had been killed."

Chief among the defenders was Lauro Cavazos, a King Ranch vaquero who would go on to become the first Hispanic foreman on the ranch. It was Lauro Cavazos who shot the horse out from under one of the leaders of the raiders, disrupting their line of attack.

The raiders lost five men and more wounded. A photographer who happened to arrive after the shooting was over took a photograph of three Rangers on horseback, their ropes unfurled and attached to the bodies of dead raiders lying in a heap in the dust. The photograph was made into a postcard and widely distributed in northern Mexico. Meant to scare off future raiders, the message backfired. It infuriated Mexican citizens on both sides of the border and inspired revenge. Years later, during a Texas state senate investigation, the father of one

Aftermath of the Norias Raid, 1915. This photograph, made into a postcard, inflamed passions on both sides of the border.

of the Rangers defended the action: "Gentlemen, those horses and those ropes were nothing but the Norias hearse. No regular funeral equipment was available." Anglos might defend it, but the picture spoke volumes about relations between the two sides. The photograph was but the latest version of Captain McNelly's dumping of the bodies from the fight at Palo Alto in the Brownsville city square.

Hatred of the rinches, already a strong current in the Mexican-American community, could spill over into a more generalized hatred, some Anglo observers felt. One Anglo farmer, for example, observed of the consequences of Ranger abuse, "No race, however ignorant or downtrodden, is going to submit to this for long without feeling an overwhelming sentiment, not only against the rangers themselves, but against the race from which they come."

Following the Norias raid and other attacks all along the border and into the interior, a state of high alert existed on the ranches of the Anglos. Rangers had to accompany a ranch worker who was going to grease the windmills; nobody dared ride fences for fear of being caught all alone; men traveled and worked in teams if possible;

automobile traffic was greatly reduced, and the driver of any automobile entering a gate would douse the lights and be extra cautious;
ranchers posted sentries at night. One night at King Ranch all hands
were alerted for a possible attack, and men with rifles mounted the
balustrades of the Main House, scanning the darkness. The night
passed without incident, and Henrietta King slept soundly in her bed.

As the raids continued, retaliation by Texas Rangers and U.S.
Army troops increased. Mexican-American citizens along the border
fled to Mexico in great numbers. They feared the Rangers, who,
fueled by their sometimes virulent racism, terrorized the innocent.
The casualties in the Mexican-American community numbered more
than three hundred deaths, compared to twenty-one Anglo deaths.
Since there were only about forty raiders, the math suggests that the
Rangers were following their old *ley de fuga* policy of summary exe-
cutions. And these facts were well known and reported in the press.
The San Antonio *Express,* September 15, 1915: "The finding of dead
bodies of Mexicans, suspected for various reasons of being connected
with the troubles, has reached a point where it creates little or no interest. It is only when a raid is reported, or an American is killed, that the
ire of the people is aroused." Rangers such as John R. Hughes were
open in their racism. "I can lick a whole cowpen of Greasers," he said.
Ranger reports contained entries like this one: "We have another
Mexican, but he's dead."

In 1916 the instigators were bought off by the Mexican government, under intense pressure from the United States, and the violence
subsided, leaving in its wake a legacy of racial mistrust and hatred that
would be slow to die along the border. Memories of the seditionists
still survive in the valley. Novelist Rolando Hinojosa-Smith remembers
how his father "would take me and show and mark for me the spot
where the Seditionists had camped and barbecued their meat half a
generation before. These were men of flesh and bone who lived and
died there in Mercedes, in the Valley."

Henrietta King lived to a great old age, ninety-two, dying on March
31, 1925. For forty years following her husband's death, she wore
widow's black, a figure at once Victorian and kindly, doing good
works, donating land and buildings for a town, a railroad, schools,

hospitals, a cemetery. Twice a year she rode in stately fashion, garbed in black, to see the roundups on the far-flung corners of the great ranch. She owned a huge gabled and turreted house in Corpus Christi, the most impressive residence in the city. She was like a public monument, and on the occasion of her death people from South Texas and from beyond came to her funeral to say goodbye to the woman who had lived so long and done so much good for the community and made her and her husband's and son-in-law's ranch a place of great hospitality.

In a grand gesture, vaqueros to the number of nearly two hundred rode their horses to the graveyard in Kingsville, Chamberlain Park, which she had caused to be built and named after her father. As the coffin was put in the ground, the vaqueros (in a "centaur dash," according to Tom Lea) paced their horses prettily around the gravesite in a stirring final act of respect to *La Patrona,* who had presided over Santa Gertrudis Acres almost continuously for over seventy years. From the old pre-rancho days, she and one of the first Kineños, Faustino Villa, lived the longest. Faustino, it is said, survived to be 118 and was still riding horseback up to two weeks before his death.

Robert Justus Kleberg died in 1932, his last years impaired by a crippling stroke that left him confined to a wheelchair. But the ranch was already in good hands, in the quite extraordinary hands really of his youngest son, Robert Justus Kleberg Jr. (actually the third).

Robert J. Kleberg and Alice King Kleberg had five children, three girls and two boys. The boys, Richard Kleberg and Robert Justus Kleberg, grew up like young princes. They were trained to rule. The oldest, Richard Mifflin Kleberg (1887–1955), was by all accounts a youth of great charm. He was an expert horseman and hunter; he spoke Castilian Spanish fluently; he took up the Mexican blood sport of fighting cocks, prompting his mother to observe: "My son Richard is the only one of my children to show an interest in poultry." He was an outstanding student at The University of Texas and acquired a law degree from there, as well. After working as head of the Laureles Division of King Ranch, he was elected to Congress in 1931. He was an old-style Texas Bourbon Democrat, a states-righter, a conservative, and especially in the latter part of his career an opponent of big government and big government programs. Much of his work in Congress grew out of his sense of the land and the need to preserve wildlife. The duck stamp law, which he wrote, was a measure designed to protect ducks from possible extinction. During his eleven-year tenure in the House, he also sponsored a bill to establish the Farm Credit Administration. The Migratory Bird Conservation Act was another notable accomplishment. He was accounted a great raconteur, a prototype of the Texas rancher and Texas personality. In Washington the Cowboy Congressman, as he was dubbed by the press, drove around town in his customized King Ranch hunting car with its cutaway doors, running boards, rifle scabbards, and, most important, beverage holders. He is probably better known today, however, for the young man he hired as his administrative aide, the young and hard-working, charming and power-hungry Lyndon B. Johnson.

Robert J. Kleberg Jr. (1896–1974) was in many respects a throwback to Captain King. A person of enormous energy—everybody says so—he spent two years at the University of Wisconsin, although he didn't really need a college education to do what he wanted to, which was manage King Ranch. He took over at age twenty-nine, precocious, obsessive, driven, very smart, and bent on doing things better. He was a ranchman all the way. He hated farming. He hated selling land. Leroy Denman noted a sharp contrast between the views of Bob Kleberg and those of his father and grandmother: "Bob, having been raised as a young boy on the ranch, really thought that they were here to own land and run cattle, and not to colonize and sell land." In 1916, when Bob was home from the University of Wisconsin for good, he argued at length that his father should not sell any more of the Laureles section to the Chapman family for what is today Chapman Ranch (not to be confused with the family or heirs of W. W. Chapman). Bob Kleberg's hatred of farming clashed with his father's interest in colonizing, in developing diversified farming. When Kleberg was sent to work on the Palo Alto district northeast of King Ranch in 1916, he grew to detest everything having to do with farming.

Bob Kleberg was always the one who was going to take over when the old guard passed from the scene. He was his father's favorite, Richard (Dick) his mother's. But Dick admired Bob as well and recognized his younger brother's capabilities. There was no rivalry over who would rule. Leroy Denman, who knew them both

Bob Kleberg's superb horsemanship skills in action on King Ranch.

extremely well, said that "Dick made a little study of everything that he liked to do; that is why I called him a great student and not a hard worker." Take roping, for example. Dick was a natural on a horse and could rope like an Argentinian or a Spaniard (he had studied both styles, you see), while Bob, who was not as good a rider by any means, rode and roped through sheer determination, without the gliding grace of his older brother.

Possessed of great intellect (and a great temper, as well), tenacity, and an absolute love of everything connected with ranching, Bob Kleberg was well fitted to become the most significant figure in King Ranch history since Captain King. By all measurements, he fulfilled that destiny.

But Bob Kleberg was not without a familiar weakness. He liked to drink—a lot. According to Denman, Bob Kleberg "drank too much probably all of his life but certainly restrained his drinking during her [his wife Helen's] life-time more than he did in the latter part of his life." A man at King Ranch in Cuba, Bob Kleberg's first international acquisition, told Holland McCombs in 1954: "*Que hombre!* He out-worked us! He out-talked us! He out-rode us! He out-gunned us! And he out-*rummed* us." John Cypher, who worked closely at Bob

Kleberg's side for many years, wrote that "Bob hit it hard all of his adult life, a malady that seems to especially affect ranchers." In Kleberg's case, he was one of those who could drink hard, work hard, and play hard, wearing lesser mortals into the ground. The alcohol never deflected him from his main goals. Cypher considered Kleberg's drinking a form of escape from the burdens of the ranch and from family pressures. Cypher remembers one of Kleberg's favorite drinks, a real morning eye-opener called *leche colorado,* composed of bourbon, milk, and honey. It sounds almost biblical, this concoction that Kleberg regarded as a "nutritious breakfast substitute."

Bob Kleberg's wife, Helen Campbell, daughter of a congressman from Kansas (she grew up in Washington and Virginia), was a woman every bit her husband's equal in fire, spirit, and intellect. Bob courted her for a grand total of seventeen days before getting married, in 1926. Their marriage appears to have been a true partnership in which each contributed something vital to the other. Edna Ferber is supposed to have based the marriage of the Texas cattle baron and the Maryland aristocrat in *Giant* (1952) on them. Kleberg gave Helen an interesting life, on the ranch, and on the East Coast, where she thrived, Helen gave him a degree of cosmopolitanism that he would likely never have possessed on his own.

Many would agree with Holland McCombs, who was simply bowled over by her: "To me she was a beautiful, composed, wise, witty, slender, auburn-haired Virginia aristocrat—at times well endowed with a patrician toughness and determination that could surmount and overcome a lot of obstacles." Leroy Denman, who vastly admired Helen, said that "through her relationship with Bob, she helped transform it [King Ranch] from a fairly provincial, local kind of an operation to an international business of prominence." Bob, too, she helped transform. "She loved to play him on a bigger and bigger stage," says Denman. They were a dynamic couple who were very self-aware of their marriage. Denman recalls a typical scene: "One time, Bob was talking to Helen about what kind of a wife she was, and he said, 'You're really just very good,' telling her all of her good qualities. Finally, he said, 'Helen, the only thing I really don't like about you, and I really have to tell you, is you're always trying to change me!' Helen replied, 'Bob, I don't try to change you, I just try to shape you up enough so that I can live with you.'"

Bob Kleberg's life's work was improving King Ranch. He did so in four areas. The first had to do with good breeding. So did the second. First, he set about upgrading the quality of cattle on King Ranch. But he did far more than that; through his vision and energy an entire new breed of cattle was brought into being, the first such new breed ever created in the New World. The Santa Gertrudis were something to behold. When his brother, Richard, described what they were seeking, he sounded like a Cubist painter defining an aesthetic: "Cattle are machines to gather and sell grass. We want a big rack to hang the grass on." The Santa Gertrudis was the big rack.

The making of the breed involved a little luck in the beginning, but it required an expert eye to see the conformation, to promote the development of the genetic line that would end in carbon-copy, Xerox-perfect duplications of a generic type. Bob Kleberg had such an eye, and he was a voracious reader on the subject of genetics and bloodlines.

The luck came in the form of a gift, in 1910, from Thomas M. O'Connor, a big rancher from near Victoria (the O'Connor Ranch is still going strong), who offered as a gift to the King Ranch a half-brahman, half-shorthorn bull. At some point this bull—the O'Connor bull, it should perhaps be called—jumped a fence to get at some shorthorn heifers on King Ranch. One of those offspring, Chemera, bred calves that seemed resistant to the unfavorable environment— heat and insects. Young Bob Kleberg thought the results of the accidental breeding looked promising, and in 1919 things looked even better when a Brahman bull, Vinotero, teamed up with a shorthorn milk cow from the Laureles division that possessed roughly one-sixteenth brahman blood from the original fence-jumping O'Connor bull and his offspring, Chemera. The result was Monkey, a playful bull with dark-red coloring and superior conformation. Monkey (1920–1932) became the king of King Ranch, siring a long line of cattle bearing three-eighths brahman and five-eighths shorthorn blood. Monkey's offspring were named Santa Gertrudis, after the most historic place-name on the property. The Santa Gertrudis were amazing. They could tolerate the high temperatures of South Texas and resist biting insects; not only that, they weighed out heavier than other breeds and produced meat of superior marbling and quality. King Ranch had long since made its brand known throughout the world of

Monkey, the genetic pioneer of a new breed of cattle, the Santa Gertrudis. Monkey never fired blanks.

cattle; now it had its own unique breed that carried the name of King Ranch to the four corners of the earth. The breed was officially recognized in 1940, and by the 1990s there were more than 3,500 breeders of Santa Gertrudis cattle.

The second thing Bob Kleberg did was to make sure that if King Ranch had any oil, it would be found, by leasing the land to Humble (later Exxon) in 1933, and using a $3.5 million loan from Humble to pay off debts. When oil hit big on King Ranch in 1939, it gave him the capital to fund other ambitious projects.

Third, if Bob Kleberg liked good cattle, he liked good horses just as much. To that end, he set out on another breeding program, working with two kinds of horses, quarter horses and, later, thoroughbreds for racing. The foundation horse for King Ranch quarter horses possessed no formal name but was called simply "the sorrel horse" or "the old sorrel." He came into King Ranch's possession by means of a shrewd purchase made by Caesar Kleberg of a sorrel colt he saw on a ranch near Alice, Texas, in 1916. Bob Kleberg, who was only twenty then, got permission from his father to breed the sorrel horse with some of the ranch's best mares. The results were outstanding. The sorrel horse—sorrel means a light red-brown color—spun out a long line of horses reminiscent in both color and quality of Monkey's progeny. King Ranch used quarter horses for work, not racing. A KR quarter horse is above all a cow horse, bred to work cattle. According to KR veterinarian Dr. James Kellog Northway, the quarter horse on King Ranch was meant to be a partner, not a slave. Good quarter horses instinctively know what to do among cattle without waiting to be told. King Ranch quarter horses made unsurpassed cow ponies, wonderful polo ponies, and even great circus ponies for Ringling Brothers.

In the 1930s Bob Kleberg went into breeding thoroughbreds in a big way, the way he did everything. He hired an expert trainer named Max Hirsch, and together they began to assemble horse talent in the same manner a big-league general manager might assemble a pennant-winning baseball team. The best horses were in Kentucky, and that is where they found Bold Venture in 1938, the first major league stud in their stable. Here again Bob Kleberg was reprising the ventures of the founder, Richard King, who back at the beginning of King's rancho had brought first-rate Kentucky horseflesh to South Texas. In the early 1940s King Ranch thoroughbreds started to win races back east, where the action was. Helen Kleberg, who named a lot of King Ranch horses, loved this side of ranching, and she and her husband cut a wide swath when they attended horse shows and races in Kentucky and on the eastern seaboard. It was only fitting that King Ranch horses would succeed in the sport of kings.

In 1943 Assault, the best thoroughbred King Ranch ever owned, was born, and three years later he won the Triple Crown, racing's crème de la crème. Assault was a hard-luck horse with a great heart. His story would be a natural for one of those old-time Hollywood films about a gallant horse that overcomes tremendous odds.

In his early youth, Assault stepped on a surveyor's stake protruding from the ground. His right front foot seemed ruined. The frog, the pad in the hoof, was destroyed, and there was other damage as well. The usual thing would be to put the horse down, because it would be crippled for the rest of its life, but because Assault was so beautiful, the ranch veterinarian, Dr. Northway, who had been with King Ranch a long time, devised a special shoe that allowed the horse to continue training. When sportswriters got hold of the story, Assault became Clubfooted Comet. After his retirement from racing, Assault was expected to sire many champions, but did not. According to Dr. Northway, "his aim was good for a hip shooter but he fired blanks." There would be no little Assaults.

In 1950 another King Ranch horse, Middleground, almost won a second Triple Crown, losing only the Preakness. With his repeated successes at the major venues of American equine racing, Bob Kleberg stood at the top of the refined world of mint juleps and expensive horseflesh.

A fourth big success awaited him: the world. Against the wishes of some of the King Ranch family, Bob Kleberg went global. Kleberg was a kind of visionary of food production, a guru of meat. He believed in red meat when red meat was king of the American dinner table. But like a true missionary, he wanted to extend the reign of red meat to the entire world, to little-bitty babies in faraway countries, to old men sitting in front of huts in Third World countries, to everybody in the whole wide world. In a 1950s interview he spoke of King Ranch's — of his—ultimate goal: "to supply human energy, to show the way to supply red meat for human energy—especially in places where it is most needed—in disadvantaged areas, the wet and dry tropics . . . in those areas where food is most needed . . . we have a big opportunity to serve mankind in this way. . . ."

Bob Kleberg's seriousness is nowhere more evident than in the way King Ranch celebrated its one hundredth year. Kleberg organized an international symposium on the problems of raising livestock and brought together scientists, nutritionists, botanists, geneticists, veterinarians, climatologists, and cattlemen from around the world. In his remarks to the glittering array of talent assembled at the Santa Gertrudis headquarters, Kleberg stated, "We wanted to mark the centenary of the King Ranch as a livestock operation, not by a big parade or pageant, or a 'blowout,' but by something that would be representative and significant of your efforts and our efforts." Kleberg's vision for the future suggested two overarching goals for the common good: "freedom from hunger . . . and freedom from oppression." The proceedings were later published under the title *Breeding Beef Cattle for Unfavorable Environments*.

The year before the symposium, Kleberg had set into motion a plan, in conjunction with the Braga family in Cuba, to raise Santa Gertrudis cattle on the lush grasslands of that country. The experiment worked well until January 1, 1959, when Fidel Castro toppled the Batista regime and confiscated all the evil foreign capitalist holdings, among them King Ranch–Cuba, worth some $3 million. King's manager, an American named Lowell Tash, after being confined to jail for several weeks, barely managed to get out of the country. He brought with him the clothes he was wearing; everything else belonged to Castro and his henchmen, pardon, revolutionaries. Some of the Santa Gertrudis herd wound up in Georgia (Russia, not America). When Bob Kleberg heard about this, he was furious.

There were other ventures, in Argentina, Australia, Brazil, and Venezuela. Bob Kleberg threw himself into these global operations with the zest and enthusiasm he brought to every undertaking, but the clock was ticking and he couldn't go on forever. At age seventy-five he could still ride a good horse and work in roundups on King Ranch, but he was winding down. He drank more and studied less. He got by on will, long years of experience, and the accustomed prerogatives of power. And there were always leche colorados when he needed a jump start in the morning.

In August 1974, he was still going strong. He had been on safari in southern Africa and bagged a trophy lion. Then in September he came down with jaundice, a liver problem, it appeared. About the last thing he did before entering the hospital was to respond to an hours-long grilling by feds who wanted to know about his campaign contributions to Richard Nixon, whom he supported and liked. He had liked Ike, too, but he didn't like LBJ anymore. None of the Klebergs did, because of the way LBJ had treated his old employer, Dick Kleberg, back in the 1944 election when Dick was defeated.

When he was in the hospital, one of the visitors who came to see him was Tom Lea, bearing in his hands a freshly minted copy of *In the Crucible of the Sun,* an account of the Australian holdings of the King Ranch and of a wonderful trip that Lea and Kleberg had made to Australia. Kleberg was too ill to do anything but acknowledge the present from his old friend.

As Kleberg lay dying, he was asked if there was anything he wanted, and he scribbled on a notepad, "Vodka tonic." This wasn't a drink that he particularly liked, but he calculated that because of its mildness, it was one he could get. But he didn't get it; the doctor wouldn't comply with such a simple request. Thus the man who had ruled an empire and was accustomed to drinking the finest liquor and wines that money could buy couldn't command a vodka tonic. It was time to go. He died on October 13, 1974, following complications caused by an intestinal tumor that impaired liver and pancreatic functions. At his funeral, per his instructions, all the finest contents of his liquor and wine cellar were served to the mourners.

In a sense, the world had already ridden out from under his saddle. He told an interviewer in 1968 that he had personally seen every inch of the ranch from horseback: "Unfortunately, I will be the last of my family to ever say that—things have changed—the younger ones won't spend a lifetime in the saddle—they won't need to."

Bob Kleberg's long tenure and dominion on horseback created resentments that bubbled to the surface following his death. There were those in the family who thought he put himself out front too much and spent extravagantly on his own pet projects, including racehorses and far-flung cattle operations in countries round the globe. "One dictator in this family is enough," said a family member after Bob Kleberg was in the ground. Although some considered him arrogant and willful— which he doubtless was—empires are not made and sustained by timid folk.

In the power vacuum following the death of Bob Kleberg, the board of directors did not choose from the most obvious candidates. Richard Kleberg Jr., a ranchman, horseman, workaholic, and hard smoker and drinker, was too weakened by emphysema to undertake the job. Standing in line to take over were two of his cousins, B. Johnson and Bobby Shelton. Both of them wanted the job, but neither of them got it. Belton Kleberg Johnson, or B. as he was always called, and Robert Richard (Bobby) Shelton were half-brothers raised from childhood by Bob and Helen Kleberg, who had one child of their own, Helenita. The boys' mother was Sarah Kleberg, Bob's sister. She married B.'s father, Henry Belton Johnson, a cowboy, in 1928, but when B. was not even two years old, Johnson died of a brain tumor; a year later, she married Dr. Joseph Shelton, who died in 1939, leaving behind a son, Bobby; then, in 1942, the mother herself died in a car wreck. Both of the men were qualified to operate the ranch, and B. had been a favorite of Bob Kleberg.

After making their cases individually to the board, both were turned down in favor of James Clement (1919–1994), a very capable man who had married one of the granddaughters of Robert and Alice Kleberg. A graduate of Princeton, he thus became the first businessman selected for the top position. He would not be the last. B. Johnson, who had always shown an independent streak, wanted out. He walked away with $70 million and started his own ranch, Chaparrosa, near Uvalde. He also became an important player in San Antonio, developing, for example, the Hyatt Regency Hotel in the old district near the Alamo and the historic Menger Hotel. Bobby Shelton hung on for three years and then left, too. Both brothers later brought suits against King Ranch, Inc., over disputes stemming from their settlements and royalties from Exxon wells on King Ranch properties. In 1981, B. figured his losses at $50 million, and Bobby Shelton figured his at $10 million. King Ranch's response was "These things happen in big successful families."

It fell to Stephen Justus Kleberg, the son of Richard Mifflin Kleberg Jr. and grandson of Richard Mifflin Kleberg, to become the next member of his family to manage King Ranch—and the last. "Tio" (uncle), as he is affectionately called, never wanted to do anything else except ride herd on King Ranch's cattle operations. He took over in 1977. For a long time, cattle had brought in smaller profits, far smaller, than other King Ranch operations. Tio burned with a passion familiar to old Kineños and those who cared about King Ranch traditions, a dedication and old-fashioned commitment that seemed to be in increasingly short supply. Most family members no longer felt the allure of living on King Ranch, where the summers, even with air conditioning, were long and barely endurable, where dust and allergens saturated the air, and where the closest town was poky little Kingsville, which could barely manage one topless bar and, as for restaurants, forget about it. For a long time the children of King Ranch had looked to Corpus Christi for entertainment and a touch of city comforts, but now, with revenues soaring from investments and profitable new businesses, King Ranch, for all its history, seemed very provincial. The biggest stockholder, Richard Sugden, who inherited all of his mother's stock (she was one of the original five Kleberg children), is a doctor who grew up in California and lives in Jackson Hole, Wyoming. Today King Ranch heirs reside just about everywhere except at King Ranch.

The line of succession that never was, that of the founder, continued on. Richard King III became a highly respected banker and civic leader in Corpus Christi. Richard King IV owns a video production company in Austin. The connection with the captain's heritage remains strong. When Richard King IV got married, he honeymooned in the captain's old suite at the Menger Hotel in San Antonio.

But Tio was a throwback to the old days. Tio on horseback was what King Ranch was supposed to be. Journalist William Broyles Jr. observed Tio in the prime of his working life, in 1980. A small man with a big mustache, Tio, then thirty-four, was riding a $4 million quarter horse, Mr. San Peppy. The horse and its rider were working cattle in the old way, in the brush and dust of a sweltering South Texas day. They were laboring on King Ranch in the time-honored manner of the old vaqueros and cowboys going back to the days of the ranch's founding. Working alongside Tio was Lavoyger Durham, head of the Norias division. If Durham's name sounds familiar, it ought to. His grandfather was George Durham, the Ranger who rode with Captain McNelly back in the 1870s and married one of Henrietta King's nieces.

To Tio and his wife, Janell, the ranch and the family were one and the same. Said Janell in 1980: "Everything belongs to the ranch, and the ranch belongs to the family. Keeping the family and the ranch together is more important than any of us." In 1986 Jay Nixon's *Stewards of a Vision (A History of King Ranch)*, a glossy, brochure-type in-house publication, stated the same point as a kind of credo: "All are dedicated to maintaining the vision. All feel the obligation to keep the dream intact and to pass it on to those who will follow."

But there was something more important than family ties to the land: profits, modern business practices, and stock options cut a lot of family ties.

And so it was that on a morning in May 1998, Tio Kleberg, with Janell by his side, read a brief but surprising statement announcing the termination of his employment as head of the four ranching operations of King Ranch, effective June 1. It was the end of an era. For the first appreciable time since 1853, there would be no member of the King or Kleberg family in charge of King Ranch. New conditions forced Tio off the ranch and onto the board of directors—meetings instead of roundups, days spent on golf carts instead of on horseback.

Tio received a kind of premature recreational retirement that happened before he was ready and on terms other than his own. But he had given his best, and that at least was in the spirit of the long tradition of King Ranch.

All Tio wanted to do was ranch. He was happiest on horseback when the worries of the balance sheet vanished in the feel of a good horse cutting off a recalcitrant calf's wayward progress. One day not too long after he was fired, he was on his horse, working with the Kineños in what would be his last roundup, when his cell phone rang (modern King Ranch cowboys carry cell phones in their pickups and saddlebags). When the caller asked where he was, Tio replied, "I'm in the middle of the Alazon pasture on a good quarter horse, doing what I love to do."

"My heart is always there," he said three years later. His numerous business and corporate interests occupy his time, but he admits that he plays "a hell of a lot of golf"—on pastoral venues far removed from those of his forebears.

Tio could look back on some real accomplishments. He increased cotton and milo farming, which was profitable, and he made more land available for hunting leases, about the only surefire source of income for many ranches in Texas today. In a move that was probably part homage and part competition with the dead giants of the past, Tio spent around $4 million developing a new breed of cattle called the Santa Cruz, which were supposed to be superior to the vaunted Santa Gertrudis. The jury is still out on that one.

As a manager, Tio had the loyalty of the Kineños and other ranch-oriented people on King Ranch, but he clashed with new CEO Jack Hunt, who in 1995 was brought in from California's Tejon Ranch Company, which he managed, to head up King Ranch, Inc. A graduate of Williams College and Harvard Business School, Hunt was—and is—the personification of the new style of corporate management. His offices are in downtown Houston, and his visits to the ranch are infrequent. Yet Hunt also has an authentic Texas ranching background. He was born in Wichita Falls and grew up familiar with the cattle business. Hunt compares himself with Tio: "I had similar experiences growing up to what Tio had. We both worked on ranches in the summer, except he went away to boarding school and I went to public school."

There the similarities ended. Hunt and Tio had several run-ins. In one instance, Hunt wanted to cut costs and proposed buying pickups without air conditioning or power locks on the doors. Tio protested, claiming the pickups were the cowboys' offices. Hunt also wanted to check the mileage the trucks were posting. He thought they might be driving too much. It was this kind of nitpicking by a man who operated out of a distant highrise and seemed to have forgotten the exigencies of the land itself, its seasons, its blistering heat, that really irritated Tio.

When Hunt looked at the balance sheets, the cattle operation did not impress him. What he liked a lot better was the sod farm in southern Florida, a King Ranch acquisition that brought in a cool $16 million a year. One of the crowning ironies of King Ranch's long investment in good grass for raising cattle was that St. Augustine grass for suburban homeowners was far, far more profitable. Besides the sod farm in Florida, King Ranch, Inc. owned properties there that produced sugarcane and rice. In 1993 King Ranch, Inc. went into the citrus business in south Florida, and now the famous Running W brand applies as equally to oranges and grapefruits as to cows. Diversification is the new world order. Since 1977 King Ranch had been in the cotton business in a big way, planting as much as 50,000 acres a year. King Ranch, Inc. owns a cotton gin in Galveston. There were leasing operations of cotton and alfafa in Arizona, other feed yard and cattle operations leased in Texas. And there were still foreign cattle operations, two ranches in Brazil that represent all that remains of Bob Kleberg's globalism.

Hunting leases—$3 million annually—were more reliable than income from cattle, which averaged $1 to $3 million. King Ranch's plentiful supply of deer yields an annual "harvest" of six to eight hundred white-tailed bucks and about twice that many does. Bow hunting for feral hogs is another source of income. Energy sources remain good, too, $12 million annually. From the corporate standpoint, cattle were definitely bottom tier, way behind sod and oil. The ranching business was becoming more and more diversified, and the terminology was new—and decidedly unglamorous, as well. Michael Rhyne, an agribusiness controller employed by King Ranch, says, "First and foremost, we are land managers."

Jack Hunt never did ask Tio to drive him around the ranch, a sore point with Tio to this day. And at a directors' meeting in Houston,

Tio's bristly irritation was obvious when he challenged a proposal made by Hunt to spend $500,000 to study environmental problems. Tio pointed out in no uncertain terms that he knew every foot of the ranch and could identify any environmental problems without having to hire a consultant. Tio's breach of corporate decorum prompted Hunt to make a rare trip to the ranch the next day to demand of Tio why he had challenged him in front of the board.

Given this difference in temperament and vision, the firing of Tio Kleberg was probably inevitable. In 1997, under Hunt's leadership, pretax profits were in excess of $32 million, with $200 million in the bank and very little debt. The money rolled in. Family stockholders (over 80) divvied up around $27 million in oil royalties in 1997, and $9 million from King Ranch, Inc. profits. That kind of money can buy a lot of corporate unity.

But in another sense the ranch was more than profits; it always had been. For the Kineños, it was a way of life. Descendants of the Mexicans who had followed Captain King out of the village of Cruillas, back in 1854, were still living on King Ranch, and their loyalties were still strong. A favored story told of King Ranch overlords from generation to generation has to do with just this loyalty. One day a visitor came to the ranch looking for Bob Kleberg and asked an old Kineño if he worked for Mr. Kleberg. "No, señora, I work for King Ranch. Mr. Kleberg, he work for King Ranch, too." An older story relates how Ignacio Alvarado, a caporal from the days of Captain King, failed at last to do his duty for the new King Ranch hacendado, King's son-in-law Robert J. Kleberg. Two days late in taking charge of a herd of cattle, Ignacio was represented by his son, who told the abogado, "My father says to tell you he was sorry he could not come. He had to die."

The Kineños had been a part of King Ranch so long that their stories and traditions were becoming part of the legend. In 1994 a musical play written by Janell Kleberg, *Tales of the Wildhorse Desert,* was produced in Kingsville. A collection of anecdotes and memories drawn from the Mexican-American families living on the King and and Kenedy ranches was published in 1997, with a Foreword by Tio Kleberg stating, "Los Kineños are my extended family. Having lived and worked almost my entire life on King Ranch, I am firmly convinced that the people and culture of this ongoing enterprise are its greatest asset."

In the patron system, the Kineños had always been provided for. Tio Kleberg understood the structure well. "When I was growing up, three were about 500 Kineño families on the ranch," he remembers. "It was in many ways like a medieval village. It was self-sufficient. People grew up to do what their fathers did. . . . If your father was a cowboy, you were a cowboy. It was like an apprentice system." In 1998 when Tio was fired, about three hundred Kineño families still lived on King Ranch. On the Santa Gertrudis section there were 108 houses called the Colony. There were forty-six houses on Laureles, thirty-five on Norias, and ten on Encino. The houses were made of whitewashed brick with tile floors and redwood doors. They were better houses than most of the Kineños would have been able to afford in Kingsville.

Until the 1980s there were no retirement or health plans. Kineños who were sick carried notes from their foremen to the Kingsville Clinic in town, where they received medical care, and the ranch was billed for the costs. Dora Maldanado, a longtime Kineño dweller on King Ranch, remembers that at Christmas, the Klebergs gave the men work jackets, the women a set of sheets, and the children toys, candy, and fruit. When Kineño couples married, they sometimes received a cow as a wedding present. The cow given to Pedro Alvarez and his bride, Carmela, was slaughtered in the backyard for a party honoring the newlyweds.

The lives of Kineño women on King Ranch were sometimes difficult. Maria Silva, seventy-nine, the daughter of a cowboy, met her husband at the Ranch School, married, and seldom left the ranch. Her husband's gravesite is close to her house. She speaks only Spanish. Silva recalls the isolation of the early days, and the memory of the birth of one of her children is vivid: "It was hard to go anywhere, because all the roads were dirt. When I was having one of my babies I waited three days for the doctor to come from Kingsville, but he didn't make it. I had my baby delivered by a midwife. Finally the doctor got here, but it was over."

The attachment to place, to King Ranch, among the Kineños is quite pronounced. Amanda Ramirez, Pedro Alvarez's daughter, says, "All the generations of our family have always lived together, and we like it that way." Her mother, Carmela, a teacher, likes having her family members buried by the front porch of the Alvarez house. That way she can visit with them. "My father really liked beer," she says, "so sometimes I take a can of beer and put it on his grave." Noelia Torrez, whose father was King Ranch butler for fifty years, makes a similar point. "It is our own little colony. We stick together."

But in the wake of Tio's departure, many of the Kineños felt insecure for the first time in their lives. Doris Guerrero, sixty-five, whose grandfather worked on Captain King's steamboat, raised eleven children in her rent-free house on King Ranch. She lives on $361 in Social Security and a pension of $96 and supplements her income by mowing the yards of other Kineños. She is fearful of change now that Tio is gone: "I feel like what Hunt is trying to do is erase history. It may not be long before the Kineño way of life is destroyed. It's like trying to say that Billy the Kid never existed."

Irene Casteneda, eighty-five, came to King Ranch from Cruillas, Mexico, following in the tradition of the first Kineños, when she was ten years old. At fifteen she met Pedro Casteneda, a carpenter who was twenty-one, and married him. When he died, Tio came to see her and took care of everything. Now, she says, "I am afraid I will be kicked out of my home and have nowhere to go."

Jack Hunt maintains that the old promises will be kept but that "we do have stockholders who expect to be successful." He foresees a future different from what the Kineños have known: "But someone starting work today for King Ranch may be looking at a different set of circumstances."

Modern technology has transformed some of the old ways of the vaqueros. Rounding up three or four hundred cows, for example, used to take about a week's work performed by fifteen cowboys. With three helicopters (contracted with outside companies), the task can be accomplished in about three hours, and the entire job of branding and doctoring the cattle can be done in two days. On the marketing side, videotapes of cattle make it possible to handle sales long distance without the buyer ever actually attending a cattle auction with the actual cattle. Chuck wagons, once a standard means of feeding vaqueros working in distant locations on King Ranch, are now museum pieces. Long gone are the days of sleeping under the stars and weeks spent camping in the brush far from comfortable quarters.

About all that is left of those days are the memories. Alberto "Lolo" Trevino, sixty-eight, perhaps best captures the age-old simplicities of the Kineño way of life on King Ranch in a story he relates of his time in the saddle: "Being a cowboy is a real dangerous job. Every day before we rode out, we would invite Jesus to come with us. Sometimes we would do everything we could to bring the cattle back around to us, but they wouldn't come. Then finally they would come. We knew Jesus had done it for us. You see, Jesus is very quiet and the cattle can't hear him."

Pedro Alvarez's son Pedro Jr., thirteen, wants to be a cowboy, but his father thinks his son ought to get an education.

In 2002 the Kineños are still on King Ranch, though their number decreases with the passage of time and the new additions to the Santa Gertrudis Memorial Cemetery. Here in 1999 were buried numerous Kineños, among them Valentin P. Quintanilla Jr., age ninety-three, a cowboy retired from King Ranch, and Lucia R. Rodriguez, eighty-six, a homemaker, employee of King Ranch, and Jehovah's Witness. The obituary pages of the *Corpus Christi Caller Times* offer a steady harvest of King Ranch dead, old-timer Kineños and Anglos all joined in that final democracy where farrier, butler, vaquero, and homemaker are as one.

CHAPTER 13

The Unquiet Past

Richard King worked assiduously at acquiring clear titles to his properties that would hold up under legal challenges. He and his lawyers did well, except in one instance, Cause No. 1279, *Helen B. Chapman v. Richard King,* filed in 1879. This was the only serious legal challenge in his lifetime, a case overlooked by many who have written of King Ranch. King prevailed in that legal contest against the widow of his friend and contested co-owner of the original Rincón de Santa Gertrudis, Major William Warren Chapman. The court decreed in 1883 that Richard King was "quieted in the possession of his lands." And so he remained, along with his heirs and assigns, and King Ranch rolled on, like the U.S. Constitution, like Texas itself, at once historic and dynamic, unchanging while ever adaptable to new conditions.

Then, in 1995, nearly 150 years after the founding of the rancho and the same year Jack Hunt's arrival augured the changes ahead for King Ranch, the old issues at the heart of Cause No. 1279 flamed into life again, and the circumstances surrounding the title, deed, and possession of the original Rincón de Santa Gertrudis would be called into question, in a lawsuit of considerable historical significance.

The case was anticipated a decade earlier, when Dick Frost, author of *The King Ranch Papers* (sensationally subtitled "An Unauthorized and Irreverent History of the World's Largest Landholders—The Kleberg Family") noted that "there never was a legal document transferring this land from Chapman to King." But Frost also stated that "the widow of Maj. Chapman is said to have acknowledged verbally what had never been written down: That it was the wish of the late major for King to assume total ownership of the Rincón ranch." Still, Frost concluded, the ambiguity of the deal between King and

Chapman, and its aftermath, was such that "A Chapman heir in modern times, however, might have an interesting claim to 7,000 acres in the heart of King Ranch headquarters." These proved to be prophetic words, because those heirs had come forward with just such a claim.

Filed on April 20, 1995, in the 28th District Court in Nueces County, Texas, the case of *William Warren Chapman, III, et al., v. King Ranch, Inc., et al.*, strikes at the heart of King Ranch sovereignty. It alleged that the 1883 judgment "was the result of a 'conspiracy' between Richard King, Robert J. Kleberg, and others to deprive Helen Chapman's children and grandchildren of their respective life estates and estates in remainder in the Rincón by using, selling, leasing for oil and gas, and otherwise disposing of, the undivided interests of these co-tenants, and concealing this fraud, both actual and constructive." At issue are 7,449 acres of prime real estate that take in part of King Ranch, downtown Kingsville, and the Kingsville Naval Air Station.

Despite Frost's observation, the case caught everybody at King Ranch by surprise, especially archivist Bruce Cheeseman. He heard about it late one Friday afternoon in 1995 when the phone rang. It was Larry Worden, a King Ranch attorney.

"Cheeseman, who the hell is Edward Coker?"

"The guy who did the book on the Chapmans. I told you about him."

"Did we grant him permission?"

"Yeah, you approved it. Why?"

"Well, we've just been served with a multimillion-dollar lawsuit."

Up until then, things had gone very well for Bruce Cheeseman. Being King Ranch archivist and historian was a dream job, though the pay wasn't so good in comparison to the wealth of the land behind it. He had the use of a company plane to travel to conferences around the state. He could quarry the archives to publish scholarly articles and monographs about the history of King Ranch. Cheeseman and his wife, Mary, even helped to put together the *King Ranch Cookbook* in 1992. And he could expect to finish out his career in Kingsville, Texas.

It was odd how things turned out, for Bruce Cheeseman had never planned to be the archivist of King Ranch. He couldn't have, because the position did not even exist until the late 1980s, when he applied and got the job and became the first one. Born in 1955, he grew up in New Jersey, far from King Ranch. With a B.A. from Pfeiffer College in North Carolina and an M.A. from Texas A&M University, Cheeseman took a job in North Carolina in the Department of Cultural Resources and then became associate archivist for Cigna Insurance in Hartford, Connecticut.

If Cheeseman did not know anything about King Ranch, the management of King Ranch, Inc. did not know anything much about archival collections. But in 1986–87, management decided that something needed to be done about its extensive backlog of records and documents. After all, things had been piling up for over a century, gathering dust, being nibbled by insects, decaying. So King Ranch, Inc. sought the advice of an expert, David Gracy, an authority on "archival enterprise" who is currently director of the Center for the Cultural Record at The University of Texas at Austin. Gracy visited Kingsville several times to view the situation firsthand. What he found was a "formidable mass" of several thousand cubic feet of King Ranch history, ancient and recent. The material was, in Gracy's opinion, "an unmanaged asset."

Some of the older records were stored in the vault in the Main House. Other extensive records relating to Congressman Richard Kleburg's tenure in Washington were stacked in rows of cardboard boxes in a defunct department store on Lee Street in downtown Kingsville. After surveying everything *in situ,* Gracy prepared a report with recommendations. In his report (September 10, 1987) he recommended four advantages to setting up a professional archival operation for the maintenance of King Ranch records: the protection of corporate interests; the reduction in cost of records storage; the speeding up of access to information in office files; and, most important, the advancement of "corporate interest through use of the records in marketing campaigns and in fostering public good will with the appropriate marking of anniversary occasions, as well as in recognizing the obligations placed upon the corporation by the unique historical status it has achieved." On this point, Gracy cited the example of Wells Fargo, which "maintains a fine museum and consciously molds its corporate image around its colorful past."

In Gracy's view, the solution to King Ranch's record problem was obvious. They needed to hire an archivist for at least two years who would set about accomplishing the twin goals of preservation and organization. But King Ranch would also need to think about what its conception of the archives would be. Gracy succinctly spelled out the possibilities: "Traditionally, the record preserved for history is more full and informative than the record maintained strictly for protection of corporate interests. Fewer records mean greater protection, according to the *Wall Street Journal* of September 2, 1987, by thwarting attorneys who, through broad actions of discovery, seek to obtain documents that, in skillful hands, can be construed to place their owner in an unfavorable light." Obviously the archive business was not without risks. At some future date, in some totally unanticipated manner, the private interests of the corporation might clash with the public interests of history and its inheritors.

Historically, King Ranch had been wary about outsiders, writers interested in telling its story, perhaps divulging its secrets. Numerous suitors were turned down. John Ashton, a journalist and professor at Texas A&M, collected material on King Ranch for many years, but was always refused in his attempts to gain the cooperation of the Klebergs to write a history of the ranch. Ashton went so far as to pen a poem upon the occasion of the death of Caesar Kleberg, longtime manager of the Norias section, but the poem, published in *The Cattleman,* a livestock trade magazine, did nothing to advance his cause. There were some exceptions. Journalists generally fared better than book authors. *Fortune* magazine, in 1933, produced a sumptuous account of King Ranch, with gorgeous color illustrations and the full cooperation of the Klebergs. *TIME,* in 1947, did a cover story on Bob Kleberg, the first and surely the last time a real rancher will be so featured.

But the main tendency was to rebuff writers. George Sessions Perry, a prominent Texas author of the 1940s, was frustrated in his efforts to write a magazine article on Assault, the King Ranch Triple Crown winner. When the Klebergs demanded final approval of what he wrote, Perry abandoned the project. J. Frank Dobie, the dean of Texas authors from the late 1920s to his death in 1964, wanted badly to write a history of King Ranch, but the Klebergs would not play ball. In 1939 Dobie, a well-known figure, visited the Klebergs at King

Ranch but failed to secure permission to write its history. Dick Kleberg, a superb horseman, challenged Dobie to a riding contest, but Dobie, who had been riding all his life, declined. A decade later, Dobie was still interested in the King Ranch assignment, but Dick Kleberg, who considered him a "pompous academician who likes to play cowboy," would not hear of it.

Years later, Texas's foremost author, Larry McMurtry, received King Ranch's approval for an article on its thoroughbreds for *Sports Illustrated,* only to have the decision reversed at the last minute. The story went unwritten. More recently, T. R. Fehrenbach, one of the most prominent historians in the state, was also turned down when he sought cooperation from King Ranch.

The one writer who was granted access to the treasures of the vault was Tom Lea, and anyone who wishes to know the history of King Ranch must begin with Lea's book. I met the man himself on two occasions. The first time was in the early 1980s when a mutual friend called and asked if I wanted to meet him. During a long conversation with Lea, I mentioned, in passing, that I was broke at that particular moment, and Lea took out his wallet and offered to lend me some money on the spot. I was touched by his generosity but, of course, declined. Years later, in 1996, when George W. Bush was in his first term as governor, my wife and I were invited to attend a small dinner at the governor's mansion in honor of Lea and the publication of *Tom Lea: An Oral History.* By then Lea's sight was failing, and I never mentioned our earlier meeting.

At that point I had only cursorily read his most famous book. Since then, I have read it repeatedly. Like the Bible, it is in two volumes. Volume I traces the life of Richard King from his arrival in Texas until his death in 1885. It is the best of the two. The second volume surveys King Ranch's history in the twentieth century and is dominated by the looming presence of Robert J. Kleberg, the man who gave Lea the coveted assignment to write the history of his (Kleberg's) beloved ranch.

Lea's usual mode in his book takes the form of epic inflation, presenting events in a heightened manner. For example, he rarely speaks of the early vaqueros who worked on King Ranch without calling them "centaurs." Once, in the space of two pages, he calls the "half-wild men" centaurs seven times. Similarly, Richard King is lionized to a Richard the Lion-Hearted status. In keeping with such heroic portraits are the romantic realism of Lea's illustrations. King's eyes, tinted blue, have a piercing quality, like an early, bearded Marlboro man. Lea, who was essentially a novelist, also had a habit of inventing dialogue to build up dramatic scenes.

If we discount the theatrics of Lea's book, what is left is a solid repository of facts. But this factual basis, underpinned by voluminous footnotes, is sometimes a problem for the latter-day historian for one simple reason: the documents from the King Ranch vault are not available for the rest of us to see. Citations such as the following share a common provenance: "Preserved in King Ranch vault"; "Letters in King Ranch vault"; "From the file of letters preserved in the King Ranch vault." Lea's researcher was Holland McCombs, a Time-Life editor who visited the ranch in 1947 to gather material for a feature article. As an integral part of the Lea team, McCombs was granted unique access to records stored in the King Ranch vault. For the researcher denied admittance to the inner sanctum of King Ranch documents, Lea's book stands as a kind of King Ranch vault once removed—a shadow in Plato's cave, as it were, not the fire but as close to it as one can get. (McCombs's research, some 1,400 pages of single-spaced material, is said to be housed in the King Ranch Archives at the Henrietta Memorial Center.)

This was the situation, then, in 1987, when King Ranch, Inc. decided to establish its archives in order to solve their document storage problem and do their duty to history. So King Ranch, Inc. placed an advertisement for an archivist in the *Newsletter of the Society of American Archivists*. Among the applicants was Bruce Cheeseman. Following a series of interviews with James Clement, chairman of the board, and other members of King Ranch, Inc., Cheeseman was chosen for the job. His experience with corporate records management at Cigna was a big factor in his favor. Little did he realize then that his new position would place him at the eye of a storm that was brewing beyond his ken, a storm that would converge on King Ranch, Inc. and that would threaten him, too, before it was over.

The quiet, behind-the-scenes job of an archivist is not well known to the general public. An archivist is charged with the orderly record keeping of the past, of old documents and books and letters and grocery bills, medical reports and X rays of ranch hands or corporate executives or livestock, all the detritus and sometimes invaluable goings-on that are involved in any one of a thousand enterprises that matter to generations to come. In this case, the archivist's documents would all be concerned with the founding, production, and preservation of the great expanse of land that was King Ranch and all the people who had made it what it was.

As its archivist, Bruce Cheeseman faced several challenges. The first big task, undertaken in 1989, was to gather a possible treasure trove, all the records and documents from the vault located at the Main House, the turreted and gabled structure rising above the trees and overlooking the land stretching away on all sides, the original domain of Captain King, held intact for nearly 150 years. The vault was a fireproof room about 12 by 14 feet, with a high ceiling. The documents were stored in oak secretaries and file cabinets. So far as Cheeseman could tell, the records were not in current use.

According to Cheeseman, the papers and documents were "generally in good shape," despite the fact that they had been stored in a room lacking the proper temperature control that is a feature of archival libraries and absolutely crucial to the preservation of documents. (The standard is 68 to 72 degrees Fahrenheit, 46 to 54 percent relative humidity.) There was some deterioration of items in the vault, caused by mildewing, staining from the oak cabinets, and pest damage from that archenemy of archivists, silverfish.

How long had the materials been in the vault? Cheeseman didn't know. Presumably they had been at the house since May 1915, when the new house had been finished to replace the one destroyed by fire in 1912, when, undoubtedly, some original records had been lost.

Cheeseman immediately began to transfer the contents of the vault to the Henrietta Memorial Center, a refurbished ice house that opened in 1989. The papers and documents were placed in acid-free folders within acid-free boxes designed to protect said documents from all the foes of historical preservation.

The King Ranch Archives were, in Cheeseman's words, conceived of as "institutional business archives." They were not open to the public, but Cheeseman urged King Ranch that there was a responsibility to make materials available to scholars for historical research. King Ranch agreed, and so the archives were made accessible on a case-by-case basis. It fell to Cheeseman to oversee the applications of those seeking admittance. "Legitimate scholarly research," he says, was the main criterion. The procedure was relatively simple. Cheeseman would evaluate the applicant's credentials and ring up Larry Worden, King Ranch, Inc.'s general counsel, saying "Larry, this is a legitimate academic." On Cheeseman's recommendation, Worden would give his approval. One applicant whom Cheeseman was proud of turning down was the celebrity reporter Robin Leech, who was looking for another "rich and famous" story.

Cheeseman threw himself into his archivist duties and came to be highly visible around the state, presenting papers at scholarly conferences and producing a steady output of publications on the lives of Richard King and Henrietta Chamberlain. He encouraged the new history being written by Hispanic scholars such as David Montejano. Once, when Montejano was in Kingsville, Cheeseman gave him a tour of the archives, and Montejano still recalls the vast scale of the documents reaching skyward from the floor, in a lofty open space unbroken by conventional ceilings.

Cheeseman initiated various outreach programs. He brought an organization of Mexican-American citizens from Corpus Christi who were interested in genealogy and showed them through the archives, a gesture that was much appreciated. Everybody interested in the history of South Texas was delighted about the rich new facility and its enthusiastic director. Tom Kreneck, archivist/historian at Texas A&M University-Corpus Christi, a friend of Cheesman's, considered him an "outstanding professional archivist" and "very much an educational player in South Texas."

One of the best public relations events organized by Cheeseman was "a Day at King Ranch," held in 1991. The occasion was to celebrate the discovery, in the archives, of copies of Tom Lea's *The King Ranch*. Not just any copies, but ones bound in a "replica of the King Ranch saddle blanket made from crushed linen." These books of "rough-hewn elegance" were the famous saddle blanket edition, three thousand copies that had been printed in 1957 and were now much valued by collectors who paid up to $2,000 for a two-volume set. There were still twelve to fifteen hundred copies in the archives. Cheeseman worked out a deal with the Book Club of Texas, an organization devoted to fine printing of rare Texana volumes. The club would print two hundred sets that would be made available to book club members at $400 a set—a terrific bargain.

On November 9, 1991, members of the book club and other Texana book lovers assembled at the Henrietta Memorial Center to hear Cheeseman read a paper titled "Tom Lea and the Writing of *The King Ranch*" and Al Lowman, historian and aficionado of fine printing, deliver a talk on "Carl Hertzog and the Saddle Blanket Edition." The two essays were made into a slender volume, printed on high-quality rag paper also left over from 1957, and titled "*The Book of All Christendom*": *Tom Lea, Carl Hertzog, and the Making of "The King Ranch*" (1992).

"It was fun," Cheeseman says of that time of celebration, one of the high points of his tenure. But in that same year, a new book about South Texas appeared. Its message would shake the quiet chambers of the archives, and Bruce Cheeseman's days as King Ranch archivist would be numbered.

Edward Caleb Coker III grew up in the Old South, in Clemson, South Carolina, where he was born in 1943. He went to good schools for his education, receiving a B.A. in economics from Stanford University in 1965 and a J.D. from Duke University School of Law in 1969. After law school he worked for a law firm in Jacksonville, Florida, through the mid-1970s, then he and his first wife started their own law firm, which ended in 1980 when the couple split up. Still in Jacksonville, he worked for a large construction company for a number of years until leaving during the big slump of 1986.

For several years afterward Coker lived on his savings, but he was by no means idle. He spent 1987 writing a series of short stories based on personal experiences—fiction rather than fact—that he envisioned as a book to be called *Carolina Rain*. It was never published. In 1988, the same year Bruce Cheeseman began as King Ranch archivist, Coker started working on a different kind of book entirely—a compilation of correspondence written by one of his ancestors, Helen Chapman, the wife of U.S. Army quartermaster William Warren Chapman. The Chapmans were not exactly legendary figures. Helen was virtually unknown outside family memory, and William Chapman was only a minor, background player, mentioned in passing, in memoirs and scholarly books that dealt with the Mexican War era in South Texas.

The Chapmans were long dead and gone, and now Ed Coker was resurrecting their lives. Why? his mother wanted to know. A southern lady, she feared that he might expose the family to the glare of public display. As Coker tells it, "I have the highest regard for her, but in many respects I think, like many mothers, she tends to look at me as a two-year-old child or whatever. And she made—expressed some concern that the only reason I was writing this book was to embarrass the family, and she wanted to have the right to look at it before it got published." Ed told her he was sorry, but he wasn't going to let anybody look over his shoulder. His way of dealing with his mother, as any son can understand, was not to talk to her about it. In his view, the letters were important because "these people were, more or less, the first citizens of Brownsville and—or at least part of the founders of Brownsville and that it was an interesting record of what happened in those early days." He continues, "And I didn't think it was a matter—something that would bring shame to us, to publish those letters. It wasn't like the letters were written by a horse thief or something like that."

The letters sort of insinuated their way into Ed Coker's possession, turning up at two different points in his life. When he was thirteen years old, in 1956, his aunt Marion Barron died in Columbia, South Carolina. Ed's mother was the executor of the estate, and she took her son with her to go through the aunt's belongings. Aunt Marion had lived in a pre–Civil War house on Gadsden Street that for some reason the Yankees had not burned. It stood kitty-corner from the governor's mansion. Helen Chapman died in that house in 1881—a date that would become very important in the postmortem history of her life.

The house was large: six bedrooms, 10,000 square feet. While his mother set about the task of putting things in order, she dispatched her son to see what was in the attic. She told him he could select one thing to keep for himself from whatever he found up there.

There were lots of old things in that attic to attract a boy's wonder. Ed found the West Point footlocker from 1837 of his great-great-grandfather, Major William Warren Chapman. He found a Colt pistol, one of the original Colts, 13 inches long. (It wasn't until many years later that he learned that Chapman and Samuel Colt had been friends.) He found Chapman's mahogany toilet kit, complete with a tube of Squibb's toothpaste, which he tasted—just the kind of thing a thirteen-year-old boy alone in an attic would find irresistible. It was still minty. He found thirty deer heads, collected by Aunt Marion's husband, an avid hunter. He found a World War I footlocker that contained a tray in which there were bullets, wild bore tusks, and hairbrushes. Beneath the tray were World War I–era girlie magazines, mild by today's standards, and in the very bottom, underneath some army blankets, was the very thing he wanted: a German helmet with a gold spike. It still had grease and grit on it, the real thing, straight from the Western Front. But that wasn't all. Still farther down in the gloom of that long-unopened footlocker, he found something that sent him reeling out of the darkened attic into the light below: a human skull, with cotton wadding in its eye sockets and nose.

There was also a trunkful of old letters. In the parceling out of the dead aunt's effects, the letters eventually found their way into the keeping of another aunt, who lived in Kansas City. Cancer ended her life—suddenly, in 1959—and the letters were sent on to Orinda, California, in 1960, to Uncle Phil Freeman, who would eventually place them in the hands of the one descendant who would read them in their entirety. (There is no evidence that anybody else in the family ever read the letters.)

In 1985, Ed attended his twentieth Stanford reunion in Palo Alto, California, and afterward visited his uncle Phil, across the bay. Uncle Phil and his wife were about to move into a condo, and he asked Ed if he would like to have some old family letters that there would not be room for in the new place. Ed said yes, and a few months later, in early 1986, three boxes, weighing a total of 165 pounds, arrived at his home in Jacksonville. Inside the boxes were thousands of letters going back to the Revolutionary War and forward to the end of the nineteenth century. A "grand mess," Coker called them.

Ed opened the first box, reached in, and pulled out a letter dated sometime in June 1851, written by Helen Chapman from Pueblo, Mexico. Ed didn't know much about Helen Chapman. He knew that a portrait of her husband, William Warren Chapman, had hung in his mother's house when he was a child, but that was all.

As it turned out, the letter from Mexico held special, accidental interest for Ed. Over a year earlier, in 1984, he had taken his oldest daughter on a vacation to Mexico City, where they had stayed at the Hotel Majestic, in the heart of the city. It was an old colonial establishment with a rooftop restaurant from which, at night, there was a grand view of the Zocolo below. As he read the letter that described Helen's last night in Mexico City, he was drawn into her world. She spoke of attending a concert at the National Palace and of meeting the president of Mexico. Tired, she returned to her hotel and went up on the roof to take one last look at the city. A thrill of recognition went through Ed. He realized it was the same hotel where he and his daughter had stayed more than a century later.

As Ed continued to read through the letters his interest increased, and he began to see that the ones written from Matamoros/Brownsville during a four-year period, 1848 to 1852, contained the most compelling information, the most interesting portraits of people, and the richest details of the lives of Helen and William W. Chapman, all sketched in vivid, readable prose.

The Chapmans, it seemed, knew or met everybody who came through Brownsville. Among the major's friends were Robert E. Lee, who was stationed in Texas at various times in the 1850s; Charles Stillman, the prime mover and shaker of early Brownsville; Harry Love, the surveyor and adventurer; Reverend Hiram Chamberlain and his family; and Richard King. Helen was a classic army wife: loyal, a good mother, interested in her husband's career, and plucky enough to endure the unhealthy climate and the dangerous frontier wildness that they confronted throughout their stay in remote Texas. Helen's letters (with a few of William's thrown in for good measure) gave a lively picture of a rousing era during a decisive period in American history.

In his spare time Ed began to transcribe the letters on his computer. This is no small task. Although Helen Chapman wrote an excellent hand on paper that possessed a high rag content, still the letters were handwritten, and transcribing pages and pages of somebody else's long-cold handwriting from another century is never easy. Anybody who has looked at the original letters, as I have, is at once grateful for the transcriptions. It took Coker three years to finish the job, producing a whopping 870 pages of unedited letter manuscript.

Coker decided the letters might be worth publishing, and he

approached the University of Texas Press to see if there was any interest. He was a little nervous about it because he had not been formally trained in history and was unsure of his qualifications. In the beginning he hoped that someone could be found who would assist him with the task.

His letter was routed to Don Carleton, director of the Barker Texas History Center (now the Center for American History) at The University of Texas at Austin. Carleton, an experienced and respected researcher and author in his own right, said he would look around for someone and a few months later recommended Janet G. Humphrey, who had published a similar project on a pioneer Texas suffragist. Ultimately, Coker chose to do the book himself, though Humphrey did provide valuable help with footnotes and editing issues. Coker had the writing bug, as he confided to Carleton: "While I am a lawyer by profession, I descend from two prior generations of college professors and somewhere lurking in my subconscious is the notion that everyone ought to publish at least one book before they perish."

By the fall of 1989 Coker had completed a draft that was ready to be sent out for "peer review"—a standard practice whereby academic presses seek the expertise of scholars in a particular field to evaluate a prospective manuscript. Peer review can kill a book, or make it better. Because of the importance of the peer review process, the standard protocol is to withhold the reviewer's identity from the author of the manuscript under consideration. Thus Don Carleton assured Coker of the value of the anonymous report enclosed with the letter: "I have masked the reader's identity, but he/she is a top notch historian specializing in the general topic of your book." Unbeknownst to Carleton or his top-notch historian, this peer evaluation was to have consequences far beyond those of the customary peer reviews one might encounter in several lifetimes of academic publishing.

The peer reviewer was quite enthusiastic about the project, stating that the Chapman letters "provide a marvelous view of nineteenth century Texas and army life." After citing some areas that needed work, the reviewer had one substantive recommendation: Coker's epilogue was too brief and skimpy. The book seemed to end too abruptly, with the departure of Helen Chapman from Brownsville to their new posting in Corpus Christi. What was the rest of the story? What had happened to the Chapmans? The reviewer offered a remedy: "Perhaps a brief 4–5 page epilogue, discussing the Chapmans' later experiences and the reasons for emphasizing only the Brownsville years, would be in order."

Coker somewhat reluctantly conceded the peer reviewer's point, partly, it seems, because of all the additional work that would be necessary. As he wrote to Carleton (March 14, 1990), "The fact of the matter is that I don't know [what happened to the Chapmans], just like I did not know about the Brownsville years until I read the letters." He also told Carleton that the book was "primarily about Helen Chapman. It wasn't really about William Chapman." But Coker, who conceded the need for a fuller picture of the Chapmans' post-Brownsville years, set to work.

The first epilogue, dated December 29, 1989, was indeed very brief, one and a third pages long, single-spaced, with another page and a third of footnotes. It contained a general overview of the Chapmans' life after leaving Texas, including a few sentences about a lawsuit brought against King Ranch by Helen Chapman: "In 1878, she [Helen Chapman] also filed suit against Richard King to recover William Chapman's one half interest in the King Ranch." Further references to the lawsuit occur near the end: "A year after her death [in 1881], her estate was victorious in the litigation to recover the one-half interest [sic] the King Ranch. However, Helen's children deemed it unwise to pursue their mother's victory against the powerful Richard King. They agreed to accept the offer made by Kleberg, Richard King's lawyer, to buy out the Chapman half interest in the King Ranch for $5,811.75 plus court costs."

In the footnotes Coker offered the first hints of a wedge between the official version, cited in Tom Lea, and Coker's developing view. Here is part of footnote 9: "It [Tom Lea's *The King Ranch*] sets forth testimony of Richard King and other business associates to the effect that Chapman had verbally released his interest in the partnership to King and that Chapman was unable to pay his share of the purchase indebtedness, namely ½ of $1575.00. (Considering the sums Chapman regularly sent to his mother-in-law as gifts, it is unlikely that Chapman would have been unable to honor his share.)" The note continues, "In an admission of startling brevity, the Lea text states, at page 34, 'The deed held up in court,' meaning, in legal parlance, that the testimony of Richard King and his witnesses was not believed nor accepted by the court as the truth."

The Chapman-King material underwent considerable expansion in Coker's subsequent revisions of the epilogue. The second version, dated September 14, 1990, was thirteen pages long, double-spaced, with new information on Helen Chapman's time in Corpus Christi (1852–1857). In fact, Coker considered putting together a second volume of her letters based on the Corpus Christi years. The last four pages of the second version offered many more details concerning the outcome of Helen Chapman's lawsuit against King Ranch, including the tantalizing fact that Robert J. Kleberg, the lawyer handling the case for Helen Chapman's heirs at the time of the cash settlement in 1883 (Helen Chapman having died in 1881), was also, *at the same time,* under a $5,000 annual retainer from Richard King.

When the same peer reviewer had an even more favorable response to the second version, Coker commented in a letter to Don Carleton (February 20, 1991): "I too am greatly encouraged by the Reader's report. He seems to have greatly matured in his insights during the last year and my respect for his professional judgment is increasing daily." The reviewer, however, never made any mention of the emerging Chapman-King narrative. Finally came the third and last version of the epilogue (dated June 24, 1991), fourteen pages, double-spaced, and the one that appears in the printed book. The most interesting new content is to be found in footnote 11, which documents information from two sources not previously cited: Helen Chapman's sworn testimony in Cause No. 1279 (*Helen B. Chapman v. Richard King,* District Court of Nueces County); and records of payments and expenditures noted in William Chapman's Record Book of Rancho Expenses, April 1 through August 4, 1856. Both of these pieces of research were undertaken as a follow-up to Coker's increasing interest in the Chapman-King lawsuit of 1879. His findings might have remained the stuff solely of antiquarian interest, an obscure, long-forgotten bit of litigation involving two former partners and a widow of one of them, except for the fact that Coker's main focus had begun to center on precisely one question: Had his long-departed ancestor and her heirs been the victims of fraud by a powerful, wealthy family, the founder Richard King and his son-in-law-to-be, Robert J. Kleberg?

Things had certainly worked out beautifully for Kleberg, who, the year after Richard King's death, married the old captain's favorite daughter, after having himself been selected by King as the man who would undertake the running of the rancho once King was gone.

How Coker came to construct a narrative of fraud is a story much misunderstood among those in Texas historical circles. According to a widely believed view, Coker visited the King Ranch archives with a double purpose—ostensibly to research facts for his book, but in actuality to ferret out documents that would buttress his case against Richard King and Robert J. Kleberg. Implicit in this scenario is a criticism of Coker's motives. The fact is, however, that Coker never visited the archives and never sought to. But he did have some professional contact with Bruce Cheeseman, first by letter and once in person. Although the two men followed quite different trails to King Ranch, eventually those trails crossed.

In wrapping up research for his book on the Chapman letters, Coker exchanged information with Cheeseman. A letter of January 9, 1990, for example, mentions several items of mutual interest. Coker wanted to know Cheeseman's opinion on the authorship of a letter signed "H Chamberlain"—was it Hiram or Henrietta? Coker also commented at some length on Pat Kelley's book *River of Lost Dreams*, which Cheeseman had sent him earlier. In the book Chapman came off rather badly, for some of his actions as quartermaster, and Coker took strong exception to Kelley's claims.

In October 1990, Coker and Cheeseman met for the first and only time. The occasion was "Women and Texas History: A Conference," a two-day event sponsored by the Barker Center at The University of Texas at Austin. Coker delivered a paper titled "Helen Chapman: The News from Brownsville," and Cheeseman delivered one entitled "La Patrona: The Moral Paternalism of Henrietta Chamberlain." (Paternalism was an interesting word to use in a conference on the role of women.) Although Coker attended Cheeseman's talk, Cheeseman did not hear Coker's the next day because he had already returned to Kingsville on the company plane. Two years later, when a book of the conference's proceedings appeared, *Women and Texas History: Selected Essays*, edited by Fane Downs and Nancy Baker Jones, neither Cheeseman or Coker was included. (Instead the book found space for, among other things, an essay attacking a professor of

English named Don Graham, for his presumed benightedness regarding the role of women in Texas writing. But that's not our concern here.)

Coker and Cheeseman disagree strongly about what happened when they met. According to Coker's account, he went up after Cheeseman's talk to introduce himself.

"Hello, my name is Ed Coker."

"We've been waiting for you to show up."

Looking back, Coker recalls, "That was the last thing I would have expected somebody to have said to me when I walked up. Before I had a chance to say anything more, he said, and I can't remember the exact words, but he began talking about are you aware that William Chapman was a crooked person. I mean, that was the gist of it." Then, according to Coker, Cheeseman summarized further details of the Chapman-King relationship and attacked both Chapmans. "I was a little taken aback by this onslaught," remembers Coker, who then said to Cheeseman: "Look, I didn't come up here to argue with you about things. I came up here to congratulate you on your talk."

Cheeseman today claims that Coker's version is "absolute nonsense." He says their exchange was brief and courteous. Coker agrees that "it ended up being a friendly conversation."

On October 9, 1990, shortly after the conference, Coker wrote Cheeseman a long, cordial letter ("It was a pleasure to meet you and to have a chance to listen to your fine talk . . .") in which he took the opportunity to suggest that Cheeseman's account of the arrival of Hiram Chamberlain's family in Texas was untrue. Following family legend as recorded faithfully in Tom Lea's book, Cheeseman had told how the Chamberlains had traveled overland from Galveston to Brownsville. But in Helen Chapman's letters there was a compelling contemporaneous account of the circumstances of their arrival by ship to Brazos Santiago at the mouth of the Rio Grande. Indeed, Cheeseman incorporated these findings in his biographical sketch, *My Dear Henrietta: Hiram Chamberlain's Letters to His Daughter, 1846–1866,* published the next year (1993). So while Cheeseman later strongly disagreed with some of Coker's conclusions, he certainly accepted some of the facts unearthed by Coker.

After detailing some other information about the Chamberlains and Richard King that he thought Cheeseman would find interesting, Coker reported that he was "intrigued" by Cheeseman's "mention of the King-Chapman dispute." He then inquired as to whether Cheeseman knew of any documents and depositions regarding King's statements against Chapman, and whether there were any depositions of Helen Chapman or letters from Ellery Brayton, who was Ed Coker's great-grandfather, Helen Chapman's son-in-law, and the attorney who handled the Chapman-King case in South Carolina.

Two months later, on December 10, Cheeseman sent Coker Christmas wishes (on Running W letterhead) along with copies of some letters "dealing with Mrs. Chapman's settlements with Captain King." He also made a remark about a letter from Mifflin Kenedy to Richard King that is sure to have rankled Coker: "It is clear from these that Kenedy & King thought Mrs. Chapman perhaps a nuisance, per Kenedy's remark in the 19 January 1867 letter to 'close up the whole business with that lady.'"

During the time when Coker was completing work on his book, he received some new documents from another family member, Anne Furman Dunn of Corpus Christi, a cousin of Coker's and a direct descendant of Willie Chapman, William and Helen Chapman's son who, following the Civil War, had returned to Texas to live. Coker had first learned of Anne Dunn on a research trip to Texas in 1989, when a reference librarian in Corpus Christi told him that there were some Chapmans living in the city. (There is also a Chapman Ranch, a huge agribusiness operation, southwest of Corpus Christi, but it is not the same family. In a nice irony, the Chapman Ranch, founded by P. A. Chapman, borders on part of King Ranch—Laureles Division— and in fact the land was sold to P. A. Chapman by Henrietta King late in her life.)

Anne Dunn is a descendant of a former mayor, McKeever Furman, who was always very proud that the Chapmans were his ancestors. Coker telephoned Anne Dunn, who mentioned that she had some Chapman materials in her possession. Nearly a year later they met at his mother's house in South Carolina. She brought with her three batches of material that Coker had not seen before: some of Helen Chapman's letters, some diary books kept by Helen Chapman in the 1860s, and, most important, William Chapman's account book. When Coker looked at the account book sometime later, he knew its contents were critical to his growing conviction that something funny, something nobody had yet explained, had happened in the Chapman-King relationship back there in the dark ages of the nineteenth century.

The News from Brownsville: Helen Chapman's Letters from the Texas Military Frontier, 1848–1852, edited by Caleb Coker, was published by the Texas State Historical Association in the summer of 1992. (Ed used his middle name for a pen name.) Like most first-time authors, Coker had optimistic ideas about the promotion and sale of his book. It is touching to look back at his attempts to promote his book. He thought the book was priced too high (most academic books are). "Even *Gone With the Wind* couldn't bear this kind of tariff and survive," he wrote George Ward, director of publications of the Texas State Historical Association. He worried about distribution, writing to Katherine Adams of the Barker Texas History Center at one point: "With no promotion, the finest book in the world will sit in boxes unbought and unread" (July 21, 1992). Yet Coker pushed on, hopeful, energetic, dedicated to the proposition that the world at large would be interested in *The News from Brownsville* if only the news could be gotten out. The world might not be interested, but King Ranch was going to be, in the fullness of time.

As with most first-time authors and nearly 100 percent of offerings by academic presses, for all of Coker's efforts, his book would fetch small sales. It was exactly the kind of scholarly volume that would be read by historians and almost nobody else. Typically, books of this nature, no matter how valuable or interesting they might be—and Coker's is extremely interesting—are reviewed in professional scholarly journals and placed on the shelves of libraries, where they await the random attention of academics or local history buffs. Such is the fate of hundreds of historical volumes published each year. They form the dense underthickets of popular history written later.

Coker at least had the consolation of receiving excellent reviews, both in the daily press and in academic quarterlies. The odd thing about the reviews, however, both those in the newspapers and those in the quarterlies, is that not a single reviewer mentioned the King subplot. Curiously, only one newspaper at the time, the *Corpus Christi Caller-Times,* took note of the explosive implications of the King-Chapman-Kleberg story contained in the epilogue and footnotes. Ron

George, a staff writer for the paper, interviewed both Coker and Cheeseman for an article on Coker's book on August 23, 1992, but the really damaging stuff appeared in an inset headlined "KING AND KLEBERG FOUGHT WIDOW FOR HER HALF SHARE OF KING RANCH." Both men were quoted. Said Coker, "Richard King made his ex-partner's widow litigate to the death rather than pay a penny. . . . And by modern standards, Kleberg should have been disbarred." This cost Coker nothing; his sympathies were clear. But what Cheeseman said would come back to haunt him—and King Ranch.

Cheeseman took strong exception to Coker's statement. Ron George reported that "Coker's version sets King Ranch archivist Bruce Cheeseman's teeth on edge, although he doesn't dispute the facts." Then, in a most damaging statement, Cheeseman observed, "Clearly, Kleberg was looking after the interest of his in-state client, versus the interests of his out-of-state client," meaning that Kleberg was simultaneously representing both Helen Chapman *and* Richard King—to the obvious disadvantage of the Chapman side. This statement would later be adduced as evidence. Cheeseman had erred rather badly, for it was easy to construe, legally, that he was speaking in an official capacity as King Ranch historian—a point that the Chapman lawyers would pound home in the legal case that would develop out of the Chapman-King affair.

In September 1992, Coker came down to Texas to promote the book. Earlier he had gotten in touch with Chapman descendants living in South and North Carolina and invited them to attend, and several did. He himself arrived a few days early and flew to Corpus Christi and rented a van. After making his presentation, he and some of the Chapman descendants drove in the van all the way down to Brownsville, where the events in the book had occurred. Along the way Ed's relatives asked questions of him about the events in the book. Coker and his family entourage even stopped by King Ranch on their way south but did not take the tour, as they arrived too late in the afternoon. Once on the border they visited Matamoros, where they saw the trees that Major Chapman had planted in one of the town's plazas, and they visited Brazos Santiago and Port Isabel, all sites of central importance in the story of William and Helen Chapman and of Texas and, indeed, of the United States itself.

They stayed at the Fort Brown Motel, the nicest hotel in Brownsville, situated near the grounds of Fort Brown, built during the Mexican War, vestiges of whose later buildings can still be seen on the nearby campus of The University of Texas at Brownsville (formerly Texas Southmost). During the evening of dining and conviviality, two members of the entourage, Marion Crane and her brother Ben Porter, both from the Carolinas, asked Ed about the Chapman connection with King Ranch. The three of them exchanged their thoughts, and Marion and Ben asked Ed whether he could find someone to represent them to see if a lawsuit to recover an interest in King Ranch would be feasible. And from that trip, that conversation, emerged the beginning of a concerted plan to bring the question of the Chapman-King relationship into the light of modern legal adjudication. They worked out an agreement among most family members, but not all. There was one branch that was not interested.

The next year, Coker hinted at his intentions in a letter to David Laughlin, a librarian at Texas A&I University (now Texas A&M University-Kingsville). Laughlin, who was writing a biographical essay on Robert J. Kleberg, requested from Coker copies of Kleberg's letters mentioned in *The News from Brownsville*. Coker replied in somewhat prickly fashion. He stated that he did not "wish to contribute to another public relations article praising the Kings and Klebergs." He continued, "As far as I am concerned those alive today are the descendants of men who made a mockery of the legal system in Texas." Moreover, he stated that Kleberg's letters were at considerable variance with the "paid-for pages" of the Tom Lea biography, and concluded, "if I have anything to do with it, those facts will be presented in a forum, of my choosing, that will allow the people of Texas to judge for themselves where the truth lies."

Those ringing final words about "a forum, of my choosing" mark an upsurge in Coker's confidence about where, in his opinion, the truth lay. What had started out as a factual chase was about to turn into a legal one. Coker's letter ended with a remark that would bother Bruce Cheeseman a good deal when the contents of the letter were brought to his attention by David Laughlin. Here is Coker's remark: "If the present Klebergs or their archival representatives have represented to you that there is a dearth of journals or personal letters from Robert Kleberg, my opinion is that they probably want to avoid further inquiry."

In a long letter to Coker dated May 4, 1993, Cheeseman sought to explain and rebut the charges Coker had made in the letter to Laughlin. Regarding Coker's comment about the "archival representatives" wanting to "avoid further inquiry," Cheeseman declared, "Nothing can be further from the truth." Then Cheeseman set out to explain his twin roles as archivist/historian: "As an archivist, my job is to preserve the documentary heritage and the cultural resources of King Ranch. To build if you will a marvelous repository of the past, carefully assembled and preserved, made available to the inquiring minds of the future. As an historian, inseparable from an archivist's duties in my opinion, my job is to interpret and attempt to understand the events of the past."

Cheeseman went on to point out "some factual errors" that Coker had made in his letter and in *The News from Brownsville*. These dealt with the price Lea had been paid to write his book ($100,000 instead of $300,000), the location of King Ranch Headquarters (on the *De La Garza Santa Gertrudis* grant, not the *Rincón de Santa Gertrudis* grant), and whether or not Lea had vilified Mrs. Chapman (Cheeseman thought not). The letter did contain two interesting admissions: "Some times King won, some times he lost. This time he lost: Mrs. Chapman had a clear interest in the *Rincón de Santa Gertrudis grant*" and, equally damaging: "It very well may be true that Robert Kleberg sold out the Chapman interests by accepting a cash settlement in lieu of 7,750 acres." Here, clearly, Cheeseman's role as historian, a searcher for the truth, put him in conflict with his role as King Ranch, Inc. historian—that is, a corporate spokesman.

The rest of Cheeseman's letter was a disquisition on the historical work that needed to be done on King and his many land transactions and of the "need for much more disciplined archival research to cut through . . . hearsay." He ended his letter with some cautionary advice: "I think that all of us can greatly benefit from a free expression of ideas. Criticism has its place, but it should be expressed in a constructive and civil manner. To suggest as you did that I would want to 'avoid further inquiry' or contribute little but 'public relations' articles is not a useful exercise." But by then the historical cat was out of the bag; it was too late. There was nothing that Bruce Cheeseman could say or do to stop whatever was coming from coming. Only he didn't know that; he still thought they were talking about history, not about something that would engulf the archives, King Ranch, Inc., and Bruce Cheeseman.

It seems clear that both Coker and Cheeseman were on the trail of the same quarry: historical truth. Only they operated from different assumptions. Coker sided with the Chapmans, naturally, and perhaps equally naturally, Cheeseman sided with Richard King. But the commitment to truth led Cheeseman into conflict with the interests of King Ranch, Inc. Cheeseman, it appears from his deposition (May 16, 1996), did not fully appreciate the implications of his position as archivist and historian of King Ranch. When he spoke publicly, he was, in a sense, speaking for King Ranch, and so he should have been careful. King Ranch, Inc. didn't hire him to speak against the interests of the ranch. His outspokenness on the Chapman/King matter would cost him a great deal. Yet it must be understood that he was never on the Chapmans' side. He considered the Chapmans carpetbaggers—an interesting viewpoint for somebody living in Texas who grew up in New Jersey. Virtually everybody in early Texas was a carpetbagger anyway. Charles Stillman, Mifflin Kenedy, and Richard King all came from the East Coast to make their fortunes in South Texas.

In the meantime, Coker was looking for "someone to represent the family to bring a possible lawsuit." If no law firm could be found, he has said since, then "I would have probably published it in book form." He approached a number of firms, but there were no takers. Attorneys thought the case was too old. Everything had happened so long ago. And there was the defendant, King Ranch, Inc., one of the most famous and powerful establishments in the state. King Ranch, Inc. could put together a stable of top-flight attorneys in a heartbeat. The case appeared unwinnable.

Then Coker visited the Edwards Law Firm in downtown Corpus Christi, an area so empty, it seems, that on most days one could fire a rifle down the main thoroughfare and not hit a soul. It costs $1 to park all day in downtown Corpus Christi. The wind blows almost constantly, and such life as there is enclosed inside buildings like the Frost Bank Plaza, where the Edwards Law Firm occupies two floors. The carpets are thick, the furniture is tasteful and heavy; huge glass windows offer a panoramic view of the city on one side, the waters of the Gulf on the other; the paintings on the walls depict scenes of local significance; everything about the Edwards Law Firm is imposing, impressive. Coker talked first to William (Bill) Edwards, a senior part-ner, an engaging, craggy, white-haired attorney with a law degree from the University of Virginia. After considering a five-page narrative by Coker, Edwards and his associates agreed to take the case. They did so on the basis of three points of law: (1) admission against interest, (2) extrinsic fraud, and (3) fiduciary relationship. The Edwards team felt that the Chapman case possessed intriguing, far-reaching implica-tions regarding land rights in South Texas. They also thought they could win the case.

In the fall of 1995, Ed Coker was in Austin again. He dropped by the Barker Center, to which, three years earlier, he had donated the original Chapman letters, where they reside today in the Edward Coker Collection. They netted a value estimate at $30,000 for tax deductions, which were divvied up among various signers of the agreement made between Ed and the extended members of his family. The tax break, plus that $5,000 in royalty earnings for Ed Coker, rep-resents to date the sum of financial benefits from the project.

At the Barker Center he saw his old acquaintances who had helped in the early days of the project, Don Carleton, director of the center, and Kate Adams, assistant director. He said jauntily upon greeting them, "Guess what?" The *what* was the lawsuit.

Meanwhile, back at the ranch, Bruce Cheeseman's career as King Ranch archivist was about to go into a tailspin. Once the suit was launched, King Ranch, Inc. declared that the job description would from now on be purely one of "records manager." Cheeseman balked at giving up his role as historian, and eventually he resigned, in July 1996, with a generous severance package. Cheeseman was unhappy about developments, though he stayed on in a consultancy role until December 1997. His job was to research Major Chapman's life, to find evidence against the major that might be useful to King Ranch lawyers. Lisa Neely (M.A., University of Texas A&M-Kingsville), whom Cheeseman had hired as his archival assistant, took over as the new King Ranch archivist.

Admission to the archives by historians and researchers was no longer encouraged. In Cheeseman's view, Coker's action had "closed up one of the most valuable archival resources in the state." Cheese-man's friend Tom Kreneck agrees, calling the closing of the archives a "shame." Every Texas historian says the same thing. And some of them are not sympathetic at all with Coker's lawsuit. The arguments against Coker are partly political: (1) The Coker lawsuit is not about Hispanic dispossession. (2) It's a case of absentee landlordism. (3) We don't know what use Chapman would have made of the land. (4) We can't know, that long ago, what really happened. Numbers three and four seem particularly odd for historians to voice, but more than one has, in my presence. Thus the major and his widow find little sympathy in the claims now being lodged on their behalf. They were carpetbaggers, absentee landlords, and they were white. Ed Coker's pursuit of justice does not persuade some historians to grant him a hearing, but the matter is not in the hands of historians now; it is in the hands of the court.

After leaving King Ranch, Cheeseman took a job as director of the Museum of the Gulf in Port Arthur, on the Texas coast near the Louisiana border. Appointed in November 1999, he left that position in July 2000 and moved to Corpus Christi, where he lives today. The bio tag line on a new book edited by Cheeseman (*Maria von Blücher's Corpus Christi: Letters from the South Texas Frontier, 1849–1879*), published in February 2001 by Texas A&M University Press, lists his current job as "independent consultant in history, archives, and cultural resources" and cites his "lengthy tenure as archivist and historial for King Ranch, a national landmark in South Texas."

When I met with him at the Corpus Christi Public Library in November 2001, he spoke of the past with a kind of smoldering anger. He believes that Coker's suit is an instance of "greenmail," a term that was new to me. "Greenmail," which obviously derives from blackmail, is a word invented by Texas entrepreneur T. Boone Pickens, Cheeseman told me, for nuisance suits, lawsuits aimed at the wealthy with the hope that the plaintiffs will be simply paid off so the defendants can avoid the greater costs of going to court.

Although Cheeseman no longer holds an institutional archivist position, he retains a highly informed knowledge of King Ranch history. After all, he has probed the inner reaches of the archives; he has seen documents that the rest of us probably never will. We talked at some length about what is in them. He scoffs at the idea of a "smoking gun" with regard to the volatile period of the 1870s, when border wars raged, land grabs flourished, and the Chapman case surfaced. He insists that the only valid study is one based on documents, but herein resides a quandary, for the researcher today is very likely to be denied access to the archives. Coker, of course, put together his case without visiting the archives—though with some help from Cheeseman. Lisa Neely, the current director, is essentially a gatekeeper. When I asked, in late 2001, for a copy of a quite innocuous document (the letter that Mifflin Kenedy wrote inviting Richard King to come to Texas), Neely replied, "Unfortunately, because of pending litigation, all of our historical documents are unavailable for research" (January 4, 2002).

Understandably, Cheeseman is frustrated by what has happened. After becoming animated telling me about some vital King Ranch information saved on his computer's hard drive, he stated that he can't get at it because the hard drive is in storage in Port Arthur and at present he is not able to reclaim it. Cheeseman's separation from King Ranch has clearly had long-term effects on his life.

He recalls with excitement the response of King Ranch officials who refused to try to settle with Coker before the lawsuit went any further and how one woman stood up in the meeting and declared, "Not a goddamn cent." He remains bitter about Coker, saying Coker "played me like a fiddle." He charges that Chapman was "politically ambitious" (as though that were a crime). He says that Tio Kleberg, whom he admires, and Tom Kreneck, his archivist/historian friend, "helped save my life." Cheeseman is trying to move forward, putting King Ranch behind him.

In March 2002, at the annual meeting of the Texas State Historical Association, held in Corpus Christi, Cheeseman attended a book signing for his von Blücher book, perhaps signaling his reemergence among the community of historians and scholars.

In 1996 Bruce Cheeseman and Edward Coker were deposed and gave extensive testimony, under oath. Tom Lea was also deposed.

At eighty-eight ("I am precisely eighty-eight," he replied to the first question put to him), Tom Lea was one of the grand old men of Texas letters, his life filled with success both as a painter and an author. His Western canvases were justly famous, and his World War II portraits of men in combat, drawn mainly for *Life* magazine, were part of the familiar iconography of that era. *Two-Thousand-Yard Stare,* for example, was endlessly reproduced. His best novel, *The Wonderful Country,* was made into a solid Western starring Robert Mitchum,

Tom Lea in Wyoming, 1958, the
year after publication of *The
King Ranch*.

with Lea himself appearing in one scene. Certainly a man of such
accomplishments never expected to have to explain and defend himself, under oath, on matters of high seriousness regarding a book he
had written some forty years earlier, involving the case of a minor
background figure whose name Lea himself admitted he no longer
remembered, versus mighty King Ranch, about which Lea had written
his best-known book.

Yet here he was at the Camino Real Hotel in his hometown of El
Paso, on April 10, 1996, facing a respectful but thorough questioning
(one hour, forty-two minutes on videotape) regarding the circumstances of the research and writing of *The King Ranch*.

Asked to explain how he came to write *The King Ranch*, Lea stated
that he had been approached, in El Paso, by a representative from
King Ranch, Inc., a Mr. Robert C. Wells, in 1950. Lea was chosen
partly on the basis of a series of paintings he had made of beef cattle—
works that the King Ranch corporate family admired a great deal.

Lea undertook the assignment "to write a monograph, not extensive, but it was to be an accompaniment to the 100th anniversary of
the founding." Asked to define a monograph, Lea said, correctly, that

it is a brief scholarly work. Lea also described the project as designed to produce "a kind of souvenir book" for seminar participants and friends of King Ranch around the world. In one year's time he was to deliver the manuscript. The task quickly mushroomed into a much more ambitious work, and Lea, caught up in the drama of the story and working only half-time on it, because he had to make a living, took five years to complete the book. He was paid by King Ranch, Inc., for the first year only. Other participants in the making of *The King Ranch* were Holland McCombs; Carl Hertzog, a well-known printer of fine books and lifelong friend of Lea's who lived in El Paso; and Frances Fugate, an English professor at West Texas State University (now The University of Texas at El Paso), who was responsible for the content and form of the footnotes. This was the team that made *The King Ranch*.

At the outset Lea wanted to get a sense of the landscape and topography of King Ranch by approaching from the same direction Captain Richard King had, a century earlier. To that end, Lea was flown over Brazos Santiago, on the coast where Richard King stepped ashore for the first time in 1847. By means of a map, Lea could get an aerial, bird's-eye view of the lay of the river and the land. Then he rented a boat and traveled upriver to Rio Grande City. From Brownsville he came overland the 130-odd miles northward to the headquarters of King Ranch, to take in, as it were, the immensity of the terrain, approximating, in a new century, with new means of locomotion, the original experience. Lea remembered how "Mr. Kleberg was rather astonished and pleased and we did all that." Lea said that Kleberg told him, "I'm placing it in your hands; you do it your way."

McCombs, the researcher, "went to King Ranch and was given access to everything," said Lea, who worked on the book at his home in El Paso, using McCombs's notes and sources. The material was massive: McCombs compiled 1,400 single-spaced typed pages on Captain King alone. Every two months or so, Lea would visit the ranch to soak up atmosphere. He was trying to write, he said, "a true account but I wanted it to have some literary value." Lea never had any reason to question McCombs's research, but Frances Fugate, the footnoter, the "fact checker," clashed with McCombs on occasion. In 1996 Lea did not know what had happened to McCombs's notes.

(Bruce Cheeseman says they are in the archives.) By then McCombs was dead; so was Fugate.

Lea vigorously denied any intervention by King Ranch and said if anybody had tried to interfere or look at any of his writing, he'd have said, "Here, take the damn stuff, I'm through."

Lea, who always considered himself an artist whether working on canvas or in words, said he was "trying to make each page of this book account for something in good prose." He always had a "literary aim," he said, which led him to rewrite some pages a dozen times.

Lea cared so much about the writing that he never worried about his rights as an author. When Hertzog copyrighted it for King Ranch, Lea felt, "It was their child; they were paying for it."

When Bob Kleberg read the first volume, he liked it so much that he thought the book should be published for a general audience, not just a select few as originally intended, and Lea suggested his trade publisher, Little, Brown. There was no editorial control at all on that end, and the book was published, in two volumes, in 1957.

When attorney Michael Terry turned to the central question, the relationship between the Chapmans and the Kings, Lea said, "I can't remember anything I wrote about the Chapmans. It has been forty years," he said. "I haven't reread the book in many years," he added. When pressed about the date when Robert J. Kleberg met his future wife, Alice King, Lea said he couldn't recall. Told that in his book he stated 1881 as the year in question, Lea observed, "I wouldn't have written it unless I believed it to be true, a fact." On a follow-up question about King and Chapman's relationship, Lea stated that he had "no recollection whatsoever and that's under oath." He remembered Legs Lewis, he said, grinning, "a kind of nifty name for a novelist," but not Chapman.

Terry asked Lea point-blank if McCombs had ever informed him about Kleberg's representing Chapman. Lea replied, "No." Another line of questioning pursued by attorney Terry had to do with the organization of the material on Chapman in the book. Details about Chapman's activities in 1856 were presented in two places over two hundred pages apart. Lea said he didn't know why he had organized the material that way.

At the end of his testimony, Lea was asked a couple of questions by King Ranch, Inc. attorney Jess Hall Jr. One had to do with an accidental meeting between Lea and Jack Hunt, CEO of King Ranch, Inc., at the governor's mansion in Austin during George W. Bush's first term. The Bushes were close friends of Tom Lea. (Laura Bush, a long-time family friend of the Leas, has declared *The King Ranch* her "favorite book.") At that meeting, Lea, who had been telephoned by Hunt regarding a possible subpoena to testify in the court proceedings, asked Hunt whether the statute of limitations was still in effect a hundred years later. According to Lea, Hunt reported that "it remained to be proved."

In conclusion, Hall asked Lea the following: "You stated earlier that you believed the facts as you wrote them in *The King Ranch* to be true. My question is, can you sit here today under oath and testify that they are true?"

Lea replied, "No, I can't. There's no way of proving that they're true. To the best of my knowledge and belief when I wrote them I believed them to be true or I wouldn't have put them down in the book. But I couldn't say, because at this late date they're not provable."

Tom Lea's heartfelt answer suggests the instability of "history." The law, by training its lens upon narrative history, is capable of causing history to be rewritten, in alignment with new facts or with a reinterpretation of agreed-upon facts. The law is a kind of literary criticism that goes far beyond the classroom into the guts and motives of how history gets made—and shaped by its chroniclers. Tom Lea's book, like its subject, would be held to intense new scrutiny.

Edward Coker and his lawyers loved Tom Lea for his sweetness, his courtesy, his old-fashioned gallantry and manners.

Tom Lea died on January 29, 2001, aged ninety-four, full of honors. A little over a week earlier, President George W. Bush had quoted words written by Tom Lea in his inaugural address.

The original drawings for the book hang in the entry hall of the Main House at King Ranch.

CHAPTER 14

Chapman v. King Ranch, Inc.

The legal process ground slowly; it was three years before a decision was handed down by the Twenty-eighth District Court. On January 5 and January 13, 1998, the trial court released a summary judgment against the Chapman plaintiffs and in favor of King Ranch, Inc.

Though obviously disappointed, Ed Coker did not waste time. He still thought he had a very strong case and intended to appeal. King Ranch had won the first round, but it wasn't over yet, not by a long shot. In late January Coker flew to Corpus Christi to confer with the Edwards Law Firm, which had taken the case, but they did not want to handle the appeal. He also met with family members, and William W. Chapman III recommended that the two of them consult with Chapman's personal attorney, Mike O'Brien. It was O'Brien who recommended Russell McMains as a "very well-respected appellate attorney." Coker, who is a member of the bar in three states—Florida, South Carolina, and Texas—entered the meeting with McMains with his eyes open. "Because Corpus Christi is a relatively small city with a close-knit bar membership," Coker said, "I wanted to make sure that there was no conflict of interest." He gave McMains a list of names of all the defendants in the Chapman case and asked him if "he had a potential conflict of interest." McMains said no, and the meeting proceeded. According to Coker, he talked to McMains for about an hour and a half—though they disagree on how long they talked and on just about everything else. In a deposition (August 30, 2001) Coker characterized the meeting this way: "Mr. McMains was cordial and responsive to my questions, and we had a wide-ranging conversation that addressed both tactical and procedural aspects of the appeal and further proceedings in the case in the event of remand for trial." At the end they discussed fees. McMains did not do such work on a contingency basis, he said, and explained that in such cases he expected to receive around $100,000 for his services. Coker said he would have to think about this in view of the fact that there were other parties to the suit that he would have to confer with. Coker said he would get back in touch with McMains, but he never did. Instead he met with another Corpus Christi attorney, Craig Smith, who agreed to handle the appeal.

Again the process moved slowly, but this time things went Coker's way. On January 11, 2001, the Court of Appeals of Texas, Thirteenth District, Corpus Christi, Texas, rendered a two-to-one decision in favor of proceeding to a trial by jury in the matter of *Chapman v. King Ranch.* Coker was elated. As he told the San Antonio *Express-News* (January 18, 2001), "We want recognition of the Chapman role in the development of South Texas and our rightful share of the property interest." King Ranch, Inc., of course, does not see it that way. King Ranch, Inc. denies any wrongdoing any time, anywhere.

The heart of Coker's case resides in the legal concept of "extrinsic fraud," one that denied a party the opportunity to fully litigate at trial all the rights or defenses that the party was entitled to assert. In the modern case, 1995 to 2001, the appellants sought to prove that Richard King committed extrinsic fraud by using Robert Kleberg to subvert the rights of Helen Chapman and her grandchildren. The decision handed down by the Court of Appeals was by a vote of two to one. Justice Federico G. Hinojosa wrote the favorable ruling, with Melchor Chavez concurring. They based the judgment on two bodies of evidence.

Under the heading "Kleberg's Representation" three evidentiary items were listed.

(1) Bruce Cheeseman's statement in the Corpus Christi *Caller:* "Clearly, Kleberg was looking after the interest of his in-state client, versus the interests of his out-of-state client." The judges quoted the entire exchange in Cheeseman's deposition regarding the quotation in the *Caller.*

(2) Tom Lea's book *The King Ranch,* commissioned by the King Ranch, which contains a "recreation of a conversation between Robert Kleberg and Richard King in 1881 in which King retained Kleberg's legal services for $5000 a year. In 1881, Kleberg was also representing Helen Chapman against King."

(3) A letter of July 24, 1881, written by Robert J. Kleberg to his parents: ". . . on the way [King] asked us to attend to his legal business for him." (Was the "on the way" a reference to the gala, much-celebrated train ride from Corpus Christi to Laredo that Kleberg took part in?) In 1881 Kleberg was a partner in the law firm of Stayton, Lackey & Kleberg, which represented the interests of Helen Chapman. This letter appears to confirm the accuracy of Tom Lea's dating of the beginning of the King /Kleberg association as 1881. Here the judges also noted: "The record also contains evidence that Kleberg represented King in March 1882 in the case of *Sobrinos v. Chamberlain.*"

Under the heading "Richard King's Fraud" seven items were cited:

(1) William Chapman's leather-bound account book with the following entries for 1856:

> Land purchased of Capt. King $100.00
>
> Acknowledgment & recording of deed $4.00
>
> ½ of Lewis interest in Santa Gertrudis $787.50

This notebook, which was not introduced in Cause No. 1279, definitely calls into question King's claim that Chapman did not pay for his half of the Lewis deed.

(2) King's inability to produce the alleged letter written by William Chapman giving up his right to land from the Lewis deed.

(3) King's inability to produce the Lewis deed requested by Helen Chapman. However, five years later, one of the attorneys for Richard King in Cause No. 1279, F. E. MacManus, sent a copy of the original deed to King's widow from "H. P. Bee administrator of Gideon K. Lewis, of the one-half of 3½ leagues to Richard King, conveyed by him to said heirs, and dated 1st day of August,

1856." The Lewis deed existed, and King's lawyer had a copy of it at the time that King denied knowing of its whereabouts. The judges concluded: "King's alleged inability to produce the Lewis deed in 1881 when requested by Helen Chapman is highly questionable when his own attorney was in possession of the deed five years later when it was returned to King's widow." This deed was not filed until 1904, nineteen years after Captain King's death. Caesar Kleberg, Robert J. Kleberg's cousin, filed it in his capacity as secretary of the newly created Kleberg Town and Improvement Company.

(4) The filing of the Lewis deed in 1904. The judges felt that if King had produced the deed at the 1879 trial, it would have "had the potential of bearing more weight."

(5) A highly technical finding that John Rankin, testamentary executor of Helen Chapman's will, failed to apply to "the probate court for permission to settle Cause No. 1279."

(6) Kleberg's letter of April 23, 1883, to Ellery Brayton, the long-distance executor of Helen Chapman's will who lived in South Carolina. Kleberg wrote:

> . . . that the suit of Helen B. Chapman vs. Richard King was disposed of at the last term of our district court which has just closed. John Rankin, Executor was made party plaintiff in the suit and judgment was rendered by consent of parties as follows, it was considered by the court that half of the land sued for which would be one half of 3½ leagues could be recovered by the plaintiff which would be 3874½ acres—also a tract of 240 acres and in consideration of a money judgment for $5811.75 against the Defendant Richard King—the title was vested to him to the 3874½ acres, and the title to the 240 acres was recovered in favor of the Estate of Helen B. Chapman thus giving Judgment in favor of the Estate for $5811.75. . . .

Thus the court in 1883 did not recognize Chapman's one-half interest as set forth in the Lewis deed.

(7) A letter of November 3, 1880, from Stephen Powers of the law firm of Powers & Wells. (Powers, longtime friend and attorney of

Richard King's, was the leading expert on land titles in South Texas.) In the letter, Powers told King, "I don't see how you are to get over Mrs. Chapman's title to the Santa Gertrudis interest. Hewlett (?) being dead, and on one _____ to any relinquishment of title by Chapman in his lifetime. It is my advice under these circumstances, to compromise if you can."

The conclusion reached by Hinojosa and Chavez stated: "The foregoing evidence reasonably puts into question Richard King's claim to the entirety of the land in the Lewis deed, Robert Kleberg's alleged inability to prove Helen Chapman's land title, and Kleberg's loyalty to his clients. Therefore, we conclude appellants have produced more than a scintilla of probative evidence to raise a genuine issue of material fact of extrinsic fraud."

In a dissenting opinion, Judge J. Bonner Dorsey concentrated on technicalities, emphasizing the "narrow" grounds upon which a petitioner could "obtain a bill of review." He summed up his view of the case in this manner: "The settlement of any lawsuit involves many difficult considerations and decisions, especially given the period in which this litigation occurred. At the time of the consent judgment both William and Helen Chapman were dead, as were other alleged witnesses. The Chapman heirs were in South Carolina and were investigating via long distance. The judgment gave the Chapman estate certain lands that King had apparently had the use of for years, and approved a sale of the land to King. The Chapmans did not take nothing by their 1879 lawsuit."

Now all Coker had to do was wait for a decision from the Supreme Court of Texas, which he was very hopeful would set a court date for a jury trial. Then, in August 2001, he saw something that made him furious. He saw the name of Russell McMains listed as one of the attorneys for King Ranch, Inc. Coker knew McMains from their meeting three years earlier. When Coker spotted McMains's name on the team of King Ranch attorneys, he had a terrible feeling of déjà vu, of history replaying itself in a new version of the Kleberg-King arrangement. Coker felt blindsided. He had revealed facts and strategy to a lawyer under the rules of client confidentiality, and now the lawyer had joined the opposing side.

The Edwards Law Firm jumped back into the fray, immediately

filing a claim to have all, *all,* of the King Ranch legal team dismissed from the case. *All* meant counsel for seven groups of parties and 120 defendants. *All* meant twenty-three attorneys who represented the defendants. For King Ranch attorneys, the Chapman case is like a South Texas Lawyer Relief Fund. The more hours in court, the merrier; this case is attorney-fee heaven.

In late November 2001, hearings were held in Corpus Christi. I attended one day of the hearings, on November 30, and for the first time met Ed Coker. He was there with his wife, Zana (her father was a big Zane Grey fan). In the gallery where observers sat, there were ten or twelve people on Coker's side, descendants of the Chapmans, most of them from Corpus Christi or nearby. William W. Chapman III, in whose name the suit is filed, is the great-great-grandson of Major Chapman. Retired from a career in electrical engineering, he continues to work on a freelance basis with various engineering companies.

Coker was immediately likable. I had thought he would be, but a voice on the telephone does not always match the person you later meet. Before entering the Nueces County Court House, I had seen a large, Santa Clause–like man, obviously a lawyer, smoking a big stogie, seemingly pleased with himself, standing, waiting to go in the building. I wondered if the man was Coker, but thought not. It wasn't; it was Russell McMains.

Coker's manner is that of a southern gentleman, courtly, thoughtful, deliberative, in short, the demeanor of an old-school lawyer. Someone once described him to me as a southern gentleman with steel beneath his velvet gloves. Perhaps so.

The judge was an attractive young Hispanic woman named Nanette Hasette, a forty-two-year-old native of Corpus Christi elected to the court in 1996 and easily reelected in 2000. Texas judges are elected by popular vote, and the pay is pretty good; Judge Hasette earns $111,000 a year. During the hearing, which stretched from about 10:30 A.M. to 5:30 P.M., she smiled a great deal and overall gave the impression of someone having her nails done. At a later continuation of the hearings, she disclosed that the sound system in the courtroom that day—a new courtroom, by the way—was so bad that she had had trouble hearing what the lawyers were saying. So she had just smiled her way through it all while the lawyers did their damnedest.

A. J. "Tony" Canales headed up the talking for King Ranch.

Canales was fresh from his big victory the previous month in the case of *Carmen de Llano et al. v. the John G. Kenedy Jr. Charitable Trust.* This was another trial involving another famous South Texas ranching family, descendants of Mifflin Kenedy. When Kenedy died in 1895, he left no will. His vast ranchland holdings at La Parra, in Kenedy County, south of King Ranch, were divided equally among four heirs, three natural ones and an adopted Mexican daughter, Carmen Morell Kenedy. When Kenedy's only surviving son, John G. Kenedy Sr., died in 1931, it was learned that Carmen Kenedy's part of the estate was under his control. No one knew why this was so. Carmen Kenedy's descendants brought a suit that ended in a mistrial in 1996, but on October 24, 2001, a seventeen-day trial held in Edinburg, Texas, ended with a judgment in favor of the trust. The winning side was able to prove that John G. Kenedy had bought Carmen Kenedy's portion of the trust and that she had spent her money pursuing a lavish lifestyle in Corpus Christi. An exuberant Tony Canales told the press: "To anyone who loves this part of the country, to anyone who loves history, this is a great case. It is a fascinating trial, because people whose names we only know from history books are actually testifying here through their old letters and words." The same applies in spades to *Chapman v. King Ranch, Inc.*

McMains testified briefly under the friendly questioning of Canales. McMains denied Coker's claims of substantive communication in their only meeting on January 22, 1998. He also stated that when King Ranch contacted him in May 2001, he mentioned, in a telephone conversation, that "there had been somebody that had come to see me, but he hadn't told me anything. He wasn't there very long, and I never heard from him again." (Coker says the meeting at McMains's office lasted an hour and a half.) McMains said that the King Ranch lawyer did not see a problem. On May 10, McMains joined the King Ranch team.

McMains stated in an earlier deposition that he had met subsequently on two occasions with King Ranch lawyers to discuss the Chapman/King Ranch case. The first meeting, on May 29, 2001, "concerned the arguments made in the Corpus Christi Court of Appeals and the manner in which the King Ranch arguments should be presented in the Supreme Court of Texas." The second meeting, on July 10, 2001, was to "discuss a draft of the petition for review."

The lawyers dueled all day that Friday when the judge couldn't hear because of the bad acoustics. Canales's style was puppy-dog friendly, Edwards's more biting and ironic. They argued back and forth on two main points: whether Coker and McMains had discussed substantive issues concerning the facts and theory of the case and whether McMains had conveyed any of the things he heard that day from Coker to the King Ranch lawyers three years later. The hearing came to an end late, around 5:30. All the lawyers wanted to go home. It would resume on Monday.

The next day, Saturday, over breakfast, I talked to Ed and Zana at some length, not an interview, just talking. I kept thinking he reminded me of someone, and then it came to me. Ed bears a passing resemblance to a younger Dominick Dunne, both physically and in his style of gregarious, engaging discourse.

The hearing resumed on Monday, December 2, but I had to return to Austin. Then the hearing was set again, for December 13. This time I was unable to attend (thanks in part to the lingering effects of the episode of the intestinal parasite that had laid me low in early November). Later, Coker filled me in on what had happened. There was more wrangling over the meeting that had taken place between McMains and Coker back in 1998, and McMains was cross-examined at length, very vigorously, and in Coker's opinion very effectively, by Bill Edwards. Coker himself testified *in camera* because much at issue was that he should not have to reveal in open court the contents of his conversation with McMains, contents that he and his lawyers maintained were substantive and crucial to the strategy and theory of their case.

Judge Hasette found against Chapman and in favor of King Ranch, Inc. The judge held that Coker did not convey any confidential information to McMains and that the phalanx of King Ranch lawyers had not received any confidential information from McMains in their subsequent meetings. Coker was neither surprised nor downcast at this ruling. He had expected it. As had I. To me, the judge lacked sufficient gravitas.

But Coker felt that no matter what the ruling, this was a sideshow to the real case, which was still awaiting a ruling by the Supreme Court of Texas. The Supreme Court was originally supposed to hand down its finding on December 20, 2001, as to whether the case would go to trial, but now, obviously, that decision would have to be delayed.

Coker also felt that a lot of good testimony had been made *in camera* and knew that the Supreme Court would have all of that material at its disposal in its deliberations. As the year 2001 ended, he remained as hopeful as ever.

Meanwhile, over at the Henrietta Memorial Center, archivist Lisa Neely and others were busy putting together a script for a new video to celebrate King Ranch's sesquicentennial, looming in 2003. It is doubtful that it will include the story of Major Chapman and Helen Chapman, so long elided from the imperial narrative.

Bibliography

Books

[Brackets indicate original date of publication.]

Allen, John Houghton. *Southwest*. Albuquerque: University of New Mexico Press, 1977 [1952].

Alonzo, Armando C. *Tejano Legacy: Rancheros and Settlers in South Texas, 1934–1900*. Albuquerque: University of New Mexico Press, 1998.

Ambrose, Stephen E. *Undaunted Courage: Meriwether Lewis, Thomas Jefferson, and the Opening of the American West*. New York: Touchstone, 1997 [1996].

Anders, Evan. *Boss Rule in South Texas: The Progressive Era*. Austin: University of Texas Press, 1982.

Atherton, Lewis. *The Cattle Kings*. Lincoln: University of Nebraska Press, 1972 [1961].

Bainbridge, John. *The Super-Americans*. New York: Holt, Rinehart and Winston, 1961.

Best, Hugh. *Debrett's Texas Peerage*. New York: Coward-McCann, 1983.

Briscoe, Eugenia Reynolds. "A Narrative History of Corpus Christi, Texas—1959–1875." Ph.D. diss., University of Denver, 1972.

Brook, Stephen. *Honkytonk Gelato: Travels Through Texas*. New York: Atheneum, 1985.

Brown, John. *Indian Wars and Pioneers of Texas*. Austin: State House Press, 1988 [1986].

Buker, George E. *Swamp Sailors: Riverine Warfare in the Everglades 1835–1842*. Gainesville: University Presses of Florida, 1975.

Campbell, Randolph B., ed. *Texas Voices: Documents from Texas History*. New York: Worth Publishers, 1997.

Cavazos, Bobby. *The Cowboy from the Wild Horse Desert: A Story of the King Ranch*. Houston: Larksdale, 2000.

Cavness, Addie Word. *La Puerta de Agua Dulce: A Chronicle of the Everyday Life of a Ranch Family Circa 1895–1913*. Austin: Shelby Printing, 1973.

Chamberlain, Samuel. *My Confession: Recollections of a Rogue,* ed. William H. Goetzmann. Austin: Texas State Historical Association, 1996.

Chatfield, W. H. *The Twin Cities of the Border and the Country of the Lower Rio Grande*. New Orleans: E. P. Brandao, 1893.

Cheeseman, Bruce S., ed. *Leroy G. Denman Jr. & King Ranch: An Oral History*. Kingsville: King Ranch Inc., 1995.

———. *My Dear Henrietta: Hiram Chamberlain's Letters to His Daughter, 1846–1866*. Kingsville: King Ranch Inc., 1993.

———. *Perfectly Exhausted with Pleasure: The 1881 King-Kenedy Excursion Train to Laredo*. Austin: Book Club of Texas, 1992.

Cheeseman, Bruce S., and Al Lowman. *"The Book of All Christendom": Tom Lea, Carl Hertzog, and the Making of 'The King Ranch.'"* Kingsville: King Ranch Inc., 1992.

Clayton, Lawrence. *Historic Ranches of Texas*. Austin: University of Texas Press, 1995.

Cohen, Saul B. *The Columbia Gazetteer of the World,* 3 vols. New York: Columbia University Press, 1998.

Coker, Caleb, ed. *The News from Brownsville: Helen Chapman's Letters from the Texas Military Frontier, 1848–1852*. Austin: Texas State Historical Association, 1992.

Cox, Mike. *Texas Ranger Tales: Stories That Need Telling*. Plano, TX: Republic of Texas Press, 1997.

Craver, Rebecca, and Adair Margo, eds. *Tom Lea: An Oral History*. El Paso: Texas Western Press, 1995.

Cypher, John. *Bob Kleberg and the King Ranch: A Worldwide Sea of Grass*. Austin: University of Texas Press, 1995.

Daddysman, James W. *The Matamoros Trade: Confederate Commerce, Diplomacy, and Intrigue*. Newark: University of Delaware Press, 1984.

Davis, Richard Harding. *The West from a Car-Window*. New York: Harper & Brothers, 1892.

De León, Arnoldo. *The Tejano Community, 1836–1900*. Dallas: Southern Methodist University Press, 1997 [1982].

———. *They Called Them Greasers: Anglo Attitudes Toward Mexicans in Texas, 1821–1900*. Austin: University of Texas Press, 1997 [1983].

Denhardt, Robert Moorman. *The King Ranch Quarter Horses*. Norman: University of Oklahoma Press, 1978 [1970].

DeShields, James T. *Border Wars of Texas*. Austin: State House Press, 1993 [1912].

De Vaca, Cabeza. *Adventures in the Unknown Interior of America,* trans. and ed. Cyclone Covey. Albuquerque: University of New Mexico Press, 2001 [1961].

Dobie, J. Frank. *The Longhorns.* Austin: University of Texas Press, 1980 [1941].

———. *The Mustangs.* Austin: University of Texas Press, 1999 [1952].

———. *Up the Trail from Texas.* New York: Random House, 1955.

———. *A Vaquero of the Brush Country.* Boston: Little, Brown and Company, 1943 [1929].

Domenech, Abbé Emmanuel. *Missionary Adventures in Texas and Mexico: A Personal Narrative of Six Years' Sojourn in Those Regions.* London: Longman, Brown, Green, Longmans, and Roberts, 1858.

Doubleday, Abner. *My Life in the Old Army: The Reminiscences of Abner Doubleday from the Collections of the New-York Historical Society,* ed. Joseph E. Chance. Fort Worth: Texas Christian University Press, 1998.

Douglas, C. L. *Cattle Kings of Texas.* Dallas: Cecil Baugh, 1939.

Downs, Fane, and Nancy Baker Jones, eds. *Women and Texas History: Selected Essays.* Austin: Texas State Historical Association, 1993.

Dunn, J. B. (Red). *Perilous Trails of Texas.* Dallas: Southwest Press, 1932.

Durham, George, as told to Clyde Wantland. *Taming the Nueces Strip: The Story of McNelly's Rangers.* Austin: University of Texas Press, 2000 [1962].

Eisenhower, John S. D. *So Far from God: The U.S. War with Mexico, 1846–1848.* Norman: University of Oklahoma Press, 2000 [1989].

Fehrenbach, T. R. *Lone Star: A History of Texas and the Texans.* New York: Collier Books, 1980 [1968].

Ford, John Salmon. *Rip Ford's Texas,* ed. Stephen B. Oates. Austin: University of Texas Press, 1987 [1963].

Foster, L. L. *Forgotten Texas Census: First Annual Report of the Agricultural Bureau of the Department of Agriculture, Insurance, Statistics, and History, 1887–88.* Austin: Texas State Historical Association, 2001 [1889].

Foster, William C. *Spanish Expeditions into Texas, 1689–1768.* Austin: University of Texas Press, 1995.

Fremantle, Lt. Col. Arthur J. L. *Three Months in the Southern States: April–June 1863.* Lincoln: University of Nebraska Press, 1991 [1864].

Frissell, Toni. *The King Ranch, 1939–1944: A Photographic Essay.* Dobbs Ferry, NY: Morgan & Morgan, 1975.

Frost, Dick. *The King Ranch Papers: An Unauthorized and Irreverent History of the World's Largest Landholders.* Chicago: Aquarius Rising Press, 1985.

Gallaway, B. P., ed. *Texas: The Dark Corner of the Confederacy—Contemporary Accounts of the Lone Star State in the Civil War.* Lincoln: University of Nebraska Press, 1999 [1994].

Gard, Wayne. *The Chisholm Trail.* Norman: University of Oklahoma Press, 1954.

Gatschet, Albert S. *The Karankawa Indians, the Coast People of Texas.* Cambridge, MA: Peabody Museum of American Archaeology and Ethnology, 1891.

Giddings, Luther. *Sketches of the Campaign in Northern Mexico in Eighteen Hundred Forty-six and Seven by an Officer of the First Regiment of Ohio Volunteers.* New York: George P. Putnam, 1853.

Goodwyn, Frank. *Life on the King Ranch.* College Station: Texas A&M University Press, 1995 [1951].

Graf, Leroy P. "The Economic History of the Lower Rio Grande Valley, 1820–1875." Ph.D. diss., Harvard University, February 1942.

Graham, Don, James W. Lee, and William T. Pilkington, eds. *The Texas Literary Tradition: Fiction Folklore History.* Austin: College of Liberal Arts, University of Texas at Austin, 1983.

Graham, Joe S. *El Rancho in South Texas: Continuity and Change from 1750.* Denton: University of North Texas Press, 1994.

Graham, Joe S., ed. *Ranching in South Texas: A Symposium.* Kingsville: John E. Connor Museum, 1994.

Grant, Ulysses S. *Personal Memoirs of Ulysses S. Grant,* 2 vols. Old Saybrook, CT: n.p., n.d. [1885].

Greene, A. C. *Sketches from the Five States of Texas.* College Station: Texas A&M University Press, 1998.

Harper, Minnie Timms, and George Dewey Harper. *Old Ranches.* Dallas: Dealey and Lowe, 1936.

Hitchcock, Ethan Allen. *In Camp and Field,* ed. W. A. Croffus. New York: G. P. Punam's Sons, 1909.

Hodder, Frank Heywood, ed. *Audubon's Westward Journal: 1849–1850.* Cleveland: Arthur H. Clark, 1906.

Horgan, Paul. *Great River: The Rio Grande in North American History,* 2 vols. Hanover, NH: Wesleyan University Press, 1984 [1955].

Hudson, Linda S. *Mistress of Manifest Destiny: A Biography of Jane McManus Storm Cazneau, 1807–1878.* Austin: Texas State Historical Association, 2001.

Hughes, W. J. *Rebellious Ranger: Rip Ford and the Old Southwest.* Norman: University of Oklahoma Press, 1964.

Hunter, J. Marvin, ed. *The Trail Drivers of Texas.* Austin: University of Texas Press, 1985 [1925].

Huson, Hobart. *Refugio: A Comprehensive History of Refugio County from Aboriginal Times to 1955,* 2 vols. Woodsboro, TX: The Rooke Foundation, Inc., 1955.

Jaques, Mary J. *Texas Ranch Life; with Three Months through Mexico in a "Prairie Schooner."* College Station: Texas A&M University Press, 1989 [1894].

Jenkins, John H., ed. *Robert E. Lee on the Rio Grande: The Correspondence of Robert E. Lee on the Texas Border, 1860.* Austin: Jenkins Publishing Co., 1988.

Jennings, N. A. *A Texas Ranger.* Dallas: Turner Company, 1930.

Kearney, Milo, ed. *More Studies in Brownsville History.* Brownsville: Pan American University, 1989.

———. *Still More Studies in Brownsville History.* Brownsville: University of Texas at Brownsville, 1991.

———. *Studies in Brownsville History.* Brownsville: Pan American University, 1986.

Kearney, Milo, and Anthony Knoop. *Boom and Bust: The Historical Cycles of Matamoros and Brownsville.* Austin: Eakin Press, 1991.

Kearney, Milo, Anthony Knopp, and Antonio Zavaleta, eds. *Studies in Brownsville & Matamoros History.* Brownsville: University of Texas at Brownsville, 1995.

Kelley, Pat. *River of Lost Dreams: Navigation on the Rio Grande.* Lincoln: University of Nebraska Press, 1986.

King Ranch: 100 Years of Ranching, 1853–1953, commemorative edition. *Corpus Christi Caller,* July 12, 1953.

Kleberg, Sally S. *The Stewardship of Private Wealth: Managing Personal & Family Financial Assets.* New York: McGraw-Hill, 1997.

Lamar, Howard R. *Texas Crossings: The Lone Star State and the American Far West, 1836–1986.* Austin: University of Texas Press, 1991.

Lane, Lydia Spencer. *I Married a Soldier or Old Days in the Old Army.* Albuquerque: Horn & Wallace, 1964 [1893].

Lea, Tom. *In the Crucible of the Sun.* Kingsville: King Ranch Inc., 1974.

———. *The King Ranch,* 2 vols. Boston: Little, Brown and Company, 1957.

Lehmann, V. W. *Forgotten Legions: Sheep in the Rio Grande Plains of Texas.* El Paso: Texas Western Press, 1969.

Longoria, Arturo. *Adios to the Brushlands.* College Station: Texas A&M University Press, 1997.

McCampbell, Coleman. *Saga of a Frontier Seaport.* Corpus Christi: n.p., n.d.

McMichael, George, et al., eds. *Concise Anthology of American Literature,* 4th ed. Upper Saddle River, NJ: Prentice-Hall, 1998.

McWhiney, Grady, and Sue McWhiney, eds. *To Mexico with Taylor and Scott 1845–1847.* Waltham, MA: Blaisdell Publishing Company, 1969.

Maril, Robert Lee. *Living on the Edge of America: At Home on the Texas–Mexico Border.* College Station: Texas A&M University Press, 1992.

Meade, George Gordon. *The Life and Letters of George Gordon Meade,* vol. 1. New York: Charles Scribner's Sons, 1913.

Meltzer, Milton. *Hunted Like a Wolf: The Story of the Seminole War.* New York: Farrar, Straus and Giroux, 1972.

Metz, Leon C. *Border: The U.S.-Mexican Line.* El Paso: Mangan Books, 1996 [1989].

Monday, Jane Clements, and Betty Bailey Colley. *Voices from the Wild Horse Desert: The Vaquero Families of the King and Kenedy Ranches.* Austin: University of Texas Press, 1997.

Montejano, David. *Anglos and Mexicans in the Making of Texas, 1836–1986.* Austin: University of Texas Press, 1987.

Myers, Lois E. *Letters by Lamplight: A Woman's View of Everyday Life in South Texas, 1873–1883.* Waco: Baylor University Press, 1998 [1991].

Nance, Berta Hart. *Flute in the Distance.* Dallas: Kaleidograph Press, 1935.

Nichols, Edward J. *Zach Taylor's Little Army.* Garden City, NY: Doubleday & Company, 1963.

Nixon, Jay. *Stewards of a Vision (A History of The King Ranch).* Kingsville: King Ranch Inc., 1986.

Olmsted, Frederick Law. *A Journey through Texas: Or, a Saddle-Trip on the Southwestern Frontier.* Austin: University of Texas Press, 1978 [1857].

O'Neal, Bill. *Historic Ranches of the Old West.* Austin: Eakin Press, 1997.

Oswandel, Jacob. *Notes on the Mexican War 1846–47–48.* Philadelphia: n.p., 1885.

Paredes, Américo. *A Texas-Mexican Cancionero: Folksongs of the Lower Border.* Austin: University of Texas Press, 1995 [1976].

Parsons, Chuck. *"Pidge": A Texas Ranger from Virginia: The Life and Letters of Lieutenant T. C. Robinson, Washington County Volunteer Militia Company "A."* Wolfe City, TX: Henington Publishing Co., 1985.

Parsons, Chuck, and Marianne E. Hall Little. *L. H. McNelly—Texas Ranger—The Life and Times of a Fighting Man.* Austin: State House Press, 2001.

Perry, George Sessions. *Texas: A World in Itself.* New York: Whittlesey House, 1942.

Poyo, Gerald E., ed. *Tejano Journey, 1770–1850.* Austin: University of Texas Press, 1996.

Ramos, Mary G., ed. *Texas Almanac 2002–2003.* Dallas: *Dallas Morning News,* 2001.

Rankin, Melinda. *Texas in 1850.* Boston: Damrell & Moore, 1850.

———. *Twenty Years Among the Mexicans, A Narrative of Missionary Labor.* Cincinnati: Chase & Hall, 1875.

Reports of the Committee of Investigation Sent in 1873 by the Mexican Government to the Frontier of Texas. New York: Baker & Godwin, 1875.

Rhoad, Albert O., ed. *Breeding Beef Cattle for Unfavorable Environments: A Symposium Presented at the King Ranch Centennial Conference.* Austin: University of Texas Press, 1955.

Richardson, Rupert N., Adrian Anderson, Cary D. Wintz, and Ernest Wallace. *Texas: The Lone Star State,* 8th ed. Upper Saddle River, NJ: Prentice-Hall, 2001.

Rister, Carl Coke. *Robert E. Lee in Texas.* Norman: University of Oklahoma Press, 1946.

Robertson, Brian. *Wild Horse Desert: The Heritage of South Texas.* Edinburg, TX: New Santander Press, 1985.

Rosenbaum, Robert J. *Mexicano Resistance in the Southwest, "The Sacred Right of Self-Preservation."* Austin: University of Texas Press, 1981.

Rubio, Abel G. *Stolen Heritage: A Mexican-American's Rediscovery of His Family's Lost Land Grant.* Austin: Eakin Press, 1998 [1986].

Sandos, James A. *Rebellion in the Borderlands: Anarchism and the Plan of San Diego, 1904–1923*. Norman: University of Oklahoma Press, 1992.

Savage, Richard Henry. *For Life and Love: A Story of the Rio Grande*. London: George Routledge and Sons, 1894.

Scott, Bob. *Leander McNelly: Texas Ranger—He Just Kept on Keepin' On*. Austin: Eakin Press, 1998.

Sibley, Marilyn McAdams. *Travelers in Texas, 1761–1860*. Austin: University of Texas Press, 1967.

Sizer, Mona D. *The King Ranch Story: Truth and Myth*. Plano, TX: Republic of Texas Press, 1999.

Smith, Diane Solether. *The Armstrong Chronicle: A Ranching History*. San Antonio: Corona Publishing Co., 1986.

Smith, George Winston, and Charles Judah, eds. *Chronicles of the Gringos: The U.S. Army in the Mexican War, 1846–1848—Accounts of Eyewitnesses and Combatants*. Albuquerque: University of New Mexico Press, 1968.

Spratt, John Stricklin. *The Road to Spindletop: Economic Change in Texas, 1875–1901*. Austin: University of Texas Press, 1970 [1955].

Stein, Gertrude. *Everybody's Autobiography*. New York: Random House, 1937.

Steinbeck, John. *Travels With Charlie*. New York: Viking, 1962.

Sterling, William Warren. *Trails and Trials of a Texas Ranger*. Norman: University of Oklahoma Press, 1959.

Stillman, Chauncey Devereux. *Charles Stillman, 1810–1875*. New York: C.D. Stillman, 1956.

Taylor, Paul Schuster. *An American-Mexican Frontier: Nueces County, Texas*. Chapel Hill: University of North Carolina Press, 1934.

Texas History Movies. Dallas: Magnolia Petroleum Company, 1956 [1928].

Tiejerina, Andrés. *Tejano Empire: Life on the South Texas Ranchos*. College Station: Texas A&M University Press, 1998.

Thompson, Jerry. *A Wild and Vivid Land: An Illustrated History of the South Texas Border*. Austin: Texas State Historical Association, 1997.

Thompson, Jerry, ed. *Fifty Miles and a Fight: Major Samuel Peter Heintzelman's Journal of Texas and the Cortina War*. Austin: Texas State Historical Association, 1998.

Thompson, Jerry D., ed. *Juan Cortina and the Texas-Mexico Frontier. 1859–1877*. El Paso: Texas Western Press, 1994.

Tyler, Ron, et al., eds. *The New Handbook of Texas*, 6 vols. Austin: Texas State Historical Association, 1996.

Utley, Robert M. *Lone Star Justice: The First Century of the Texas Rangers*. New York: Oxford University Press, 2002.

Vielé, Mrs. [Teresa Griffin]. *"Following the Drum": A Glimpse of Frontier Life*. Austin: Steck-Vaughn, 1968 [1858].

Villareal, Roberto M. "The Mexican-American Vaqueros of the Kenedy Ranch: A Social History." Master's thesis, Texas A&I University, 1972.

Wallace, Ernest, David M. Vigness, and George B. Ward, eds. *Documents of Texas History*, 2nd ed. Austin: State House Press, 1994.

Walton, George. *Fearless and Free: The Seminole Indian War 1835–1842.* Indianapolis: Bobbs-Merrill Company, 1977.

Webb, Walter Prescott. *The Texas Rangers: A Century of Frontier Defense.* Austin: University of Texas Press, 1965 [1935].

Weber, David J., ed. *Foreigners in This Native Land: Historical Roots of the Mexican Americans.* Albuquerque: University of New Mexico Press, 1973.

Williams, Docia Schultz. *The History and Mystery of the Menger Hotel.* Plano, TX: Republic of Texas Press, 2000.

Williams, J. W. *The Big Ranch Country.* Lubbock: Texas Tech University Press, 1999 [1954].

Winfrey, Dorman H., and James M. Day, eds. *The Indian Papers of Texas and the Southwest 1825–1916,* 5 vols. Austin: Texas State Historical Association, 1995.

Winkler, John K. *The First Billion: The Stillmans and the National City Bank.* New York: Vanguard Press, 1934.

Woodman, Lyman L. *Cortina: Rogue of the Rio Grande.* San Antonio: Naylor Company, 1950.

Wooster, Ralph A., and Robert A. Calvert, eds. *Texas Vistas: Selections from The Southwestern Historical Quarterly.* Austin: Texas State Historical Association, 1980.

Zamora, Emilio, Cynthia Orozco, and Rodolfo Rocha, eds. *Mexican Americans in Texas History: Selected Essays.* Austin: Texas State Historical Association, 2000.

Articles

Apcar, Leonard M. "Behind the Wheel: Ford King Ranch F-150 SuperCrew, Sizzle from a Branding Iron." *New York Times,* December 9, 2001, Section 12, p. 1.

Ashton, John. "Render Unto Caesar." *The Cattleman* 33, no. 2 (July 1946): 43.

Barragy, T. J. "The Gathering of the Texas Herd." *Journal of South Texas* 11, no. 1 (1998): 1–17.

Benavidez, Rachel. "River Weeds Choking Rio Grande Waters." *Brownsville Herald.* April 16, 2001, pp. A1, A12.

"Big as All Outdoors." *Time,* December 15, 1947, 89–98.

Brezosky, Lynn. "Jurors Reject 420 Million Kenedy Suit." *San Antonio Express-News,* October 24, 2001, pp. B1, B5.

———. "Weeds Choking Rio Grande, Border Cities' Water Supply," *Austin American-Statesman,* May 31, 2001, p. B7.

"Brownsville Fights Weeds for Its Water." *Austin American-Statesman,* May 17, 2002, p. B6.

Broyles, William. "The Last Empire." *Texas Monthly*, October 1980, 150–173, 234, 236, 238, 240–242, 244–253, 255–258, 260, 262–264, 266, 268–269, 270, 272, 275–276, 278.

Burnett, John. "King Ranch: Times Changes All But Legend." *San Antonio Express-News*, August 15, 1982, pp. 1A, 16A.

Chamberlain, H. "Report of the Raid on King's Ranche." *Tri-Weekly Telegraph*, February 1, 1864.

Cheeseman, Bruce S. "'Let Us Have 500 Good Determined Texans': Richard King's Account of the Union Invasion of South Texas, November 12, 1863, to January 20, 1864." *Southwestern Historical Quarterly* 101, no. 1 (July 1997): 77–95.

Coker, Caleb, and Janet G. Humphrey. "The Texas Frontier in 1850: Dr. Ebenezer Swift and the View from Fort Martin Scott." *Southwestern Historical Quarterly* 156, no. 3 (January 1993): 393–413.

Coker, Edward C., and Daniel L. Schafer, eds. "A West Point Graduate in the Second Seminole War: William Warren Chapman and the View from Fort Foster." *Florida Historical Quarterly* (April 1990): 447–475.

Cox, Mike. "Recalling the King of Ranches." *Austin American-Statesman*, October 11, 1996, p. F2.

Cox, Patrick L. "'An Enemy Closer to Us Than Any European Power': The Impact of Mexico on Texan Public Opinion Before World War I." *Southwestern Historical Quarterly* 105, no. 1 (July 2001): 41–80.

Davis, Rod. "The Tip of Texas: A Rio Runs Through It: Part 1." *San Antonio Express-News*, June 3, 2001, pp. L1, L6–7.

"Deep Roots Keep Texas Ranches Together." *Dallas Morning News*, November 25, 1979, p. AA1.

Delaney, Robert W. "Matamoros, Port for Texas during the Civil War." *Southwestern Historical Quarterly* 58, no. 4 (April 1955): 473–487.

Dobie, J. Frank. "A Giant Among Texans." *New York Times*, September 15, 1957, p. 6.

Dugan, Frank H. "The 1850 Affair of the Brownsville Separatists." *Southwestern Historical Quarterly* 61 (October 1957): 270–287.

Ellis, L. Tuffly. "Maritime Commerce on the Far Western Gulf, 1861–1865." *Southwestern Historical Quarterly* 77, no. 2 (October 1973): 167–225.

"Empire of Cattle: The King Ranch of Texas." *Fortune*, December 8, 1933, 49–61, 89–90, 92, 95–96, 98, 103–104, 106, 109.

Erramouspe, Roxanne. "Today's King Ranch." *The Cattleman* 82, no. 4 (September 1995): 10–32.

Falgoust, Neal. "Commemoration of Mexican-American War in Limbo." *Corpus Christi Caller-Times*, February 18, 2002, pp. A1, A6.

Fehrenbach, T. R. "San Jacinto Fight Changed History." *San Antonio Express-News*, April 15, 2001, p. 65.

Friend, Llerena B. "The Texan of 1860." *Southwestern Historical Quarterly* 62, no. 1 (July 1958): 1–17.

Gard, Wayne. "The Impact of the Cattle Trails." *Southwestern Historical Quarterly* 71, no. 1 (July 1967): 1–6.

George, Ron. "King and Kleberg Fought Widow for Her Half Share of King Ranch." *Corpus Christi Caller-Times,* August 23, 1992, p. D4.

———. "Letters from the Edge." *Corpus Christi Caller-Times,* August 23, 1992, pp. D1, D4.

Gibbs, Nancy. "A Whole New World: The New Frontier/La Nueva Frontera." *Time,* June 11, 2001, 34–79.

Gloria, Rene. "Santa Gertrudis: The Best Breed Under the Sun." *Texas Historian* 60, no. 2 (November 1999): 9–12.

"Gone South and West." *Wall Street Journal,* December 29, 2000, p. A16.

Graf, Leroy P. "Review of *The News from Brownsville.*" *Journal of Southern History* 59, no. 2 (May 1993): 367–369.

Grant, Mary Lee. "At Old Kenedy Ranch, Visitors Find Peace Within the Silent Halls." *Austin American-Statesman,* October 7, 1999, p. B7.

———. "Uncertain Future—Kinenos' Way of Life at King Ranch Threatened by Corporate Change." *Corpus Christi Caller,* September 6, 1998, pp. A1, A12.

Greaser, Galen D., and Jesús F. de la Teja. "Quieting Title to Spanish and Mexican Land Grants in the Trans-Nueces: The Bourland and Miller Commission, 1850–1852." *Southwestern Historical Quarterly* 95, no. 4 (April 1992): 445–464.

Gregor, Alison. "Experts Say Kenedy Suit Not Much of a Precedent." *San Antonio Express-News,* October 26, 2001, pp. B1, B8.

———. "Rio Gurgle." *San Antonio Express-News,* June 24, 2001, pp. A1, A11.

Grisales, Claudia. "Action Urged to Help Boost Border Counties' Economies." *Austin American-Statesman,* March 18, 2001, pp. D1–2.

Haley, James L. "San Jacinto Victory Should Be Celebrated by All Texans." *Austin American-Statesman,* April 20, 2002, p. A11.

Havins, T. R. "Texas Fever." *Southwestern Historical Quarterly* 52, no. 1 (July 1948): 147–162.

Hollandsworth, Skip. "When We Were Kings." *Texas Monthly,* August 1998, 110, 113–117, 140–144.

Jacobs, Janet. "Heir to King Ranch Tempered His Determination with Humor." *Austin American-Statesman,* May 22, 2001, p. B5.

Kilgore, Dan E. "Corpus Christi: A Quarter Century of Development, 1900–1925." *Southwestern Historical Quarterly* 75, no. 4 (April 1972): 434–460.

"King Ranch Moving Offices to Houston." *Dallas Morning News,* June 19, 1989, p. D4.

Larralde, Carlos. "J. T. Canales and the Texas Rangers." *Journal of South Texas* 10, no. 1 (1997): 38–68.

———. "Juan Cortina's Spy: Elena Villarreal de Ferrer." *Journal of South Texas* 11, no. 1 (1998): 104–124.

Leggett, Mike. "Draining Life from the Rio Grande." *Austin American-Statesman,* June 15, 2001, pp. 1A, 10–11A.

———. "Eagle-Eyed Guide Takes Birders on Flights of Fancy at King Ranch." *Austin American-Statesman,* April 19, 2001, p. C7.

———. "Game Warden's Death a Shock to Tightknit Group." *Austin American-Statesman,* August 9, 2001, p. C7.

Lewis, Mark. "Don't Indict 'Popular History.'" *Wall Street Journal,* January 22, 2002, p. A20.

Lowman, Al. "Remembering Tom Lea, Fellow, Texas State Historical Association." *Southwestern Historical Quarterly* 105, no. 1 (July 2001): 1–13.

McGraw, Dan. "A Fistful of Dollars: The King Ranch of Texas Rides into a Profitably New Business Era." *U.S. News & World Report,* July 24, 1995, pp. 36–38.

"Man Finds Car Lost Twelve Years in King Ranch." *Corpus Christi Caller,* November 6, 1948, p. 1.

Markus, Kurt. "The King Ranch Today: Working Cattle on Norias." *The Western Horseman,* May 1980, 37–45.

Martin, Gary, and John Tedesco. "Texans Court Navy Bombs." *San Antonio Express-News,* June 23, 2001, pp. 1A, 14A.

Martinez, Deborah. "Nanette Hasette Wins Second Term as Judge." *Corpus Christi Caller-Times,* November 8, 2000, p. 83.

Martin, Gary. "Navy Sinks Texas Bomb Site," *San Antonio Express-News,* July 12, 2001, pp. A1, A8.

Milloy, Ross E. "In Courtroom in Texas, Engrossing Bit of History." *New York Times,* October 25, 2001, p. A16.

Murphy, Charles J. V. "The Fabulous House of Kleberg: A World of Cattle and Grass." *Fortune,* June-July-August, 1969, 2–28.

Myers, Kit. "The King of Ranches." *San Antonio Express-News,* November 30, 1999, p. 3M.

Payne, Darwin. "Camp Life in the Army of Occupation: Corpus Christi, July 1845 to March 1846." *Southwestern Historical Quarterly* 73, no. 3 (January 1970): 326–342.

Pinkerton, James. "Health Care: Crisis at the Border." *Houston Chronicle,* May 5, 2002, pp. H1, H20.

Pohl, James W. "Review of *The News from Brownsville.*" *Southwestern American Literature* 18, no. 1 (Fall 1992): 95–96.

Rayburn, John. "Rainmaking in South Texas, 1891." *Journal of South Texas* 10/1 (1997): 3–19.

Reinhold, Robert. "Texas' King Ranch Works to Overcome Difficulties." *Dallas Morning News,* September 6, 1987, p. A53.

Rhoad, A. O. "The Santa Gertrudis Breed: The Genesis and the Genetics of a New Breed of Beef Cattle." *The Journal of Heredity* 40, no. 5 (May 1949): 115–126.

Rhoad, A. O., and R. J. Kleberg Jr. "The Development of a Superior Family in the Modern Quarter Horse." *The Journal of Heredity* 37, no. 8 (August 1946): 227–238.

Rippy, J. Fred. "Border Troubles Along the Rio Grande, 1848–1860." *Southwestern Historical Quarterly* 23 (October 1919): 91–111.

"Robert Richard Shelton, Heir to King Ranch, Dies." *Houston Chronicle,* January 7, 1994.

Russnogle, John. "Why Cotton Is King at King Ranch." *Top Producer,* December 1991, 18–20.

Schwartz, Jeremy. "South Texas Homelands: Ballis' Win May Inspire Other Land Struggles." *Corpus Christi Caller-Times,* August 13, 2000, pp. A1, A4.

Sharpe, Patricia. "Where Are They Now?" [Stephen J. "Tio" Kleberg]. *Texas Monthly,* September 2001, 125.

Shockley, Martin Staples, and A. Ray Stephens, eds. "J. A. van blerk 'Met President Reitz deur Texas,'" trans. Natalie Alice van Blerk. *Southwestern Historical Quarterly* 74, no. 1 (July 1970): 81–98.

Sibley, Marilyn McAdams. "Charles Stillman: A Case Study of Entrepreneurship on the Rio Grande, 1861–1865." *Southwestern Historical Quarterly* 77, no. 2 (October 1973): 227–240.

Spong, John. "Hooked." *Texas Monthly,* June 2002, 40, 42, 44, 46–47.

Tanner, Ogden. "The Wild-Horse Kingdom of Richard King." *NRTA Journal,* May–June 1981, 38–41.

Tedesco, John. "19th-Century Claim on King Ranch Still Alive." *San Antonio Express-News,* January 18, 2001, p. 7B.

Tinsley, Anna M. "King Ranch Visionary Clement Dies at 75." *Corpus Christi Caller-Times,* January 3, 1994, pp. A1, A12.

"Tio Kleberg Leaving Day-to-Day King Ranch Operations June 1." *Livestock Weekly,* Internet edition, February 9, 2002.

Tyler, Ronnie C. "Cotton on the Border, 1861–1865." *Southwestern Historical Quarterly* 73, no. 4 (April 1970): 456–477.

Vertuno, Jim. "Official Says Water Deal Is Insult to Texas Farmers." *Austin American-Statesman,* July 3, 2002, p. B7.

Warburton, L. H. "The Plan of San Diego: Background and Selected Documents." *Journal of South Texas* 12, no. 1 (1999): 125–155.

Webb, Walter Prescott. "Tom Lea's Powerful Portrait of Fabled King Ranch." *Dallas Morning News,* September 15, 1957, section 2, p. 3.

Wooster, Ralph A. "Wealthy Texans, 1860." *Southwestern Historical Review* 71, no. 2 (October 1967): 163–180.

———. "Wealthy Texans, 1870." *Southwestern Historical Quarterly* 74, no. 1 (July 1970): 24–35.

Yardley, Jim. "Longer Horns Hook Big Bid." *Austin American-Statesman,* April 29, 2002, p. B6.

Documents

Chapman Document Report. One hundred and thirty-nine items including probates, deeds, letters, etc. relating to *William Warren Chapman, III, et al., v. King Ranch, Inc., et al.* Edwards Law Firm, L.L.P. Corpus Christi, Texas.

Cheeseman, Bruce S. "La Patrona de Santa Gertrudis: The Moral Paternalism of Henrietta M. King." Paper read at Conference on Women in Texas History in Austin, 1990, pp. 1–26.

"A Day at the King Ranch." Program Announcement: The Book Club of Texas, November 9, 1991.

Deposition of Bruce Smith Cheeseman. Videotape. May 16, 1996. 3 vol. Tape 1: 92 minutes. Tape 2: 98 minutes. Tape 3: 21 minutes.

Deposition of Edward C. Coker, III. June 5, 1996. Vol. 1: Typescript, 148 pp.

Deposition of Edward C. Coker, III. June 6, 1996. Vol. 2: Typescript, 146 pp.

Deposition of Tom Lea. Videotape. April 10, 1996. Vol. 1: 102 minutes. Vol. 2: 10 minutes.

Gracy, David B., II. "The Archives of the King Ranch, Inc.: A Report and Recommendations," September 10, 1987, pp. 1–10.

Jose San Roman Sobrinos et al. v. Chamberlain et al. Supreme Court of Texas, March 25, 1890. 76 Tex. 624, 13.S.W.634.

"King Ranch Saddle Shop—Casual Comfort from the Ranch—A Tradition of Quality for over 100 Years." Brochure. Kingsville, TX: King Ranch Saddle Shop, Fall 2000, pp. 1–38.

Kleberg, Robert J. Jr., "A Review of the Development of the Breed." Pamphlet, n.d.

Number 01–1430 in the Supreme Court of Texas. On Appeal from the Thirteenth Court of Appeals, Corpus Christi and Edinburg, Texas. Response to Petitions for Review.

Report of United States Commissioners to Texas. May 7, 1872. U.S. Congress Executive Document. 42nd Cong., 3rd Sess., 1872–1873.

Richard King-Charles Stillman Correspondence. Stillman Collection, Houghton Library, Harvard University.

"Texan Frontier Troubles." 44th Cong., 1st sess., HR Report No. 343, February 29, 1876.

Tijerina, Andrés. "Major Factors in Tejano Land Dispossession: A Paper." Presented to Annual Meeting of the Texas State Historical Association, Austin, March 4, 2000, pp. 1–13.

"Unedited Rough Draft Only": Hearing on Cause No. 95-2273-A, *William Warren Chapman, III, et al. v. King Ranch, Inc., et al.* 28th District Court, Nueces County, Corpus Christi, Texas, November 30, 2001.

"William Warren Chapman, III, et al., Appellants, v. King Ranch, Inc., et al., Appellees." Number 12-19-163-CV. Court of Appeals. Thirteenth District of Texas, Corpus Christi, pp. 1–25.

Interviews by Author

Bruce Cheeseman. Corpus Christi, Texas, November 2, 2001.
Tom Krenick. Corpus Christi, Texas, October 31, 2001.
Al Lowman. San Marcos, Texas, November 17, 2001.
David Montejano. Austin, Texas, February 18, 2002.

Miscellaneous

Lisa Neely, letter to author, June 9, 2000.
Lisa Neely, e-mail to author, February 4, 2002.

Index